I0461325

Copyright © 2022

All rights reserved.

To contact the author or to book an event, please email info@mattball.org

For more information about the book, please visit LosingMyReligions.net

To peruse material cut from earlier drafts of this book, see new pictures, and read new essays, please visit MattBall.org

Book design by Mandy Tucker, Anne Green, and Matt Ball.

Cover design by Mandy Tucker (MandyTuckerDesign@gmail.com).

Published by One Step for Animals, Inc., a 501(c)(3) nonprofit.

All proceeds from this book that would normally go to the author will instead go directly to One Step for Animals.

ISBN – Color Paperback : 979-8-9869565-2-7
ISBN – Amazon B&W Paperback: 979-8-9869565-0-3
ISBN - eBook: 979-8-9869565-1-0

First Edition: October 2022

For AMG

<Snape*>"*Obviously*"</Snape>

Every writer has an ideal reader,
and it was just my good luck
that mine wanted to sleep with me.

–*Michael Chabon*, Wonder Boys

*Alan Rickman as Snape being reviewed by Dolores Umbridge in
Harry Potter and the Order of the Phoenix. Anne is a big Rickman fan.

Matt Ball is the author, co-author, secondary-author, ghost-author, and non-author of countless articles, speeches, book chapters, and even *entire books!* The most recent (before this one) is his blockbuster* *The Accidental Activist*. Currently, he is President of One Step for Animals; previously, he was shitcanned from so many nonprofits that we can't list them all here. Before Matt's unfortunate encounter with activism, he was an aerospace engineer who wanted to work for NASA (to impress Carl Sagan).

His hobbies include photography, almost dying, and ███████. (*Hey! This is a family-friendly bio!*) He lives in Tucson with his soulmate and reluctant editor Anne Green, along with no dogs, no cats, no guinea pigs, and only the occasional snake and scorpion.

*JK

There's no such thing as no regrets
But baby
It's all right.

–Mary Chapin Carpenter

It's sad
So sad
Why can't we talk it over?
Oh, it seems to me
Sorry seems to be the hardest word.

–Elton John

The point is, there is no point. Choose your own!

–Ann Leckie

Writing a book is hard!
You have to go long stretches
without looking at social media.

–Faith Salie

Table of Contents

I'm choosing my confessions
Like a hurt, lost, and blinded fool, fool.

Oh no, I've said too much.

-R.E.M. "Losing My Religion"

When you are in the middle of a story
it isn't a story at all,
but only a confusion....
It's only afterwards that it becomes
anything like a story at all.

–Margaret Atwood, Alias Grace

When I write something
I usually think it is very important
and that I am a very fine writer.
But there is one corner of my mind
in which I know very well what I am,
which is a small, a very small writer.
I swear I know it.

But that doesn't matter much to me.

–Natalia Ginsburg, My Vocation
(Translated by Dick Davis)

The next thing I remember
is coming to with my head against something
hard and cold and wet. I don't know where I am.
There is no noise, only formless light.

I can't move and I can't feel my legs.
It dawns on me: "Maybe I'm paralyzed."

Then I realize my head is in a pool
of my own blood.

My soulmate is on the other side of the door.

She doesn't know if I'm alive.
She will have to save my life.
She will bring me back again.

Anything for Her Laugh
+ Warnings & Notes

When I'm 40 years older,
when I'm wrinkled and wise
I will trade all my liberty
for that look in your eyes.

–Tears for Fears, "The Tipping Point"

To spare my hands, much of what you'll read here was spoken into my phone. (Huzzah for voice recognition!) This also makes sense because I am looking to have a conversation with you. Yes, a sadly one-sided conversation for now, but the non-memoir portions of this book have been developed through decades of discussions with hundreds of friends and acquaintances and enemies, including some of the most brilliant and astute individuals you could ever hope to meet. Their ideas and insights, reproaches and rebuttals have stretched my mind, leading me down paths I never imagined and very often resisted.

The conversation is as honest as possible. Not fictionalized, not dramatized, not sugarcoated, not exaggerated, not glorified. It goes to some dark places. And my humor is often dark, too. I read Anne one bit and she laughed. I exalted: "That's what I'm going for." "Oh, no, no, no," she replied. "You can't say that."

Oh, yes, yes, yes.

I was born a cranky old man. You've been warned. Keep in mind large swaths of this book are much, *much* worse for Anne.

PS re: conversation: Books, including memoirs, are generally presented as fully-formed, perfectly-polished pieces of coherent narrative. But that is not how they come about. Writing takes place within a life, with much else going. If you and I were sitting down to talk, that conversation would obviously take place within the context of our lives, our moods, and the broader world. So in these pages, I'm going to tell you at least some of the context, to let you know what is going on as I write. I'll also share some of my thought process. Really, this isn't a *book* as much as a *window* into one month of the interesting life of an uninteresting person.

Throughout the book are random photographs by me and EK Green; sorry they are reproduced in lower quality in this print version – printing in high-rez glossy color would cost ~3x more; you can get better color ebooks (with active links) for free at LosingMyReligions.net. There are travelogs, too, as the book was written during the month of May 2022, while Anne and I were traveling together for the first time in over three years. (Of course, editing went on for *many* months after the first draft was finished.) Believe it or not, being written during our travels makes the book much happier than it would have been otherwise.

PPS: This book may *seem* substantial, but you can skip some chapters – e.g., many of the animal, philosophy, Worsts, and *SportsBall!* I will note those as they come up.

The general arc of the book's narrative – the "Days" – runs as follows: 100% chance of shitty, then partly sexy, then beautiful with gusts of lust, concluding with dangerous, near-fatal shitstorms interspersed with periods of bright sun.

You will find the non-Day chapters of varying interest and usefulness.

There are three Perfect times and three Worst times.

Some names have been changed. Some have not.

Two events and one picture were determined to be too gross and embarrassing even for me. Apologies to my beta readers.

If you wonder if something is serious or not, assume I'm joking.

There are 47 (not 42) typos – catch them all!

Also, after failing to get the interest of any literary agent – yeah, I know, another old white guy <snore> – I've added links for the ebook / pdf versions. (If you don't already, *please* use **AdBlock**. Your life will be better.) When I'm reading, there are often things I don't know or would like to investigate more, so just a quick click over to Wikipedia or YouTube or Amazon. ██████████████ ████████████████████████████████ ████████████████ Obviously, though, links don't work in this print version. Sorry. Again, please see LosingMyReligions.net for the ebook.

Finally: Even as a conversation, it has been extraordinarily hard to write a memoir for *you*. Most of it was easy to write for *me* – every person, every place, every event is rich with memories, images, sounds, associations. Even the shitty Before Anne times were easy to write, as those stories have been repeated many times and I no longer associate with Young Matt.

(However, the chapters covering Plague Year 2021 and The Last Worst – Day 29 Concluded and Day 30 – were much harder for me to write than they will be for you to read.)

But for the book as a whole, the question remains:

Why would you give a shit?

I've wondered that every day I've worked on this.

On the other hand:

> If you're not telling a story
> with all the classic ingredients that hold people:
> love, war, sex, conflict, tragedy....
>
> *–Trish Hall,* Writing to Persuade

Well, for better and for worse, I've got all those for you.

Here we go.

Day 1: One Love, One Hate + Carl Sagan

Welcome to your life.
There's no turning back.

–Tears for Fears, "Everybody Wants to Rule the World"

Growing up, I had one great love and one great hate.

For as long as I can remember, I loved everything to do with airplanes and space. (You might say that would be two loves, but: aerospace.) Although I didn't get to fly until 1979 (an American Airlines 727, DTW-STL-IAH) I had visited the Smithsonian Air & Space Museum in Washington DC the previous year with my maternal grandfather. Robert had served in the Pacific during WWII, so he appreciated the naval aviation exhibit and quietly

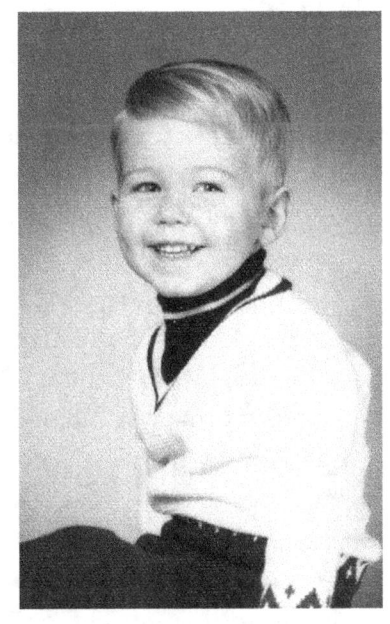

tolerated the ten-year-old's endless excited explanations on everything from the Wright Flyer to the X-15.

(This is still a problem today. Anne often walks into my office and catches me watching "plane videos" while I'm doing physical therapy. Even worse, the local Air and Space Museum is free for us the first weekend of the month, so she has *repeatedly* heard of the F-102 Delta Dagger's failure and how aerospace engineers fixed it with the F-106 Delta Dart. If you are dozing off already, imagine what it is like to be my spouse.)

Northern Ohio winters, on the other hand, I *loathed*. This made for particularly bittersweet Octobers, when the light was brilliant and pure, the leaves luminous, and the air crisp and scented with the season's first woodsmoke. But even the festivals, with their enormous grills of savory meat, cauldrons of sweet apple butter, piles of greasy fried dough ("elephant ears") and flagons of warm spiced cider couldn't completely suppress the dread of what was about to descend.

At the time, I thought it was just the temperature. I was cold from October through April. Anne and EK would later dub me "Big Frozen Feet" during our winters in Pittsburgh. (I'm *still* a baby when it comes to the climate. The first time all three of us came to visit Tucson Arizona, we snickered when my young cousin Peter put on a knit hat and heavy jacket while we were in shorts and t-shirts. Now, though, I'm just like him.)

It turns out the problem was more than the cold. It was primarily Seasonal Affective Disorder (SAD) which I wouldn't learn about until I was an adult. Eventually I found an SSRI anti-depressant that helped me avoid so many listless hours on the couch during the depths of January and February. Finding a mind medicine that worked was a difficult process, though. Years before, just after it was introduced, a doctor prescribed Prozac (for major depression, not SAD) and I didn't sleep for three days. It was one of the times I literally thought I was going to die.

Anne is the same way about grey days. After we had lived here in Tucson for a while, she came with me on a work trip. Starting in Portland and heading north, I gave a series of talks and interviews throughout the Northwest. On the morning of the third consecutive dreary day in Vancouver, she muttered, "If I don't see the sun today, someone is going to get hurt."

For us, sunshine can be even more powerful than any SSRI. When we first escaped Pittsburgh's winter gloom for Arizona's brilliance, it was the best high I'd ever experienced. It was shocking, a revelation: We didn't have to be depressed all winter long!

However, I didn't understand the physiology of this as a kid. I just felt a fear and loathing of winter's coming.

Of course, I wanted to be an aerospace engineer. My goal was to design planes or work on NASA's missions to the other planets. Carl Sagan had planted this seed with his original public television series, *Cosmos*. Every episode enthralled me. His shows and books transported me away from my wretched terrestrial experience. This may read like melodramatic nostalgia, but I was once out with a girl – a desperately-desired but exceedingly-rare occurrence – who was visiting her Ohio relatives across the street. Even then, I insisted on cutting our time short so I could get back in time to see that night's *Cosmos* episode. It was a rerun, but worth it.

I talked about Carl Sagan so much that teachers referred to him as "Uncle Carl" – "I saw Uncle Carl on Carson last night." Much like Neil deGrasse Tyson had done a few years before (and would talk about on the first episode of his 2014 version of *Cosmos*) I wrote to Uncle Carl, pleading to be allowed to visit. Unlike NdGT, I was refused. Carl did write me a very nice letter, though, telling me that if I wanted to study the planets, I should go into physics, not engineering.

Letter:

CORNELL UNIVERSITY

Center for Radiophysics and Space Research

SPACE SCIENCES BUILDING
Ithaca, New York 14853-6801

Telephone (607) 256-4971   Laboratory for Planetary Studies

9 December 1985

Mr. Matthew Ball
32 Walnut Street
Tiffin, Ohio 44883

Dear Matthew:

The enthusiasm evinced in your letter meant much to me --
especially after a long hard day of work. I'm sorry that my
schedule is so supersaturated that I am unable, at this time, to
arrange a meeting.

Let me urge you to work as hard as you can towards your professional goal, and unless you are much more comfortable in
engineering than in physics, let me urge you to major in physics as
an undergraduate. With physics you can go into any of the sciences,
and even aerospace engineering. But if you want to <u>study</u> the planets,
then the proper route in through physics.

With every good wish,

Cordially,

Carl Sagan

CS/ey

However, I wanted to actually help build something, rather than just look at data. I'm very much an engineer by nature. There is an old joke:

> A physicist and an engineer are asked to prove all odd numbers are prime. The physicist says, "One is prime, three is prime, five is prime, seven is prime, nine is not prime, eleven is prime, thirteen is prime. Nine is experimental error, all odd numbers are prime." The engineer says, "One is prime, three is prime, five is prime, seven is prime, nine is prime, eleven is prime, thirteen is prime, all odd numbers are prime."

The joke is that we engineers don't care about "proving" anything. If you ask for a proof, it means we already know it is true. Stop wasting time and let's get to work solving real problems.

(The better joke is that I need to explain the joke. Engineer humor!)

That letter from Uncle Carl hung framed on my bedroom wall until my parents sold the house. I still have it today. (The letter, not the house. Never going back there.)

Later, as an adult, I had a debate through the mail with Uncle Carl about the nature of ethics. He disagreed with me, saying sentience couldn't be the basis for ethics, because it extends down [sic] through many creatures. I wrote back that sentience's prevalence couldn't be an argument against it, especially since sentience was the only thing that made sense. Intelligence couldn't work, because it varies widely within humans, but our fundamental human rights shouldn't vary. I don't know what he thought about that, because he died soon after. (Does that mean I won by default?)

From what I've learned, it seems like Ann Druyan, his final wife and co-author on the very pro-animal *Shadows of Forgotten Ancestors*, is the one more concerned with other creatures. However, even in 1977's Pulitzer-winning *The Dragons of Eden*, Sagan had written:

> The cognitive abilities of chimpanzees force us, I think, to raise searching questions about the boundaries of the community of beings to which special ethical considerations are due, and can, I hope, help to extend our ethical perspectives downward through the taxa on Earth and upwards to extraterrestrial organisms, if they exist.

(Just FYI, you'll get no Pulitzer-length Sagan sentences like that from me in this book.)

In an effort to get to warmer winters, I spent eighth grade looking into aerospace engineering programs in better climates. I was too timid and provincial to consider moving all the way across the country to California. (During my first year of college, someone mildly asked, "Do you wanna get high?" I totally freaked out. Much more on drugs to come.) MIT was way too cold, so Georgia Tech was it. More research into Tech showed that my path to the sun would be their President's Scholarship.

From then on, I tried to curate my (horrible) high school experience to fit the President's Scholarship's criteria. This involved more than just retaking the SAT when Tech raised the minimum score required from 1350 (my first score was 1370) to 1400 (second score: 1410). I also had to show "leadership."

So I cheated.

During my first year of high school, in one of many incidents of bullying during 12 years at Catholic schools, a former "friend" pried open my locker and dumped milk over all my possessions. He was caught and then "wanted" (read: "was forced") to make amends. In order to show Georgia Tech their desired "leadership" skills, I had him get me elected to Student Council.

The locker incident precipitated what I think was my first significant mental break. I had always been anxious and high-strung: A toy aircraft carrier breaking, a painting mistake on a Pinewood Derby car, an inability to swallow pills – these and more brought on major meltdowns. When I was 14 or 15, I fell apart in the principal's office, having been busted for assisting a cheating ring in an attempt to be less despised. However, the locker incident put me in bed for an extended period, simply unable to function.

After my locker was ruined, I was given space at the end of the juniors' hall. This created an entirely new cohort of bullies. One kid ran for the President of Student Council with the slogan "Matt Ball out of our hall." That was it. Those were his signs. That was his campaign speech before the entire school.

At least I was too tall to be crammed inside that locker.

Like the teachers in grade school, the teachers in high school hated me. (Except my 12th grade art teacher. Foreshadowing!) One petty example: they didn't grant me membership in the National Honor Society until I was in my cap and gown about to give my valedictory address at graduation, and then only because my mom had gone ballistic.

Grades 1-12 suuuuucked.

My parents knew this was coming, right from the bitter beginning. Dad told me the story after I had left for college:

When I was in first grade, my folks went to the parents' night where they were given the results of our standardized tests. My mom sat beaming, holding out the sheet with all my 99th percentiles like a trophy. When the test expert got to the part of his presentation about gifted students, he noted that kids at the very top often had significant problems fitting in. He even mentioned troubles with teachers.

Goddamn was he prophetic.

As he painted this gloomy picture, mom's face slowly fell. She pulled the sheet in closer and closer and sank down lower and lower, trying to hide.

My parents did try to help. When I started high school, mom insisted that I take Biology instead of "General Science." The school had a strict policy that no first years take Biology, but as would eventually be the case with the National Honor Society, she beat them into submission.

I worked my butt off in Biology – one of only two classes that required effort until Kent State. (The other was Mechanical Drawing, which turned out to be a waste of time since engineering was moving to computers. Mech D was incredibly hard because even before I broke my neck, I could hardly control my hands. In second grade, the nun – who was shorter than me, no joke – singled me out for bad handwriting.)

At the end-of-year awards ceremony, the principal explained that the school recognized the top student in all three science classes. ("General Science" didn't count.) "But this year, we're giving out a special award to Jane...." (Jane was clearly the smartest in the class ahead of me.) I turned to the kid next to me in the bleachers and started bitching. "I'm sure I did as well as she did!" My whining continued until I heard:

"...*Matt Ball.*"

I had no idea what was going on. I looked around. There was silence and people staring at me, so I decided to walk up. (What else to do?) There, the principal handed me a medal. Some of the upperclassmen hissed at me as I walked back.

It turned out that I *had* won the Biology prize, but Jane's grade was so close to mine that they gave her an award, too.

The next year, I totally choked on a Chemistry exam. To this day, I don't know what happened. (The teacher was also flabbergasted.) Of course, I sobbed. Jane would win the Chemistry prize that year, and, after being valedictorian of the class of '85, she would go on to major in Chemistry. Coincidence?

Chemistry was the one academic award I failed to win there in Redneckistan. I won the Physics prize the next year. I even won the English prize at graduation.

This was long expected of me. At the eighth-grade awards program, Father Shiffler said, "You might as well just stay up here." (That kinda thing made me *exactly* as popular as you would think.)

Starting in sixth grade, Shiffler was the only person around who was taller than me, teachers included. In the "Can you imagine?" column of the grade-school paper, they once asked, "Can you imagine ... Matt Ball ever looking up to someone?" To this day, I wonder if they intended the double meaning, if they knew just how right they were about me in that cow-forsaken cowtown.

Random Photo #1: Moon and Half Dome, Yosemite.

A pale imitation of Ansel Adams.

Parentheticals & Grammar & Memory

"If you didn't know what it was about,
why'd you keep writing?"

"I couldn't stop."

–Wonder Boys
(the movie based on Michael Chabon's novel)

Much of my life has been spent writing and editing to official style guides and conventions. However, the bottom line shouldn't be rules or consistency. The bottom line should be communication. I want this book to be an easy, fun, and helpful read.

Well, at least two out of three.

One example:

I've never seen a good way to deal with ideas that are not directly part of the linear narrative. A footnote immediately draws your eye down, and then you have to find your place again. (Even worse on a Kindle.) Endnotes are mostly ignored; to read them in context is even more disruptive than footnotes.

For this reason, I'm leaving parentheticals in the text. There will be plenty, because that's how it goes. Recounting a life doesn't happen linearly.

You'll notice that I'm also breaking other rules. Like complete sentences. We don't always talk in complete sentences, so why must we when we write? I want this to read as though I'm talking with you, not to pass muster with The World's Best Editor.

Another example: when there is an adverb modifying an adjective – e.g., tightly-tuned, fantastically-funny, incredibly-insightful, hunkily-handsome, amazingly-alliterative – I hyphenate them, even though Anne complains. *But the words read together to modify the next word!*

Also: No need for a comma after a parenthetical – the parenthetical creates the necessary pause for the reader.

I'm not repeating the song title if it is already in the quoted lyrics. The repetition looks silly.

Microsoft Word (where I'm laying this out) doesn't have good hyphenation or tracking and kerning controls (sorry) so the text isn't fully justified. But white space is a reader's friend. Seriously – if you were to design a book from scratch, would it look like a book from hundreds of years ago? No! Let's stop doing things just because that's how they've been done before.

I'm creating this for you, not a designer or editor or professor. I want you to experience reading it as I did writing it – as me talking with you, sometimes happy, sometimes sad, sometimes pissed off.

And with digressions. Many, *many* digressions.

Finally:

The author doesn't have the energy
or, more importantly, skill,
to fib about this being anything
other than him telling you about things,
and is not a good enough liar to do it in any competently
sublimated narrative way....

–Dave Eggers, A Heartbreaking Work of Staggering Genius

Everything here is true to the best of my memory. I would testify to it under oath in court, "So help me Dog." Yet of course memory is incredibly fragile and fallible. Every time we recall a memory, we rewrite it.

I've told these stories (mostly to Anne) so many times that there is no way any of these memories is pristine. Of course, I know my memoir-writing ego wants me to be the hero, so my synaptic connections have often been reweighted to make me better than I am. However, there is no option but to tell you what I remember.

Well, except not to tell you anything. But where's the fun in that?

Yellowstone Falls and part of Yellowstone Canyon.

Day 1 Continued: Up Shit Creek

GET OUT!

–Sister Rita

Before I went to Kent State University in 1985, the only smart person I ever knew was Paul. (There are two Pauls in this book – three if you count McCartney – plus four Marys, two Brians, two Carolines, two Kens, two Aarons, two Lovetts, and many variations of "Anne.")

Paul the First was in my first-grade class of 18 kids at Saint Pius School in Toledo Ohio. He and I would go up to second grade for reading and math, making us absolutely *beloved* by the teachers and kids in both classes. After that year, the school skipped him right to third grade. (I later found out my parents wouldn't let them do that to me; at the time, however, I assumed I wasn't quite as smart as Paul.) Then his family moved away.

After I finished fifth grade in 1979, the five Balls moved 58 miles south-east to the town of Tiffin Ohio, population: 15k. Phillip, the classmate who drew my St. Pius going-away card, had to prompt our classmates: "Say something nice about Matt." Most wrote "you tall" or "your tall."

In Tiffin, I went to St. Joe's grade school, where I had Sister Rita for math. She loved math. She *especially* loved the funky math problems that were part of the annual northwest Ohio math competition. She lived for that event.

I didn't really think much about it when I first competed in seventh grade. But a few days later, while I was shooting hoops on the playground, Sister Rita came struggling across the blacktop (she wasn't the most fit person) yelling something. Turns out I had won. She was far more excited than I was.

Actually, she was more elated than I'd ever seen *anyone*. She also enjoyed the awards banquet far more than I did, given that no one from St. Joe's had ever even placed before. (In a photo from the banquet, my dad's tie is hilariously short.)

At the competition the next year, I was only interested in sneaking away with fellow trumpeter Caroline the First, my sole girlfriend between grade one and grade twelve. (The math competition was on the campus of Bowling Green State University. More foreshadowing!) She and I successfully sneaked, so I was pretty happy and ... distracted ... when it came time to take the test. On the bus ride back, Sister Rita toddled over and eagerly asked me how it had gone. (The test, not the sneaking). When I told her, "I feel like I did better last year," she deflated. But I won again.

Pluses, minuses

Among pluses and minuses recorded this week were:

PLUS — A commendation to "Kardiac Kapers"and everyone connected with the production, and also to the audiences, whose contributions boost the Tiffin Area Physician's Placement Fund.

PLUS — Matthew Ball, St. Joseph School eighth grader, ranked first over hundreds of others in two recent regional math contests — and first for the second year in a row in one of them. His school won first place in a six-county region in one of the tests.

MINUS and PLUS — Unemployment locally may be dropping, but 15.1 percent for March is still far too high.

Note: 15.1% unemployment!

Winning didn't keep me in Sister Rita's good graces, though. One time I yawned in class – I almost never slept well – and she screamed at me, "If you're bored, get out!" I looked around, truly bewildered. Yelling even more loudly than she had after I won the math competition, she bellowed, "If you're bored, get out!" Now I realized she was talking to me but was paralyzed.

"GET OUT!"

I had no idea what to do. After another moment, I stood up, left the classroom, and went to the boys' bathroom. In a few minutes, John came down to get me: "You're up shit creek, man."

While school sucked, it's not like things were awesome at home. For example: After what felt like many failures (only two, though – time is different to a kid) I finally won the Pinewood Derby – where Cub Scouts build and race little cars. Those winning wheels were modeled after a 1958 Formula 1 race car (the previous year's had been a rocket). In the victorious photo, I'm in my uniform and hat – I almost always wore a hat – holding the red-and-yellow car and first-place medal.

Back home in a celebratory mood – this was *definitely* better than winning a math competition – I was horsing around with my younger brother. We accidentally knocked a plastic bottle of Johnson's Baby Shampoo into the tub. Mom erupted, shrieking at us to GET OUT! and go to the Villa – the orphanage a half-mile away that was her go-to threat.

This time proved to be no threat, so we got out. It was dark and cold and wet. My memory is that my brother didn't have anything on his feet, so I gave him my slippers. My recollection also includes snow, but I wouldn't bet lots of money on that.

Instead of the orphanage (too scary!) we went to neighbors a few doors down, ringing their doorbell while sobbing hysterically. The neighbors called my folks, who eventually came to get us and told us to come up with our own punishment.

For spilling a bit of No More Tears shampoo.

Nothing about this post-derby incident is fictionalized or exaggerated. But this isn't a "check out how my dysfunctional family ruined me" book, so let's stop there. I'll also skip the shitty slave-labor jobs that fueled my horrible relationship with money…

…except the one when I was fifteen (so young that I could be paid less than minimum wage) in an unventilated factory where the paint and solvent fumes were terrible. Add that to growing up during Peak Lead – leaded gasoline, leaded paint – and it's amazing I can even tie my shoes.

By the way, my mom better never find out about this book. (And our kid should never read it either. No one should have to think of their parents as sexual beings. *Ewww.*) Twenty-five years ago, I was quoted in the Wall Street Journal saying my mom wasn't supportive when I stopped eating animals. (Because she *wasn't*, and the article was about how vegetarianism causes family stress.) Even though no one she knew read the Journal, she is *still* angry about that. A quarter-century later!

I'm still angry about several things (OK, more than several) but mostly about what happened last year, in July 2021. I've let most of the rest go to at least some extent, although not with forgiveness. As you'll see.

Germany foreshadowing

Day 1 Concluded:
The Tyranny of Money

Push the button.

–The Chemical Brothers

After Paul the First, I didn't meet any other smart kids my age until 1985. That's when I discovered many colleges run summer programs for kids they want to recruit. I was invited to Harvard, which provided one of my few fun non-basketball memories from Tiffin Calvert Catholic High School:

During a class change, as I walked by the principal on my way to my locker, I very casually mentioned, "Oh, I need a letter from you – I've been invited to Harvard." When I walked back, he was still stunned and could only say one word: "Harvard?"

I'm pretty sure life would have been significantly different if I hadn't turned down Harvard. But their program cost a bit of money, while I could go to Kent State for free.

This might have been the first time my unhealthy relationship with money made a very important decision for me. It wasn't because I viewed money as an end in itself. Rather, I saw money as freedom.

One thing I realized as a kid was that the true golden rule is: Those who have the gold make the rules. Even then, I didn't want to be ruled. I wanted to be free, free of all these people. Nearly everyone wants something, and – maybe intentionally, maybe subconsciously – they will use any possible leverage, including debt, to get what they want.

It might sound like I was rebellious, but in reality, I was an obedient Catholic boy, serving mass when others wouldn't – even while sick, barfing in the vestibule. Like PETA co-founder Alex Pacheco a few years before me, I thought I might want to be a priest. (The local girls seemed to think I should be celibate.) Luckily, Father Ted looked me straight in the eyes and said, "No. No, you don't."

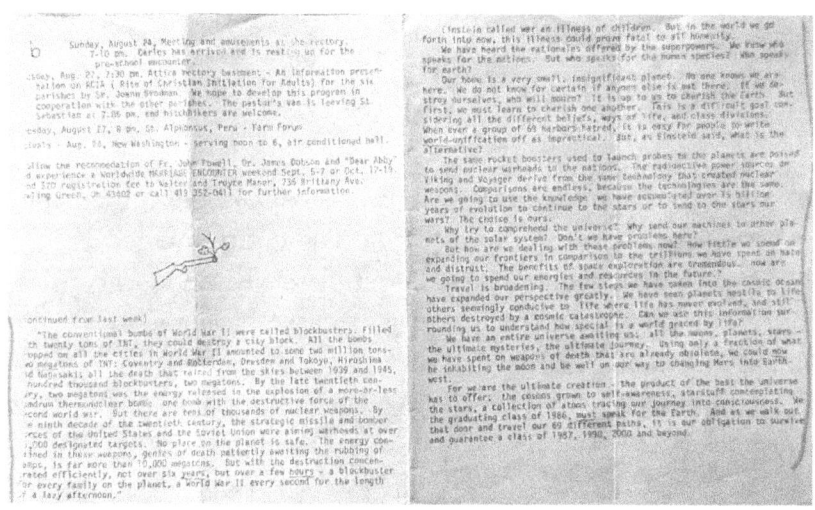

Ted was the only person who liked my valedictory speech in 1986. He reprinted it (above) in two parts in his parish's bulletin (not our parish – St. Joe's certainly wouldn't have allowed that) with a lovely introduction and a funny note at the end of the first half: "What a cliffhanger!"

If anyone else at graduation listened, it soared over their head like the Concord. One classmate, Ricky, came up to me after and said, "Bally, someday you'll have to tell me what that was about."

The school administrators were just relieved. That year, they changed the rules so that the valedictorian had to submit their speech for approval. (For those keeping score: the school would let an upperclassman mock and vilify me with campaign signs and his speech to the entire school, but I could not even mention my experiences at the school.) Everyone thought I was going to use the speech to take my vengeance and document how hellaciously I had been treated for four years.

I wanted to. I *yearned* to. For years, I had dreamt of doing so. In my head, I wrote speech after speech after speech. I visualized that moment in great detail, when I would finally have my revenge.

But they had me boxed in, and I wasn't brave enough to pull a bait-and-switch. So instead, I basically stole Chapter 13 of Uncle Carl's *Cosmos*, "Who Speaks for Earth?"

A quick Googling finds this summary:

> A climactic wrap-up where Carl Sagan summarizes both the nightmarish behavior of our species and the possible alternatives to that behavior. This episode is "a prognosis for Earth" that weighs humanity's successes and failures. The episode opens by juxtaposing the actions of respectful European traders in Alaska with those of the conquistadors, and goes from there to a wrenching description of a dream of Sagan's. In that dream, he is exploring space, and comes upon a planet as it snuffs out, only to return to find Earth snuffed as well. That leads to an impassioned discussion of nuclear weapons.

Like Uncle Carl, I spoke about the ever-present possibility of nuclear war. This threat cast a pall over my childhood and adolescence.

(In fact, my first specific memory of suicidal thoughts is tied up with nuclear war. During seventh grade, we were tasked with writing a story about the end of the world. [Nice, huh?] I wrote mine with two alternating plots. The first started with current world events followed by fictionalized events leading to DEFCON 1, with the President getting out "The Button." The second plot followed events in my life that eventually drove me to get out one of my father's guns. The last chapter was simply: "He pushed. I pulled."

I got an "A" on the assignment and totally freaked out my teacher.)

Graduation was my first, utterly nerve-wracking public speech. At one point I lost my place and almost panicked. Early on, I threw in one of Douglas Adams' jokes from *The Hitchhiker's Guide to the Galaxy*:

This planet has – or rather had – a problem, which was this: most of the people living on it were unhappy for pretty much of the time. Many solutions were suggested for this problem, but most of these were largely concerned with the movement of small green pieces of paper, which was odd because on the whole it wasn't the small green pieces of paper that were unhappy.

This joke – *a Douglas-Freaking-Adams joke* – got *zero* response. And that isn't just my recollection – I've seen the videotape.

Ever since I gave that valediction and got the hell out, Calvert has tracked me across the country, futilely sending me newsletters and pleas for money. Anne says someday she's going to write back that I left her and ran off with a priest.

More random: Saguaro cactus arm

Harold and Ed

Is God willing to prevent evil, but not able?
Then he is not omnipotent.
Is he able, but not willing?
Then he is malevolent.

–Epicurus

I sent my pal NASA Brian the book's initial working title and first chapter. He wrote back: "I hope you don't rush through growing up. You've shared so many helpful stories with me of that period and it would be nice to read the long version."

Hopefully helpful, but not "nice." Sorry.

In all the time I've been conscious, my dad has had one good friend. Harold was a fellow pharmacist who would occasionally come over to Toledo from Cleveland for a few days, where he would sleep on the pull-out sofa bed in the family room.

When Harold was there, my brother and I would hurry downstairs, jumping on to the bed to wake him up. He also delivered the rebuke I remember most from Toledo, even more than mom's "GET OUT!" I had failed to unload the dishwasher the night before, and the next morning Harold said, "I'm very disappointed in you." It burned.

Unlike dad, Harold (being hugged in this picture) was single. Like dad, he was a smoker. (You can guess where this is going.) Unfortunately, most of my memories of him are of his slow death.

One summer night in '79, I had the deep realization that Harold was going to die. I had known this in the way a smart eleven-year-old knows anything, but I hadn't internalized it until then. That evening, though, it was like peering into the abyss. If Harold was going to die, I was going to die. And that would be that. (By this point, I no longer truly believed in Christian heaven.) I sobbed and sobbed.

We moved to Tiffin at the end of that summer. That winter, we drove to Cleveland to see him, but he was now too sick for us kids to be allowed in. Driving back, we hit a terrible snowstorm on the Ohio Turnpike. My brother, mom, and I all piled into the far back of the station wagon (the one I would get five years later when I turned 16) so there was more weight over the back tires. (How crazy unsafe was that?) We eventually made it to a motel.

When we got back to Tiffin late the next morning, the sun was out, brilliant on the fresh snow. As we walked in, the phone was ringing. It was the news that "Harold is no more."

I remember weeping, but also that everything was colorless, dark, and blurry. At the funeral, I didn't feel like crying – I felt all cried out – but did when everyone else did. At some level, I thought, "This is weird." It was my first conscious experience of emotional contagion.

Sometime in the next year or so, my brother, dad, and I watched *Brian's Song*.

<spoilers>

Based on a true story, this 1971 ABC "Movie of the Week":

> recounts the life of Brian Piccolo (James Caan), a Chicago Bears football player stricken with terminal cancer after turning pro in 1965, told through his friendship with teammate Gale Sayers (Billy Dee Williams). Piccolo's and Sayers's sharply differing temperaments and racial backgrounds made them unlikely to become friends but they did, becoming the first interracial roommates in the history of the National Football League. The film chronicles the evolution of their friendship, ending with Piccolo's death in 1970.

</spoilers>

After the movie ended, dad turned to us, crying. I don't remember what he said, but we started crying, too. It was the only time I ever saw him cry – he hadn't cried when we got the "no more" news, nor at Harold's funeral. He hasn't cried in front of me since.

Anyway, back to my childhood in Toledo.

The couple my folks spent the most time with were Ed and Nancy down the street. Mom and dad would go over to play cards and drink, and one of their daughters would babysit us. My brother and I had huge crushes on Jeannie, the red-haired younger daughter who was not that much older than us. (My first girlfriend, not counting Molly, would have red hair. Coincidence?)

Ed was super-friendly, helpful, and kind. His last name ended in "-ski," but he didn't get upset when six-year-old Matt unknowingly told a Polish joke. He calmly explained why it wasn't a very nice thing to do. (I would later have a classmate, Cass, who would act like a walking Polish joke. Thanks to Ed, I never commented on it, but it was so true!)

An example of how kind Ed was: He once joined us for a family vacation on Ocean Isle. The chili I made was way too spicy, even for me. Ed, however, ate and ate, saying how great it was, sweat rolling down his bald head.

Ed's fortunes were the inverse of his kindness. For instance: in a short amount of time, both his mother and wife died. (Just like Teddy Roosevelt.) Yet Ed continued to seem good-natured through it all. His oldest daughter Cathy was severely injured in a horrific freak car accident. Ed persisted, as kind and giving as ever.

He would tell a joke: "They told me 'Cheer up! Things could be worse!' So I cheered up and things got worse."

That would be my 2014 and 2021.

SportsBall!

And father had had such hopes
For a son who would take the ropes
And fulfill all his old athletic aspirations
But apparently now there's some complications

–The Decemberists, "The Sporting Life"

I had another basketball dream last night. For every seven or so dreams I remember, one will be about basketball. You would think this wouldn't happen, since I've not actually played a game since 1985. The mind is a strange thing.

When I started this book, I didn't think I'd write about basketball, as it isn't interesting, important, or funny.

So instead: *Baseball!*

As if to karmically balance my intellectual gifts, my natural athletic abilities were less than zero, much to the chagrin of my dad and grandpa Virgil, both baseball stars. My dad pitched through college, and grandpa worked his way onto the small-time circuit with a bunch of guys who "cudda played pro ball." Into his nineties, he could still recall their names. (Not me! There are two young women with whom I was naked and intimate [not at the same time] whose names escape me entirely.)

My lack of any talent, combined with the fact that I was flopping around like a tube man, led to some awkward and painful moments for the three of us. (Dad, Virgil, and me, not me and the young women.)

I tried to play baseball, but I *suuuuuucked*. This isn't false modesty. (I'm writing a book about myself – how modest can I be?) I was just *terrible*. I sat on the bench until my one superpower was needed: a walk. Since dad had taught me to bat left-handed, just as Virgil had taught him (we're all right-handed in everything else) I would freak out the eight-to-ten-year-old pitchers, who would then not be able to get the ball over the plate. Thus, I walked even more than I struck out.

Trying to at least *look* the part, second from right.
My one friend Mike is smiling on my left.

There were only two highlights from my hundreds of horrible hours on the baseball diamond. Once – and only once – I made a catch in the outfield. Virgil would describe this for years as though I was Willie Mays in the '54 Series.

The second highlight, believe it or not, was at bat. This pitcher was able to throw good pitches, but only slowly and cautiously. I fouled off three, thinking to myself, for the first and last time ever, "I can hit this guy!" Then I rapped a shot right over the third-base bag. Surprisingly, I didn't just stand there in shock; the foul balls had prepped me to think I just might not strike out. I ran out a stand-up double. Then I stood on second for the rest of the inning, cheering encouragement to my teammates at bat: "C'mon! Even I can hit this guy!" But I was left stranded. <sniff>

No one ever looked at me and thought "Sports Star!" But I was always tall and always asked if I played basketball. I started in fifth grade while still in Toledo. I was – you guessed it – terrible. But it was actually *worse* than baseball, which was just a lot of sitting on the bench punctuated by standing stiffly at the plate until ball four or strike three. On the basketball court, I was clearly and embarrassingly the slowest in all the drills, but only because an even less athletic kid was excused from them. That pissed me off – I desperately wanted someone to finish the wind sprints behind me.

Although I would block the occasional shot – I was a head taller than some of these kids – I could only do that if I got down the court in time. I only scored twice the entire season, both in the same game. Someone threw the ball to me – usually a big mistake – at the top right of the key. I pivoted and shot ... and it went in, all net. The next time we had the ball, the exact same thing!

What the hell?

Right after that (again: not making this up) dad got to the game. He asked one of his friends in the crowd how it was going, and the other dad excitedly told him, "You should have seen it! It was amazing!"

I honestly don't remember anything about my sixth-grade season after we moved to Tiffin, except that I started to kinda like basketball. That was also when I was diagnosed with the back deformity scoliosis. (In both planes! Thanks, Intelligent Design!) I was worried that this would interfere with basketball, but even with ongoing back issues, I was about to get three memorable years.

Seventh grade is where things got good. (*SportsBall!*-wise, that is.)

That year, St. Joe's hired a new coach for seventh and eighth grade boys' basketball. Ferretti (who I always knew as "Freddy" – it was only later that I learned his last name was Ferretti) was a fat, crude asshole. He would insult one of us, then loose his uproarious, ugly laugh. His cackles would fill the gym, which was the smallest court I ever saw. (This was good, since I had less distance to plod.) He would snap naked boys with towels and flush the toilets to burn us while we were in the showers. (I avoided showering as much as I could.)

I was never once molested by a priest, even though I was around them a lot – often alone when I was the only server. I guess the priests thought of me the same way as almost every girl in Ohio. But Freddy tormented us all. In retrospect, it was *really bad!* I was used to corporal punishment – although not to the same extent as my brother – and "humor" based on insults, but Freddy took it to a new level.

Yet Freddy did know how to coach my group. We had Aaron, the All-American boy who would be varsity quarterback in high school. There was also Jim, a scrappy player who lived near me, so we practiced all the time in my driveway on our crooked hoop. We still have a picture of the two of us, crouched down against the winter wind.

Our practice paid off. I was "good" in as much as I could often get down the court in time to rebound. I could also put offensive rebounds back in. Eventually. I could sometimes shoot, miss, and get my own rebound three times before finally putting it in. So my stats – number of rebounds – went up, even if my shooting percentage went down.

But my main contribution was blocking shots, because we were a pressing team. That is, instead of running back and waiting for the other team to dribble the ball down, we would start playing defense as soon as the other team had the ball. Jim and especially Aaron were athletic and agile, often stealing the ball from the other team for a quick layup. And I could just stand back and cheer them on from under the other hoop.

(During a game we were losing in ninth grade, Aaron stole the ball toward the end of the third quarter. The coach yelled "One shot!" One minute and twenty-six seconds later, we had scored 18 unanswered points and put the game away. And I, standing alone at the other end of the court, hadn't moved a muscle.)

The press was especially effective on our tiny grade school court, where the other team had no room to maneuver around our guys. But even on bigger courts, if they broke the press, there was a gangly goofus guarding the basket, ready to block their shots without even jumping. (Which was good, because I couldn't and still can't jump. I could never dunk more than a softball, and that was only once.)

We didn't lose a single game in seventh grade (next photo), and most were not even remotely close. Yet even in the blowouts, Coach Freddy kept the starting five in. It was the same for the regular season of eighth grade, although we lost to our cross-town rivals in the finals of the playoffs, despite having beaten them twice in the regular season. That last day, though, St. Mary's Mark and Nick effectively harassed Aaron, and their Pete just shot the lights out.

But the next year, Pete, Nick, and Mark were with Aaron and me in high school, along with a new kid from Michigan, Cass. (Who really was a walking Polish joke! For example, he insisted a quarterback at the University of Michigan had won the Heisman Trophy twice. When we proved to him that this QB had never won the Heisman even once, Cass would just not believe us. Fake news!)

By this time, basketball was my life. (There was no nerd community in Tiffin – before the internet – and I had no social life.) After Boy Scout camp the summer of 1982, I went to basketball camp at the University of Toledo, where I played against a future college star (I think it was Jimmy Oliver). I wasn't even in high school yet, and this guy was being recruited by colleges. In one game, he came down with a rebound and put his elbow into my mouth. (My poor mouth – its abuse continues to this day. I'm currently wearing retainers to undo some of the latest damage [Day 29].) I went down then got back up and ran down the court. The referee stopped the game after he noticed blood all over the floor. (My front teeth had gone through my bottom lip, so it was a gusher. You can still see the scar.) (This was not the most embarrassing wound I ever suffered at a camp, but I won't tell you about *that* one.)

Mr. B, the high school's varsity basketball coach, had noticed the talent in my grade and was salivating at the prospect of actually having some success. (I didn't recognize it at the time, but Mr. B was clearly tired of being in the football coach's shadow.) Mr. B coaxed Bud, a former varsity coach, to come out of retirement to lead my ninth-grade team.

You can see our team at www.bit.ly/3w6Dzyr with future stud number fifty in the center of the back row. (Also slapping the glass as number 41 at the bottom of the page – they deliberately cropped off my feet to hide that I'm only two inches off the ground.) You can also see me on page 76, along with Caroline the First, who would be Salutatorian, in the row below. On page 81, you can see Cathy, who was on the women's varsity team. I had a crush on her, so I would often ask if she wanted to practice together. It was the closest I would get to a girl until senior year. Cathy looks a *lot* like Mary, my first college affair.

My first high school game that winter was a win but not a blowout. Our next game, home against Margaretta, was tight and hard fought. Their center was a bit shorter than me but more athletic (duh). Right at the end of the game, we were down by two when Aaron was fouled. He hit the first free throw but missed the second. I watched in despair as the rebound sailed over my outstretched fingers...

And right into Aaron's hands. He proceeded to sink the go-ahead shot with only two seconds left. Margaretta got off one last full-court shot that almost went in, but we had won.

I was exhausted. After two years of easy wins, I wondered if this was what high school basketball was going to be like.

It wasn't. The rest of the first round of games were all blowouts, some by as much as forty humiliating points.

Coach Bud was thoughtful and analytic and generous with his knowledge. We would chat frequently. For example: heading to the locker room at halftime during another blowout, I asked him what he would say in the other coach's position. He replied without hesitation: "I wouldn't ever be in that position."

He also told me that while Aaron, Pete, Nick, Cass, and I were the best athletes he could put on the floor, putting Mark in for Cass was the best *team* he could put on the floor. It took me a minute to figure out what he was saying, but after that, I saw that dynamic. I later found out that Kareem Abdul-Jabbar – the player I most revered – had said, "Five guys on the court working together can achieve more than five talented individuals who come and go as individuals."

But Bud was coaching us like a varsity team, not a ninth-grade team. To him, there was no future, just this game. He only ever played the six of us, swapping Mark and Cass, no matter the score.

When we went to Margaretta for our second meeting, they had gotten better. Their center was as tall as me now, and stronger. (More duh.) They were beating us by seven at halftime, with the crowd cheering them on and our bench silent. During halftime, the coach made adjustments for us six, and then implored the rest of the team to get into it. For some reason, they did, and cheered us on to a comeback victory. (That was the "18 points in 1:26" game.)

It didn't last. By the end of the regular season, the benched eight openly seethed. They would hurl basketballs at the six of us, and we would throw them back. I had never experienced anything like it. When we faced Margaretta in the finals of the tournament, I thought we would win. I had only lost one game in three years and that was to three of my current teammates.

The championship match was close. Even though they led the entire time, I just knew we would come back. But by now, their center was clearly taller than me. In one exchange, we went up together and I blocked his shot. He went up again and I blocked again. He went up yet again and I was called for a foul. And our bench was actively rooting against us, mocking us during time outs and at halftime.

After the game, I sobbed, along with several others. The non-starters smirked and celebrated. Mr. B came in and exhorted us to remember how we were feeling, and then commit to doing the work so we would never feel that way again.

I was elected to speak at the awards banquet, ready to tell the "eighteen points in less than ninety seconds" story. Then Coach Bud told that story right before me, adding, "It was the most amazing thing I've ever seen." I never saw Bud again.

That summer of 1983, Mr. B took four of us to a five-star basketball camp out east. At the camp, I played against Jeff Lebo, who would be a star at North Carolina, play in the NBA, and return to NC to coach. Shockingly, I was also one of the top jump-ropers in the camp – I made the finals three of five days, even more than Lebo. And that – *ta-da!* – is the most useless fact in this entire book.

Not as useless: they taught us "Practice doesn't make perfect. *Perfect* practice makes perfect." Just dinkin' around with a basketball isn't going to make you any better – you must train and do drills specific to skills you want to hone. This obviously applies to the rest of life as well.

The camp was also my first time around Black kids. (I honestly don't know if I had ever spoken to a Black person since my Kindergarten teacher during my only year in public school.) Two kids from Philadelphia took to eating with me and sometimes Aaron. They called me "The Doctor," saying it real smooth: "The Dahhhk-tahhh!" Unfortunately, it wasn't because I played like Dr. J, the best basketball player in Philly ever. It was because of all the prescription and OTC drugs I had. (I am the offspring of a pharmacist and a hypochondriac.) (Illicit drugs come later.)

An example of how sheltered we were: Mr. B drove us through South Philly – he had gone to school at Temple – which was our first experience of an inner city. Tom, who would soon shoot past me in height and become the starting Varsity center, literally cowered in the middle of the van.

JV: My last year as a starter
#33 in the back with glasses, a black eye, and a fading concussion.

The next year, Mr. B moved Aaron up to varsity, but not Pete or
Nick. (Or me, obviously.) Pete was pissed off and never played
again. Aaron had always made Nick better, but they were now
separated. Despite my daily efforts – including many humiliating
hours in the weight room – I was not improving, while everyone
else was getting stronger and taller. For the last time ever, I was
the starting Junior Varsity center, and we ended up winning only
half our games.

   The highlight was an away game at Old Fort. It was a very low
scoring game – Jim and I were pretty much the only ones who
scored for Calvert – and the game was tied at 25 with nine
seconds remaining. Someone took a shot and missed, and I got the
rebound. I went up and was fouled.

   Before I could line up for the free throws, Old Fort called
time-out to try to "ice" me – i.e., give me time to think about the
shots and freak out. As we went over to the bench, Brian ran up to
give me encouragement. I waved him off, saying, "No sweat, I got
this."

Coach Rombach, who I also really liked, very wisely chose not to talk to me at all. (This is an extremely vivid memory, as I was supercharged with adrenaline. And the outcome was in the paper the next day to verify my memory.) Instead, he looked at the other four and said, "OK, after Matt makes the shots, I want you..." and then described the press he wanted to run out the last seconds.

We ran back onto the court before a full crowd, already there for the upcoming varsity match. I stepped to the line, dribbled three times, and shot. (From camp: BEEF: Balance, Elbow [under ball], Elevation [release at the top], Follow-through.) It hit the front of the rim, the back of the rim, and then went in.

The second was nothing but net.

> In junior varsity action, Matt Ball dropped in a pair of free throws with nine second left to give Calvert a 27-25 triumph. Ball finished with eight points and Jim Ruehle added nine. Jeff Abbott tossed in 11 to pace Old Fort.

After we showered and got back into our shirts and ties, we went out to watch the varsity. Their injured mountain of a starting center (a bigshot on the football team) was sitting in the stands with the star of the girls' varsity squad. (She was easily the best basketball player in our school that year.) He called out to me and waved me over. Still grinning like the cat that caught the canary, I was sure he was going to congratulate me for winning the game under such pressure. But he only said my collar was crooked.

Coach Rombach was at least three inches taller than me and had actually played college ball. He was soft-spoken, thoughtful, and honest, like Bud. But unlike Bud, he knew he wasn't coaching a varsity team. Coach Rombach could laugh.

In one close game, I was playing well but in foul trouble. He took me out after my fourth foul. With only a few minutes left, he called me over to sit next to him. Without looking at me, he stated, "Matt, I need to put you back in. But you can't foul out. Do you understand me?" I nodded and he turned to look me dead in the eye. "Do you understand?" I firmly told him Yes.

I went in when we had the ball. After we scored (or not, I honestly don't remember) we went back down the court and I – say it with me – immediately fouled out. As I walked off, Coach just looked at me, shook his head, and laughed.

The next year, I rode the varsity pine for a losing team. Mr. B was not happy. He was a big guy, a "locker room motivation" guy. After the first half of an embarrassing game, he exhorted us in part by hollering, "I know we only use ten percent of our brain. Bally might use more, but none of you are even using five percent now!"

At the downbeat banquet, I got the academic award and never played basketball again. Mr. B was let go after that year.

(Also, it is not true that we only use ten percent of our brain. That myth needs to die.)

And that was my (organized) *SportsBall!* career. I took up tennis after I got back from Kent State and was actually not horrible. Brian and I played and beat the Wagner twins, Julie and Jenny, who went on to be state champions the next spring. But then I got mono and lost my chance to try out for the boys' team. During college, I played Guido a number of times, and he almost always won (but kindly never humiliated me).

On a family vacation once, dad took me to a golf course. We went to the driving range while waiting for our tee time. There, I proceeded to top the ball, shank the ball, and sometimes entirely whiff past the *teed-up ball*. After I hit one almost exactly sideways, dad said, "Maybe you should just walk along."

Eventually, I was not awful enough to play a quick nine (by myself) dozens of times around Pittsburgh. This included many times at Oakmont East, the public course right next to fabled Oakmont Country Club, the only place I saw Tiger Woods in person. The first hole at Oakmont East was right along Oakmont Country Club's third hole. That is where Tiger gave the 2007 U.S. Open to Angel Cabrera by airmailing the third green on Sunday. (Winning didn't help Angel; he is currently in an Argentinian jail for assaulting his ex-wife.)

(Update: Today, our neighbor was wearing a hat from that very 2007 U.S. Open. I commented on it, and he gave it to me!)

I've not played golf since we moved to Tucson, as it is quite expensive here and, more importantly, you can't just go and hack away *alone*. Also, my degenerative osteoarthritis isn't super conducive to golf. So now, in addition to Tae-Bo, I walk, hike, and sometimes jog with Anne. It is lovely.

PS: As Steve Jobs would say: "One more thing." I know this chapter is already way, way too long (sorry) but this story just occurred to me:

After my JV season ended, the varsity team didn't have a full 12 to take to the tournament. Mr. B told me I'd move up for at least the first game. But the day before, I got really sick, so Jeff took my spot. Brian and I listened to the game on the radio. It wasn't close, so Mr. B started putting in the younger guys. Then we heard: "And coming in for Tim is Matt Ball." Brian and I looked at each other, mouths agape. We then figured out they hadn't changed the program, and Jeff was wearing the jersey that had been set aside for me.

"Matt Ball" did pretty well. Better than any varsity game I actually played. Thanks Jeff!

Sunset in the desert (better bigger, but so it goes)

Three tips for you
but not my enemies
(you know who you are)

These things
That I've
Been told...

–Tears for Fears, "The Working Hour"

1. Ask people about themselves.
Only answer questions.
Rinse, repeat

Except maybe our kids, we are each our own favorite topic.

(Yeah, I know that is laughable, coming from an egomaniac expecting you to read a book about himself. Sorry.)

Aaron Ross, a selfless, dedicated, globe-trotting animal advocate (not my super-jock basketball teammate) is the best I've ever met at this. Once, I asked him a question, which he answered very briefly. Then he asked me a question. I did the same. We went back and forth like a tennis match. It was hilarious.

Very few people are truly present in a conversation. As Trish Hall notes in *Writing to Persuade*: "Sometimes people appear to be listening, but they are just trying to figure out where to jump in."

One way around this is to never respond to something said; only reply to direct questions. That way, you can focus on what the person is saying.

Corollary: Feelings matter more than facts.

In spring 2016, our then-21-year-old offspring flew to DC for interviews at the Science and Technology Policy Institute. Paul met EK for dinner and gave them this advice:

> It isn't what you *say* to an interviewer,
> it is how you make the interviewer *feel*.

This, of course, sucks, as it just perpetuates the entrenched power structure – upper-middle-class white dudes hire more of the same. But it is important to know how the game is played, especially when you're coming in as the only vegan being interviewed.

EK did get the job, which led to beating a Republican in the White House's bowling alley. (Yay!) But also meant shaking Newt Gingrich's hand. <shudder>

2. Always ask, "What is the alternative?"

Something might *seem* good – e.g., Pad See Ew – but there might be something better – green curry. (Or vice versa!) Something might *seem* bad – e.g., voting for and working for Hillary. But the alternative – millions of women losing the right to basic bodily autonomy – is far, far worse. (Yes, I'm still bitter. And Hillary is great!)

3. Things won't always be this way.

From your depth of despair to your most orgasmic high, things *will* change. I know this won't always *seem* possible, especially in the bad times. But things *do* change. No one goes through life in the same mental state.

This isn't to say that it isn't hard, often frustrating work to get out of a bad mental state. I really do understand. You'll see.

Ball

Day 2: Bullet in a Bible

Tin soldiers and Nixon's coming
This summer I hear the drumming
Four dead in Ohio

–Crosby, Stills, Nash & Young

By the time of my valediction in 1986, Father Ted probably knew I was agnostic. He had helped on that path, starting my disillusionment with the Catholic Church. I hadn't known the reason priests weren't allowed to marry. (So they had no legitimate heirs who would then have potential claims to church land.) Or why the Church originally declared male masturbation a sin. (The man contained the life [of course] the woman just incubated it, so spilling one's seed was "murder," just like Mifepristone today.)

Unfortunately, the latter stricture had been well and fully beaten into my head for seventeen years, causing me – and countless others – unnecessary suffering. But the Church's prohibition on contraception has caused so much hardship and misery that it is impossible to fathom. ("Untold numbers of women and children have died, will die and are dying right now as a direct consequence of Humanae Vitae.")

(And of course, all the child abuse. In short, the Catholic Church is a criminal enterprise. Google "NSFW Priest jokes." Example: Two priests are driving one day and get waved over at a traffic stop. A cop approaches the priests' vehicle and says to the driver, "Sorry to pull you over, Father, but we're looking for a couple of child molesters." The two priests share some private words, then the driver turns back to the cop and says: "Alright officer, we'll do it!")

Going to Kent State the summer of '85 also pushed me further down the road of freethinking. It was the first time I wasn't surrounded by fellow Catholics. It was the first time I had knowingly met a non-Christian. It was my first time around college students. And despite years of studying wars, it was the first time I really faced history.

The latter came like a thunderbolt. We were touring Kent's campus when the guide pointed out a hole in a metal sculpture. It was from May 4 1970, when the National Guard fired into the crowd of protesting students, killing four, paralyzing another, and seriously wounding many more.

This may seem silly, given that today we are aware of so many incidents of state-sponsored violence. By the 2020s, we've watched, for example, Officer Derek Chauvin slowly, almost casually take George Floyd's life while others looked on, including someone filming the murder.

But in 1985, I wasn't aware of anything like this. (Remember: small town, Catholic schools, no internet.) It was only when I saw the bullet hole that I realized agents of the state had turned military rifles on fellow citizens, mowing them down with bullets so powerful they passed right through thick metal.

This stopped me cold. I stood there, my right hand on the back of my sweating neck, staring at the hole in the sculpture even as the tour moved on.

(I am re-reading this just after Uvalde, the latest slaughter of children. This is our world now. As much as anyone, Newt Gingrich is to blame. In 1996, he released a set of words for Republicans to use against Democrats. It doesn't matter that they are false, just use them anyway! A selection: "betray, cheat, corrupt, disgrace, failure, greed, hypocrisy, incompetent, insecure." This marked the final break from politics as a competition of ideas. Because of Newt, politics fully became war. For more, please read Ezra Klein's *Why We're Polarized*.)

Other than three basketball seasons and a visit to the Air and Space Museum, my life had been pretty crappy until that point. Hated by fellow students, resented by teachers, having met my sole peer at age seven only to have him taken away a year later.

Kent State marked a turning point. I met peers; I stayed friends with Dan for years. I would never again lack for someone thoughtful and intelligent in my life. And I would try new, embarrassing-in-retrospect things which I'd rather not talk about.

Seeing the clean hole left by a bullet aimed at kids just like me –well, that broke me out of one innocent, cloistered cocoon.

The Kent State crew. Dan is third from left.
Your dashing narrator is lower right in his Carl-Sagan jacket.

Day 2 Concluded: Zero to Sixty

Sex and drugs and rock and roll
Are very good indeed

–Ian Dury

After Kent State, the new, hippie, divorced art teacher was about to break me out of another cocoon.

Although I spent much of my day taking classes at Heidelberg College (named for a very beautiful and touristy German town where Anne would soon live, pictured here) I also needed to finish a few things at Calvert. Art was one requirement, and the teacher quickly recognized me as a fellow outsider. In a move she would soon regret, she introduced me to her daughter.

Gretchen was a sophomore at the aforementioned Bowling Green State. She lived with her mom in a big farmhouse about an hour away from Tiffin, a route my Chevy Citation soon knew well. In one of those "small world" moments, her father and uncle had attended St. Francis High School in Toledo with my dad. Dad described her uncle as "the Matt Ball of the school. But this wasn't Calvert – this was Toledo's premier all-boys school." (That is: Gretchen's uncle stood out among other smarts, not just hicks.)

Up until this point, I was the quintessential loser when it came to the opposite sex. Although six foot two with luscious blond hair and sky-blue eyes, I had long been considered a freak by the girls of Tiffin. The only break in my long loserdom was an eighth-grade fling with our future salutatorian – furtive fondling and clumsy kissing in stairwells and abandoned classrooms, including at Bowling Green State. (And the bandroom, to complete the nerd cliché – although you won't ever mistake me for Wynton Marsalis, who, as shown here, I met in 1985.) But that was it, other than in first grade when Molly told me "You have sexy legs" while we watched Bugs Bunny.

Gretchen was also a smart person who had grown up trapped in the small-minded Midwest. We talked in torrents when we couldn't get somewhere with a modicum of privacy, and didn't talk much when we could. My Catholic programming was pretty quickly shoved aside by my evolutionary programming in an embarrassing first time that started and finished well before the conclusion of Side One of Wynton's *Black Codes from the Underground.* (Hey, cut me some slack – I had never even been *awake* for an orgasm before.)

She then took me from zero to sixty in one torrid season: in a field; alongside a road; in a graveyard during an ice storm; four times in four places in eight hours; before a space heater on the floor while my brother pounded on the door.

It was a life that I couldn't even have dreamt of six months before, my imagination having been stunted by Catholicism and the petty people of Podunkville.

(Not every adventure worked out, though. Gretchen once drove us to the edge of some local woods, and we scurried in until we figured we couldn't be seen. While *au natural* on the forest floor, we heard a door slam. Stopping to peek out through the trees, we saw a pickup truck behind her van – a local farmer had come over to investigate the strange vehicle. It turned out Gretchen had left her keys in the van, and Cletus took them and drove off. Oops.)

All this was to the great and ironic chagrin of my mother, who for years had prayed I would find a girlfriend. (Way to go, Jeebus!) She even went to a parish priest with worries that I was gay. (Reminder this was the mid-80's, at the start of AIDS, in conservative rural Ohio.) I was told much later that the priest was sympathetic but reassuring, telling her during another of their conversations, "Matt wants answers to questions the rest of us don't even know exist."

But in the fall of '85, there was only one thing I wanted.

Gretchen's mom also came to regret her matchmaking, commenting disapprovingly to Gretchen about how "sexually active" she was *relative to their dog.* (I am not making this up.) What to say to that other than "*Mother!*"

As if to prove neither of us had a fully-functioning prefrontal cortex, Gretchen and I also took "artistic" double-exposure fully-exposed photos. I forgot about them until Anne was going through some of my childhood stuff. Oops.

Sadly for teenage me, those few paragraphs above all the sex there will be for a while. (At least with another person – Gretchen also released my block on free soloing.) My drugs come later. Here's the rock-and-roll, with peripheral drugs:

At family dinner one night in early '86, with my brother on my left, I turned to my sister on my right and made a dig about how our brother's ears were crooked. The next thing I knew, I was on the floor with blood everywhere. With one sucker-punch, he had laid my nose onto the right side of my face.

Who's crooked now?

(Unfortunately, this was just the start for my poor nose.)

Once the swelling had gone down, the break required surgery, my first time under general anesthesia. Coming out, I had something like sleep paralysis – my mind was awake, but I couldn't move my very nauseous body. It was exceedingly disturbing. I was starting to panic when bodily control very slowly started to come around.

(This was not the first time I'd been in the hospital, just the first time I remember. I almost died from scarlet fever when I was four – score another victory for modern medicine. Scarlet fever will come up again in a future death and near-death.)

Under coercion, my brother bought me a ticket to see Simple Minds at an arena in Cleveland. (Their big hit was "Don't you forget about me," from the magnificent movie *The Breakfast Club*. If you haven't seen it, please stop reading now and watch. If you are a decade or more removed from college, please also watch *The Big Chill*.) The Call ("The Walls Came Down") opened and were surprisingly good. (Most opening acts I've seen have been terrible.)

They would later record "Let the Day Begin," the unofficial anthem for Al Gore's 2000 campaign.

Both bands were *really loud.*

Between acts, there was a strange, unfamiliar smell in the air. I asked Brian (pretty much my only friend in high school) what it might be. He laughed: "It's weed!"

Brian had a burnout older brother, so he had different experiences. Except for my frenzied few months with Gretchen, I was still pretty freaked out about anything "against the rules." For example, I didn't drink at all. (I've made up for it since.)

But others sure drank, there being nothing else to do there in Hicksville. Julie, one of our class's tennis-playing identical twins, asked me to senior prom, supposedly because her college art-student boyfriend couldn't attend. At a party after, while Julie was off playing quarters, I sat out on the porch by myself. My former basketball teammate Nick came out and said, "Bally, there's something I always wanted to do – offer you a beer." I politely declined (it was very nice of him, although he was wasted) and soon left. Julie spent the night with the Spanish exchange student.

What's Dick Got to Do with It?

I wanna get with you
Only you, *only you.*
And your sister
I think her name's Debra.

–Beck

That Beck song cracks me up *every time* I hear it. Anne sings a modified version of the last line quoted above whenever my sister comes up.

For two weeks after Gretchen made clear what she wanted, I was engaged in an epic internal struggle: Catholicism vs Genes. But after I wised-up and we had been at it like crazed rabbits for several months, I would regularly tell her, "I love you."

You're probably thinking: "You were 17. You knew nothing about love." But I *did* know everything I needed to know, at least from natural selection's point of view.

Natural selection is why you and I are here. We are each the result of an unbelievably long and unbelievably unlikely string of successful copulations. Think about it: Starting when sexual reproduction evolved two *billion* years ago, *every single one* of your ancestors was successful in creating a fertilized egg. And then each one of those fertilized eggs successfully made it to reproductive age. And each one of them successfully reproduced. Each and every one of those events was, to be a broken record, highly unlikely.

So, every one of your ancestors was good enough to beat out all the competition for that particular mate at just the right time. And then the offspring was strong and resourceful enough to be able to repeat the cycle. Everything – and I mean *everything* – about your ancestors had to be increasingly refined and relentlessly optimized for reproductive success. Otherwise, that less-than-optimized individual would have been tossed from the gene pool. If *just one* of your ancestors had taken their eye off the ball for even a *second*, someone more single-minded would have gotten in on the action. And then, sadly, someone else would be enjoying this entertaining and insightful book. (But they wouldn't be nearly as smart or good looking as you.)

Ignore billions or even millions of years of evolution. Look back just 27 generations, to the fourteenth century (where the current U.S. Supreme Court is taking us) and you have over a *hundred million* ancestors. (2^27) For those of us with European ancestry, that number is about twice the population of Europe at the time. To put it bluntly: we're all interbred if we look back far enough. This is how one in every 200 men alive today are direct descendants of Genghis Khan. Unbelievable, huh? But you can look it up. Go ahead, I'll wait.

"KHAAAAAAAAAAN!"

Khan left his legacy via methods we don't particularly admire today. (Except Supreme Court "justice" Sam Alito, given his love of marital-rape-defending Matthew Hale.) But for generations, many of our great^n-grandparents' successful couplings were not the result of the man fighting his way to alpha status and "owning" the woman. Rather, most of our recent ancestors convinced their mate to get with them – at least for those few minutes, but often for enough time to successfully raise our great$^{(n-1)}$-grandparent to reproductive age.

So the question is: How to convince someone that they gotta get with you, only you, *only you*?

According to one hypothesis, self-awareness evolved so we could understand and thus manipulate others. At some point in evolutionary history, an animal not only experienced their own thoughts and feelings, but also became cognitively aware that their allies and rivals and potential mates *also* had thoughts and feelings. They could then attempt to exploit that awareness to convince others to do what needed to be done, which was, ultimately, to get their genes to the next generation.

But if *you* let yourself be duped by that wily other, you wouldn't do so well. Thus, bullshit detectors evolved, creating an impasse.

What to do, what to do?

Let's go back a ways to take Catholicism and other recent societal norms out of the picture. Paleolithic Matt is introduced to Paleolithic Gretchen. (Dropping "Paleolithic" from here, but keep picturing us in our fine cave-dwelling attire.) By dint of being there, natural selection has left both of them adept at getting their genes to the next generation – being able to get with a mate but not be taken advantage of. Because reproduction is vastly more costly – and risky! – for the female of our species, Gretchen's and Matt's motivations and incentives differ. (Again, I'm speaking only in evolutionary terms, not moral or normative terms; this is how things are, not how they should be.) Without seventeen years of relentless anti-sex programming, Matt is motivated to use one of his trillions and trillions of sperm cells, from one of his thousands and thousands of ejaculations, to fertilize one of Gretchen's precious few eggs. (He's not consciously thinking of fertilization, of course. He's only motivated to copulate.)

On Gretchen's end, she wants to get as much from a potential mate as possible – e.g., food and shelter for a successful pregnancy as well as help raising the offspring to reproductive age. Successful parenting as a human is a real challenge, unlike back in the day when froggy Matt and froggy Gretchen could just dump their gametes in the water and then hop away. (Good luck, kids!)

Matt knows he's not the only suitor around, although he is, by far, the tallest and smartest. What can he do to convince Gretchen to get with him? He could promise things – a big hut, plentiful rabbit meat, warm pelts. But Gretchen doesn't have to believe his promises. He's not some stranger from 60 miles away. She knows his prospects – the two of them live in a relatively small band.

What can Matt do? He could assume she wants to hear professions of his undying love and devotion. But natural selection has left Gretchen with a finely-tuned bullshit detector.

There *is* a better way Matt can convince Gretchen that he truly loves her, that he will devote himself to "only you, *only you.*"

That way is for Matt *himself* to fully believe what he says.

This is why people who sneer, "He's just being led around by his dick," aren't quite right.

He's being led around by his *genes*.

This is also why, when a spouse (usually a man) leaves (usually for a younger woman with more reproductive potential) and says of his previous mate, "I loved her, but we grew apart" and/or "she changed," he truly and sincerely believes it. She did change – she approached (or hit) menopause.

This is also why, when Woody Allen runs off with one of his adopted daughters and says, "The heart wants what it wants," he means it, even while the rest of us think, "*Ewww*."

Again, this is not not *not* to say this is how things should be. It is not even to say this is how things always are. Thousands of years ago, 1985 BCE Gretchen and Matt successfully but *unknowingly* negotiated a way for their genes to get on down the line. In contrast, 1985 CE Gretchen understands reproduction and has The Pill. She now can enjoy sex in isolation of the genetic imperative to reproduce. (And yes, I know 1985 BCE is not Paleolithic.)

And 1985 Matt didn't *start* by telling Gretchen he loved her. Right from the start, everything his genes wanted was sitting right there, ready and eager. It was later that I started to feel and express my love for her. This happened when Gretchen started pulling away, once getting with her became my only goal. (She may love sex, but there are other things to life!) I wanted to keep the party going, and my genes would have me say – truly *believe* – whatever might get things back to the four-times-a-day frenzy of the month before.

Anyway, this is a rich if fraught topic. Later, I'll have a bit more to say in the "Fight the Power Part 1" and "How to be a Stud" chapters, but keep in mind that people have hang-ups and political and/or religious agendas that they bring to any discussion of anything to do with sex. This has led to some truly awful and absurd "scholarship" on human sexuality and sociology. An excellent, honest starting point for this topic (other than this book) is the previously-mentioned *Shadows of Forgotten Ancestors*.

But the best book on understanding these dynamics is Robert Wright's *The Moral Animal: Why We Are the Way We Are: The New Science of Evolutionary Psychology*. I have gifted this more than any other. When our kid hit eighth grade, I gave it to them. One evening, EK came into my office, holding the book and literally bouncing up and down with excitement: "This explains so much!"

Yes, yes it does.

PS: I met Bob Wright at Princeton with EK when the latter was in sixth grade (story to come) and Bob and I kept in touch. Two years later, I told him about our offspring's reaction to *The Moral Animal*, which he was grateful to hear.

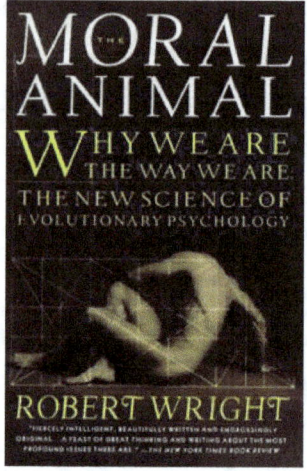

Day 3: Funeral Suit

If you're looking for sympathy,
you'll find it between shit and syphilis in the dictionary.

–David Sedaris

Gosh, I've forgotten how much I enjoy writing. For my first book, I took apart existing pieces of writing and put them into a narrative arc. Anne took later essays and speeches and created *The Accidental Activist*. So this is my first time actually creating a book-length piece from *nothing*. But the pain is pretty bad this morning. I wonder if it is correlated with typing yesterday.

You have to wonder what I would be like if I had grown up with other smart kids, like Gretchen's (absent) father and uncle. And with teachers who had qualifications beyond being a nun or a former jock who couldn't get another job. But from the time I set foot on Kent State's campus in June 1985 until Gretchen and I broke up that winter, I tried to live as much of that "with other smart kids" life as I could. It left me with mono and severe depression along with Seasonal Affective Disorder. I missed fifty days of school senior year, dropped classes at Heidelberg College, and was too sick to fly to Atlanta for my scheduled and long-awaited President's Scholarship interview.

The summer prior to Kent State, on our way to Disney World, my family stopped at Georgia Tech. There, I met the Aerospace Engineering department head. Professor Summers was friendly and enthusiastic, talking with me alone before meeting the rest of my family. He made me want the President's Scholarship even more.

So in the late winter of '86, I dragged myself to the second weekend for finalists, despite being too sick to even enjoy flying. I had a new suit just for this occasion, which I kept for decades as my "funeral suit." I don't really remember a whole lot from that trip except eating in a converted church and having a hush puppy for the first time – even better than tater tots! (Anne vehemently disagrees with me on this.)

However, I *do* remember the interview. There were two engineering professors (men, of course; I don't remember seeing any women at all) in a small, poorly-lit room. They sat together facing me across a table. Their second question was why I wanted to come to Georgia Tech. Years of yearning overcame my illness, and I spoke with great fervor about Tech for maybe a minute. When I excitedly got to my meeting Professor Summers in '84, one of the interrogators cut in: "You know he's dead, right?" The room darkened further as a pall descended; he correctly took my stunned silence as a No. "Brain cancer." Then the *coup de grâce*: "Yeah. He was my best friend."

That's when it became my funeral suit.

I honestly don't remember anything at all of the interview or trip after he said "best friend."

That cruel coin toss, that flap of a butterfly's wing, that imperceptible tweak to a chaotic system. I can't know for sure what would have happened had I drawn a different interviewer. But it is damn easy to imagine that I would never have learned about factory farms, would never have become an activist, would never have met Anne, never helped create EK. I could be living the life of Brian, an engineer at NASA who designs instruments that explore the solar system, who is husband to an atheist wife and father to a smart, high-strung child.

But fate *did* give me Professor Summer's best friend.

So a month after my trip to Atlanta, on a bright spring day, I opened the cruelly-thick and inviting envelope. My parents and I were standing in the living room where we learned, to my great sorrow but not surprise, that Georgia Tech's "Congratulations!" was for a *partial* President's Scholarship. Not the full-ride. Not the prize for which I spent four long years contorting myself.

Since my National Merit and other scholarships would cover *all* the costs of attending the University of Cincinnati, the next thing I knew, I was stepping off the elevator in UC's Calhoun Hall, looking down the hall at a young man hesitating at the door of our Summer Orientation dorm room.

(Looks like I lied about no Sagan-long sentences. Sorry. Also, I obviously don't believe in fate. Just a literary device.)

This picture *might* make sense at the very end of the next chapter.

Ball

Day 3 Concluded: Ready ... Aim ...

Enjoy the silence.

–Depeche Mode

Guido was relieved to see me walking down the hall. He had been debating whether to go to other rooms to be social, or just wait for his roommate (me) to show up. His would be my last close friendship not based on animal advocacy or *amore*. He was smart (the son of two PhDs) athletic (tennis champion in Akron, won a mixed-doubles tournament with my girlfriend a few years later) talented (good enough at the violin to be chosen for the regional youth orchestra) and funny (Moo). He had dual citizenship with Italy, where his parents had grown up and with whom he spoke fluent Italian. He was the oldest child and had, of course, been raised Catholic.

We weren't assigned the same dorm that first year, but shared apartments the following four. (Engineering at the University of Cincinnati was a five-year program, because we worked every other quarter. Those $7/hour jobs were how I was able to stay financially independent.) We shared a love of food (his mom made the best pizza I've ever had) Spenser novels (the winsome smile of a modern-day knight) and sense of humor (Moo – a long story not worth telling here but also the title of a fantastically-funny novel by Jane Smiley).

Guido was there when I met Mary, my '87-88 / '91-92 infatuation and wudda-cudda-shudda everything-but lover. When Diane, the aerospace grad student who became my partner and *de facto* but never-*quite*-official fiancée, first met Guido, she thought he and I were a couple. (Moo.) She seriously questioned me about it even after I had given her plenty of reason to know I was straight. (This pattern would repeat six years later.)

But for that first year, Guido was in a different dorm. I was back in the all-male Calhoun Hall as the result of a switch that, like Professor Summer's best friend, would alter the course of my life.

I had requested the quiet floor, as I have always had crazy trouble sleeping. (Even as a baby!) When I got my room assignment, though, they had put me on the engineering floor.

This upset me greatly – quiet was *way* more important than geekery. Phone calls got it switched to the quiet floor, which, it turned out, was requested by pretty much no one else.

Instead, the floor was populated with overflow students whose housing requests came in late. As far as I could find out, nobody had actually requested quiet but me.

Next door was Ed, another first-year aerospace student, and Jim, Ed's high school friend who was starting UC's high school remediation program. Jim was a brute of a fellow who was not, shall we say, interested in discussing Kierkegaard or listening to Shostakovich. One time I heard a series of loud noises from their room. Turned out they were hurling records (vinyl – again, this was 1986) into the cinder-block wall, covering the room with shards of Bruce Springsteen and Run-DMC.

In the spring, Jim invited me to drive him to Miami University, a lovely campus an hour away where his girlfriend Amy was also starting college. I was happy to get out of town, to get away from the city's bright lights and see the stars. (Photo at end of chapter by Kevin Drum. with permission.) Amy was on dorm door duty when we got there, so she squirreled us away in her room, even though we weren't supposed to be there unaccompanied. (Sneaky!)

Jim started working his way through the twelve-pack he brought (why he needed a driver) while I sat and read Thoreau. Eventually, he *really* needed to pee but didn't dare venture into the hall. Instead, he was refilling the now-empty beer bottles when the door opened. It was Amy's roommate. With her parents. And Jim panicked, which didn't help his aim.

Kevin Drum's picture of our home galaxy, viewed edge-on from our corner in the outskirts of an arm, far from the center.

Day 4: Losing My Religion

I wish I was a christian, knew what to believe
I could learn a lot of rules to put my mind at ease

–Rosanne Cash, "World Without Sound"

An early start today – 3:30 a.m. The pain is … sub-optimal; probably a day of extra physical therapy.

Our offspring had a hard time in eighth grade the year after we moved to Tucson. A gaggle of boys, all of whom had been in advanced classes together for years, were not pleased to see EK: "We had a good thing going until you came along."

That same year, the Social Studies teacher did a rather subversive unit on comparative religions.

At the end of the unit, in the one class I wish everyone would have in grade school, the teacher asked her students why they believed their particular religion. The kids, having been primed by studying other religions, eventually realized that their religion was what their parents taught them. It wasn't because they, at age 12, had happened upon and chosen the One True Faith.

One of the kids then piped up: "I think EK would be an atheist even if their parents weren't atheists."

(At the time, EK did not go by EK or they/them. But now that they have grown into who they really are, there's no point using their former name or identifiers.)

Gila Monsters are nicer than 8th grade boys.

That class came to mind two Wednesdays ago. I was feeling upset in the late afternoon and didn't understand why. It had been a good day, as hump day tends to be. Then, when I was trying to get myself in a meditative mood by reading Robert Wright's book *Why Buddhism Is True*, I could not focus on the words. I was just so agitated.

Thanks to Bob, I was able to step back and query my mind as to what was going on. After a minute, I realized the pain was even worse than normal. I checked my Old Man Pill Containers and saw that I had taken neither my afternoon pain medicine nor my antidepressant.

There will be more to say about the mind later on, but the punchline is simple: We are just a walking bag of chemicals.

Since we are just a bag of chemicals without control over our mind, at the whim of any external force, what could the soul be?

As mentioned, I went through twelve years of Catholic school, which was more than enough to show me Catholicism's absurdity. (I only discovered later how criminal the Church is.) Christianity itself is fully ridiculous, of course. (God sacrificed god to appease god. WTF?) Only when I really internalized that there were other religions (which took many, many years, given that I grew up surrounded only by Midwestern Catholics) did I realize that my beliefs were just a product of when and where I was born.

Uh-oh.

But I still felt that there was *something* special about me, that I wasn't simply the product of evolution.

I didn't enjoy the process of becoming an atheist *at all*. (This is why I always have deep sympathy for others' struggles.) I kept trying to grasp at any potential landing spot between where I started and where logic was leading me.

In high school, I considered becoming a member of the Bahá'í faith. To simplify in a way that is insulting, they believe an amalgam of various religions, understanding that much truth is to be found in all traditions.

But when I learned more about the origins of religions, I realized an amalgam didn't make sense either.

Of course, some good ideas *do* exist in many religions. The Jefferson Bible is a good example. Thomas Jefferson basically removed God from the New Testament, using razor and glue to create *The Life and Morals of Jesus of Nazareth*. In this telling, Jesus is a pretty good guy: love thy neighbor, help the needy, share your wealth. (Jesus really is against the rich!) Nothing about killing Jews, throwing homosexuals off rooftops, forcing women to give birth, or persecuting Trans kids.

Yet none of this means there are any gods.

Hmmm.

In the winter of '85-86, I picked up my study of Russian literature that started the previous summer at Kent State. *The Brothers Karamazov* proved a bigger lift than *Crime and Punishment*, especially reading it on my own. I took a break about halfway through *Brothers* and devoured Uncle Carl's newly-released novel, *Contact*. I don't want to give away too much, but the book's ending is very, *very* different from the movie's. (I love Jodie Foster, so I

won't say anything bad about the movie, which didn't come out until July 1997. I was tagging along with Anne at a workshop at *freezing* cold St. Olaf College in Minnesota [did I mention it was *July*] when we saw the movie on opening weekend. But seriously – Matthew McConaughey? Did anyone even *read* the book?)

OK, a *small* spoiler. The book's ending made me think that it was possible to believe in something like a god. There was *evidence*.

Bill Nye The Science Guy once debated a Christian preacher, taking questions from the audience. One of the last questions was, "What would make you change your mind?"

The preacher said, "Nothing." [Holy Shit!]

Bill said "Evidence."

That says it all. Definitely put me on the side of evidence. (Seriously. *Yeesh.*)

Sam Harris and Richard Dawkins were once asked what evidence would make them actually believe in god(s).

Note that this is a different question than "What would make you change your mind?" I could easily change my mind on evolution, if, for example, a fully-formed rabbit skeleton was found in the Silurian Period. (And if I was convinced it is not a fake, a la Piltdown Man.) The Standard Model, Dark Matter and/or Dark Energy, quantum mechanics – I could change my mind on all these theories.

But none of that would entail believing in a *god*.

Harris and Dawkins answered, "Nothing." They elaborated along the lines of Arthur C. Clarke's third law: "Any sufficiently advanced technology is indistinguishable from magic."

This was shown quite well in the *Star Trek: The Next Generation* episode "The Devil's Due." In that episode, someone with advanced technology convinces a less-technologically-advanced society that she is the Devil. Captain Picard then replicates and explains all of "the Devil's" miraculous powers, freeing society from the con.

("Who Watches the Watchers" is another great episode touching on religion. After season two, *Star Trek: The Next Generation* is an amazing series. One of Carl Sagan's billions and billions of kids wrote for the show at one point.)

We call this photo "Warp Speed."

Knowing that "any sufficiently advanced technology is indistinguishable from magic," I honestly can't imagine what would make me completely believe in any specific god. The more plausible explanation would always be sufficiently advanced technology. (Want magic? Search YouTube for Shin Lim Fool Us. That ten minutes from 2015 is just incredible!)

But if what happened in the novel *Contact* happened during my life, I would change my beliefs at least somewhat. (Update: Hervé Le Tellier's newish book *The Anomaly* presents a similar-ish scenario. Please avoid reviews or spoilers on that one!)

After I finished reading *Contact*, I was totally amped up. I remember going down to the family room, literally bouncing up and down with excitement, unable to explain to dad why I was so excited.

Of course, *Contact* is fiction.

Once I started digging into "subversive" texts – thankfully, the book banners weren't yet in Tiffin Ohio – I discovered that many of the great minds in history were atheists and freethinkers.

While reading a biography of Bertrand Russell, I watched someone go through what I was going through – losing his religion. He realized that everything going on in the brain is strictly following natural laws – the laws of physics. Since that is the case, there is no need for a soul and no need for a god. (And, importantly, no room for free will.) (I know that the question of gods is different from the question of free will, but they were entangled for me. We'll discuss free will and other aspects of the mind later.) Old Bertrand also came to The First Cause / Cosmological argument, which Carl Sagan had already dealt with for me: If we don't currently understand how the universe started, we can stop there. We don't need to invent a god, whom we can never understand at all.

Or as I like to say:
"Don't replace the unknown with the unknowable."

(Copyright 1988, Matt Ball)

Day 4 Concluded:
"Just one more."

Whatever the explanation for consciousness is,
it might always seem like a miracle.

And for what it's worth,
I think it always will seem like a miracle.

–Sam Harris, Waking Up app

Another (possible) unknowable is consciousness – subjective experience. Philosopher (but not logician) David Chalmers calls it the Hard Problem. Chalmers can imagine a world exactly like ours, except no creature has consciousness. Like computers and robots, we animals would still process data and interact with the world and each other. We would react to negative stimuli but without experiencing suffering. We would seek out calorically-dense foods without experiencing the feelings of hunger or the pleasure of feasting on frosting. We would court and mate and raise children without passion or lust or love. There is *seemingly* no reason we need to have conscious, subjective experience, the "feeling of a feeling," to use neuroscientist Antonio Damasio's term.

At this point in the process of losing my belief in god(s), I kept thinking along those lines. Why would it possibly feel like something to be alive, if not for the existence of something in addition to matter and energy? Something that made me special?

It was 1988 when I had my breakthrough. I was working for Booz, Allen, and Hamilton, living quite alone and getting through a lot of books. One was 1976's *The Origin of Consciousness in the Breakdown of the Bicameral Mind* by the psychologist Julian Jaynes. As I would find out, his book is considered a joke by many. When I tried to discuss it with a professor back at the University of Cincinnati, he scoffed and said, "Don't read that book. Read *my* book!" (His book was not useful.) But Jaynes has kind of a cult following on the edges of psychology and the study of consciousness.

I have no opinion if Jaynes was brilliant or a quack. What I found useful was a working, non-mystical theory of how consciousness might come to be. That was all I needed to move from squishy agnostic to level-six de facto atheist, to use Dawkins' scale from *The God Delusion*. Level seven is the top, where, like the mirror of Bill Nye's preacher: You are *completely sure* there are no gods. It is hard to be level seven, because there is seemingly no way to definitively prove that there are no gods. Proving a negative is hard!

On the other side, though, it also appears impossible to logically be level one: absolutely sure there *is* a god. (Not that logic ever stops anyone.) Level six seems to be where the current evidence leads.

Consciousness is a topic where a lot of wishful thinking gets puffed up with a lot of big words and passed off as "deep thought." For example, Chalmers takes his imagined consciousness-less zombie world to claim that consciousness must be an "epiphenomenon." He then jumps to believing in panpsychism, which claims that consciousness pervades the universe and is a fundamental feature of it, like gravity. (This will come up again in the later Lontermism chapter.)

However, the very first postulate in Chalmers' argument is clearly wrong. There couldn't be a zombie world exactly like ours, *because zombies wouldn't write books about zombies while trying to explain consciousness.*

Just because Chalmers' can *imagine* a consciousness-less zombie world exactly like ours doesn't make it *possible*, just like my imagining a 747 flying backwards doesn't mean the laws of aerodynamics are false.

This topic has been explored much better by people much smarter than me. Possibly the best is the book by Richard Dawkins I mentioned, *The God Delusion.* (Like *Why Buddhism Is True*

the title is meant to capture attention rather than accurately reflect the contents of the book.)

Dawkins (who is problematic in other ways) also had the pithiest summary of this entire section. On Stephen Colbert's previous show, Dawkins explained to Stephen: "You're an atheist when it comes to the Norse Gods, the Greek and Roman Gods, the Hindu Gods. You're an atheist on hundreds of gods. I'm simply an atheist on just one more."

PS: Regarding books: If you go to Amazon and search on "Atheism," you'll find dozens and dozens of books trying to attack the idea. Now think about that. If you were truly confident that there is a god and you were truly secure that you know who god is and what it wants, why would you care about attacking morons like me who don't think the way you do? You're not going to save our souls.

And in case you were wondering, I'm writing a book attacking religion because religion causes unfathomable suffering. In comparison, we Freethinkers are saints.

Also, as George Carlin put it: "I saw religion as the first big betrayal." Only one of many, Mr. Carlin.

Worse than Hitler

In the beginning the Universe was created.
This has made a lot of people very angry
and been widely regarded as a bad move.

–*Douglas Adams,* The Restaurant at the End of the Universe

You might be familiar with the Simulation Hypothesis, which says, in short, that we are likely living in a computer simulation. (If that just sounds like gibberish to you, please skip ahead.)

My argument against the Simulation Hypothesis is that anyone who ran such a simulation would be directly responsible for creating every war, genocide, and atrocity in human history. They would have directly caused unimaginable numbers of individuals – human and non-human – to be brutalized.

If someone created a simulation of our world, they would be, by unfathomable orders of magnitude, more evil than any human that has existed. Even if the creator mercifully turned off the simulation right now, they would have been the cause of every crime and every atrocity so far.

Today, we outlaw child abuse, torture, and rape. Wouldn't an even-more-advanced civilization also outlaw the creation of people who torture, rape, and abuse children? Silicone-based or carbon-based, the suffering of sentient beings is still suffering, and causing it is wrong regardless of the substrate of consciousness.

One counter-argument is that the people of the future will be so far beyond us that they won't care about the suffering of "inferior" animals in a simulation, just as we don't currently concern ourselves with the welfare of ants. But I would think this wouldn't be the case, since we incredibly-flawed human beings are (generally) expanding our moral circle, even while living in our limited, competitive, and often zero-sum world.

It seems very unlikely to me that an advanced civilization will:

1. Care about simulated lives enough to use some of their limited computing resources to create those, but
2. Not care at all that they are creating immense suffering in those simulated lives.

Consider also that instead of bringing into existence vast torture and brutality, this future computational power could instead create happy individuals.

Regardless, I'm not sure how any of this matters. Talk of simulations only serves as a harmful distraction. We have every reason to believe individuals around the world are suffering right now. (I can attest, with 100% certainty, that this is true for at least one individual.) Digital or physical, suffering is wrong, and we should do whatever we can to alleviate it.

(If there is a creator reading this right now, please turn the simulation off and use those resources to simulate more dogs. Lots more dogs. Thanks!)

Update, June 6 2022 (anniversary of D-Day):

These ideas had bounced around my head for a while and were first published on my blog on April 7 2019. I thought that this chapter and the later chapter "Biting the Philosophical Bullet" were my contributions of original thought. But Yuval Harari beat me to it in his 2018 book 21 *Lessons for the 21st Century*:

> Perhaps we are all living inside a giant computer simulation, Matrix-style. That would contradict all our national, religious and ideological stories. But our mental experiences would still be real. If it turns out that human history is an elaborate simulation run on a super-computer by rat scientists from the planet Zircon, that would be rather embarrassing for Karl Marx and the Islamic State. But these rat scientists would still have to answer for the Armenian genocide and for Auschwitz. How did they get that one past the Zircon University's ethics committee? Even if the gas chambers were just electric signals in silicon chips, the experiences of pain, fear and despair were not one iota less excruciating for that.

So say we all.

The base of Upper Yosemite Falls

Day 5: The End of Innocence

Remember when the days were long
And rolled beneath a deep blue sky
Didn't have a care in the world

–Don Henley, "The End of the Innocence"

Back to Calhoun Hall, University of Cincinnati, 1986:

It wasn't "interrupted flow" Jim or even Guido who changed my life. It was my first-year roommate Fred, an older transfer student from New York.

By this point, I was well used to being the tallest person in any room, but Fred was two inches taller and probably eighty pounds heavier.

Fred was also a vegetarian. In the previous 18 years, I'm pretty sure I had never met a vegetarian before.

Knowing no one else in our dorm, Fred, Ed, Jim, Gene (a goth-y kid on the other side of Ed and Jim) and I would eat together in the cafeteria. Fred made me his special project, ignoring the others when it came to digs like "How's your murder burger?" Since we roomed together in a tiny box, he had ample opportunity to regale me with the details of slaughterhouses and factory farms.

The latter was not a term I had heard before. Back in Tiffin, I had gone to pig roasts and sausage-making parties. My family would regularly buy half a cow at slaughter time, stuffing the bounty into a full-sized freezer in the garage. Growing up, when St. Matthew's Day (September 21) came around and I got to pick the restaurant for our family outing, I always picked a steakhouse. My paternal grandparents had a chicken coop, and I was just fine with eating their legs and wings (the chickens', not Grandma and Grandpa's).

Suffice to say, I love meat.

(Most meat, that is, but not all – growing up, Midwestern frugality put some *truly disgusting* pieces of animals on my plate.)

This isn't a "Go Vegan!" book, so I'm not going to get into the details of how animals raised for food live and die. But there are probably not many kids in college today who grew up around what can truly be called family farms. Things have changed fast. In Grandma Clara's time, about half of the people in the U.S. were involved in agriculture. Now, fewer than two percent of Americans are farmers. In 1872, a U.S. farmer fed about four other people. Today, the average farmer feeds more than 150 people!

(And one quick non-gruesome animal fact that will be important later; feel free to avert your eyes: A chicken today bears almost no resemblance to her ancestors. Chickens my grandparents raised would not even weigh a kilogram at two months. Today, the average chicken weighs well over four kilograms at two months. The rate of growth is so fast that the industry struggles with "woody breast syndrome." Sounds delish, doesn't it?)

Given my Midwestern comfort with killing and my deep love of (most) meat, Fred found me a difficult and exceedingly reluctant sell. But even in the face of my obvious attempts to tune him out, he persisted. Eventually, I accepted his logic. The Smiths were right with their album the year before, *Meat Is Murder*.</lecture> (The first song you'll hear at the link, "The

Headmaster Ritual," is the most ... bizarre collection of bouncy, happy pop music and dark, horrible lyrics.)

Let me assure you: There weren't specific vegetarian options at the cafeteria, let alone a vegan station. I lived on the cafeteria's Cap'n Crunch, cheese sandwiches, and french fries. Piles and piles of flaccid, forlorn french fries.

Not surprisingly, I wasn't particularly happy. My mom was sure I was doing permanent harm to my health. I couldn't really argue.

So after a few months, I went back to eating meat. (Didn't see that coming, did ya?)

But I was never able to completely forget what was being done to animals. I had lost the bliss and innocence of ignorance.

The next year, Guido and I shared a funky (if often cold) apartment in a big converted Victorian house. This was my first time really living on my own – paying rent, trying to minimize the phone bill, warming myself in front of an open gas oven. I was also directly responsible for my own food choices. One sunny early autumn day, I was looking in the mirror while shaving. (Before Anne, I only grew a beard in the cold months.) The thought just came to me: "How can I consider myself a good person if I continue to eat animals?" </lecture> (Really. I'm serious. I mean it this time. No more lecture.)

And then, right at that moment, and this is entirely true, the medicine cabinet started shaking, and a deafening "Bam! Bam! Bam!" filled the room.

I have never eaten (animal) meat since.

(Well, *almost* never. Damn you, Florida!)

(It turns out that our neighbor on the other side of our bathroom mirror was pounding in a nail to hang a picture. But at the time, it almost seemed like a sign, one of two in my life. The second sign, as noted by ... let's call him "Judas" ... after Anne and I got together: "That you met your soulmate is kinda an argument for god.")

PS: Watch in amazement as I unite the previous two chapters:

If we were living in a simulation,
how would we know it was a simulation? ...

My hunger is a simulation, I told myself,
but I wanted a cheeseburger.
Cheeseburgers are a simulation. Beef is a simulation.

(Actually, that was literally true.
Killing an animal for food would get you arrested.)

–*Emily St. John Mandel,* Sea of Tranquility

God, the Greatest Murderer of All Time

At school they taught me how to be
so pure in thought and word and deed.
They didn't quite succeed.

–Pet Shop Boys, "It's a sin"

Many years before Fred prodded me to stop eating animals and Phil prompted me to go to anti-fur protests, Ardyth Anderson, my maternal grandmother, brought me into activism. Unfortunately, it was on the wrong side and denied me a lot of pleasure.

(I hate reading biographies where there are a bunch of backstories about grand-parents and other relatives. I don't care about them! But this one has direct bearing on why I ended up so very broken and yet so very witty.)

Ardyth did not have a happy life. You would recognize that immediately upon meeting her. She was basically orphaned at a young age when first her father and then her mother went to an asylum. She basically had to raise her two younger brothers, against whom she held grudges unto the grave.

In some ways, she was a feminist. She played basketball when that was not acceptable. (Three-on-three half court, so the girls wouldn't "exert" themselves.) She also went to work when that was frowned upon. (Many people today don't realize how repressive things used to be. Women were only allowed to run in the Boston Marathon in 1972, when Anne was nine years old. Before she was a judge, Ruth Bader Ginsburg – also one to buck traditions and norms – did a lot to give girls and women more opportunities. It still kills me that RBG undermined so much of her legacy by staying too long and being replaced by Justice Amy Handmaid's-Tale.)

But holy chicken Ardyth was definitely anti-feminist in other ways. Unlike my paternal grandparents, she wasn't raised Catholic. Upon meeting Robert, though, she converted and became *über*-Catholic. More Catholic than the Pope. Ardyth went to Mass every day and never ate meat on *any* Friday. (Which is why I always pushed to visit her on Fridays, to get Joe-Joe's pizza, OMG. This was especially true during Lent, when mom's offering was tuna noodle casserole made with cream of mushroom soup. <blech>)

Ardyth's true mission in life, however, was to deny women legal access to abortion. Even before the cynical right-wing ploy got rolling (see postscript below) she was on board with Catholicism's crusade against bodily autonomy and reproductive freedom.

She didn't get the memo that we should be *less* like the Taliban, not *more*.

It was a pretty compelling logic to a very religious and unpopular kid who, once puberty hit, had nearly-zero luck with the opposite sex: If you wouldn't kill a newborn baby, you wouldn't kill an about-to-be-born fetus (baby!). At no point going back the previous nine months was there any change in kind that would alter the morality of killing the fetus (baby!). The only change in kind happens at fertilization; life starts at fertilization; QED, abortion is murder. And murder in *all* cases – there was no exception based on what led to fertilization (e.g., rape or incest). A baby is a baby, full stop.

I was committed to this logic for many years, although my seventeen-year-old self set it aside like a hot potato after Gretchen told me she was on The (99% effective) Pill that frenzied fall of '85. (And if The Pill had failed ... I don't even want to think about it.)

My first (barren) year of college, after I had declared my allegiance to the "abortion is murder" logic in the school newspaper, a professor mentioned that it was possible that The Pill might sometimes prevent the implantation of a blastocyst (baby!). To which no-girlfriend-Matt replied, "In that case, The Pill is murder." He shook his head sadly and said, "Well, I guess I admire your commitment to your position."

All this messed me up. I adopted a Clintonian rule of "no sex before marriage" – i.e., nothing that could risk pregnancy. I regret this more than I can tell you. Right from the start, Mary, my first girlfriend in Cincinnati (Day 6) drove me absolutely wild with lust. We ended up rolling on my floor on our first official date, naked in her king-sized bed the second. Years after we had last seen each other, we ended up in bed again shortly after she walked through the door. But because of my commitment to faulty logic, that relationship was never consummated.

Ugh.

Ardyth's influence and the Catholic Church's fucked-up views on fucking continued to plague me and my (surprisingly numerous – I wish my teenage self could have known) relationships, right up until the day Anne and I wed in the smallest possible wedding. I refused to "go all the way" with three other willing and eager young women I won't get into here. (But Mary plus those three *would* have brought me into the average range of sexual partners. Take *that*, Tiffin girls!)

Although I wouldn't fully see the flaws in my logic until after Anne and I wed (god*damn* am I slow) I reluctantly started to see some flaws in my stance while in Cincinnati – at least as law (as opposed to for myself). One person asked me what the difference was between a second-month abortion and killing a mosquito. I stammered something about "humanity" and tried to forget the question. (Fellow engineer Phil, who held the same position as I did – we met when he sought me out after reading my bitter and simplistic anti-choice piece in the school paper – was intellectually braver. Immediately upon hearing the mosquito question, he took it seriously.) But I did realize it was absurd to ban The Pill on the basis of an extremely unlikely event that involved a microscopic sphere of cells. Banning The Pill would certainly lead to many more *actual* abortions, *even if* legal abortions were banned.

Hmmm.

I also became *very* uncomfortable with the idea of forcing women to bring a pregnancy to term after rape and incest.

Hmmm.

Obviously, my logic at the time was fatally flawed. *Of course* there are morally-relevant changes in the development of a human. A blastocyst doesn't have the ability to feel pain, let alone have interests. In retrospect, hanging your entire case on the word "potential" is just pathetic – even worse than insisting the unexplained is proof of the unexplainable.

Once I realized that policy could only be dealt with logically by dealing with trade-offs, I was able to recognize that these questions were actually very complicated. When I read Peter Singer's second edition of Practical Ethics, I was well onboard with letting a woman and doctor make these complicated decisions.

It's none of my fucking business.

It was only in 2020 that I learned this jaw-dropping statistic from *New Scientist's* article, "The real reasons miscarriage exists – and why it's so misunderstood":

> For women in their early 20s, 50 per cent of pregnancies end in miscarriage; in their early 40s, it is 80 per cent.

And then reading Carl Zimmer's *Life's Edge* in 2022:

> Scientists have come up with estimates for how many pregnancies are lost naturally, and they are enormous.... All told, from conception to birth, the researchers found the figures may rise to 40 to 60 percent. If a country were to declare that life begins at conception, and that fertilized eggs have the legal rights that all persons are due, it would have to treat these losses as a medical catastrophe. Worldwide, it would mean the deaths perhaps more than 100 million human beings every year, dwarfing deaths from heart disease, cancer, and every other leading cause.

Policy questions aside, that means that if you believe in a God that has anything to do with human affairs, then God is the greatest abortionist ever. If you also believe that abortion is murder – the unnecessary taking of an innocent life – then God is, *by orders of magnitude*, the greatest murderer of all time. They created billions upon billions of what anti-choice people proclaim to be the purest, most innocent life, only to snuff it out before it had its first wish.

Also, if you truly and sincerely believe that abortion is murdering an innocent life, then a miscarriage is, at best, manslaughter. No woman should ever try to get pregnant ever again.

What really got me off abortion as "a thing" was realizing just how misogynist and nasty and downright evil many "pro-life" folk are, especially politicians who say things like "If it's a legitimate rape, the female body has ways to shut that whole thing down." I wish your mother had shut you down.

I apologize this was so sober. (And angry.) If you're interested in a deeper and more thorough examination of this and similar questions, please check out the latest edition of Peter Singer's *Practical Ethics*. (The latest version because Peter has changed his mind on some things – imagine that!)

Finally, I'd like to encourage everyone to try to recognize and overcome the damage our religions and Puritanical society has done to us. Sex can be an amazing – even transcendent – way for two (or more! or one!) consenting adults to experience great pleasure together. (Or not! Sex is not necessary for a good life.) It doesn't have to mean love, it doesn't have to mean commitment, it doesn't have to mean anything other than you want to enjoy each other for a while during a life that otherwise generally contains much frustration and suffering.

PS: I had a separate chapter expanding on the sentence, "It is none of my fucking business," but I cut it down to this:

Abortion is awesome. It isn't icky. It isn't a "necessary evil." It isn't "I personally oppose abortion, but…." It isn't something non-politicians should shy away from.

Anything that can help women have more control over their reproduction is awesome. Anything that can help make every baby a wanted baby is awesome.

Just consider what the other side is saying: They, through the powers of the state, want to control when a woman can reproduce. They *don't* want every child to be a wanted child.

We want every child to be a wanted child.

Think about it: take two pills and expel a tiny clump of cells with less sentience than a cockroach. The world is spared yet another unwanted child, and on average, poverty is reduced. The woman regains control of her life, and in the future, can bring a *wanted* and provided-for child into the world.

Furthermore, consider examples of what they want.

Some states are banning all abortions in all cases. Imagine a 10-year-old child who has been raped. It is discovered after only six weeks. Despite Republican lies, *this really happens*. It happened hardly a month after SCOTUS overturned Roe. Republicans want to force raped 10-year-olds to carry to term and give birth, rather than let her have a 10 mm clump of cells removed. *This is not a joke.* The Family Research Council has a 50-page document saying why a raped woman must carry the pregnancy to term.

Those who ask, "Well, how often does that happen?" are missing the point. (But again: it does happen! The world sucks more than you know!) This example clearly shows that there is complete asymmetry between the woman (a child, in this case) and the blastocyst.

Or consider an ectopic pregnancy. The pregnancy can't come to term – the pregnancy will *kill* the woman before viability.

But Republicans would rather *kill an actual human being* rather than let her take a safe drug to save her life. Indiana state Rep. Davisson explained: "[None] of us are guaranteed tomorrow. We must accept death as a consequence of life."

That is just completely nuts. Cuckoo-bananas.

Banning abortion isn't about protecting life.
It is about expressing hatred and exerting power.

PPS: I'm not saying that it is awesome to get an abortion. I want to live in a world where consenting adults could have sex however they want, and conceive only when they want. Given the world as it is, however, abortion is "awesome" *compared to the alternative.*

Note: I don't want to return to the pre-Dobbs era. I want everyone to be able to live a rich, full life and only bring a new person into the world when they are sure they want to *and* are physically, psychologically, and materially able to provide that child a fair start.

We're the ones pushing for every child to be wanted and be given a fair start. The other side contends that "a lot of 13-year-olds do phenomenal" as mothers. The choice is clear.

PPPS: States are now banning Methotrexate, one of the safest, least expensive and most effective treatments for roughly a dozen autoimmune conditions, from juvenile idiopathic arthritis to Crohn's disease. Millions of Americans depend on it. But it is being banned because it is also used to safely end deadly ectopic pregnancies.

PPPPS: Note the modern religious right didn't start from some moral stance. It started as a racist political ploy. From Dartmouth Professor Randall Balmer's article, "The Real Origins of the Religious Right: They'll tell you it was abortion. Sorry, the historical record's clear: It was segregation":

> [T]he abortion myth quickly collapses under historical scrutiny. In fact, it wasn't until 1979 – a full six years after Roe – that evangelical leaders, at the behest of conservative activist Paul Weyrich, seized on abortion not for moral reasons, but as a rallying-cry to deny President Jimmy Carter a second term. Why? Because the anti-abortion crusade was more palatable than the religious right's real motive: protecting segregated schools. So much for the new abolitionism.

Day 6: Adventures in Wine, Wings, and Women

You live above your dad's [five]-car garage
With your vinyl and [many-suitor] entourage.

–Barenaked Ladies, "Alternative Girlfriend"

Another 3:30 a.m. start. The pain is about average so I am again strolling in the dark, talking to my phone.

My first year of college, 1986-87, will set no records for ... anything. I did not like sleeping three feet from a giant who was hounding me to give up meat, especially since I had discovered onanism *less than a year before*. I did not like not having a girlfriend. I was still sick. I was depressed. School was ... hard? Is that what that was? I got something called a bee? Is that even a grade?

The summary event of that year: Near the end of my first quarter in the fall of '86, I was in such agony that in the middle of the night (it's always the middle of the night with me) I dragged myself to the RA's room and ended up in the hospital.

However, my *second* year of college, 1987-88, *does* set records. It was when "Bam! Bam! Bam!" happened while shaving in the converted Victorian. Guido and I listened repeatedly to Peter Gabriel's *So* and George Winston's *Autumn*. (I have a vivid memory of standing at the bottom of our outdoor access steps and hearing "Red Rain" pouring down from our windows. It was a magnificent autumn day – one of those indelible moments.) He (Guido, not Peter Gabriel) taught me about classical music, and we played tennis.

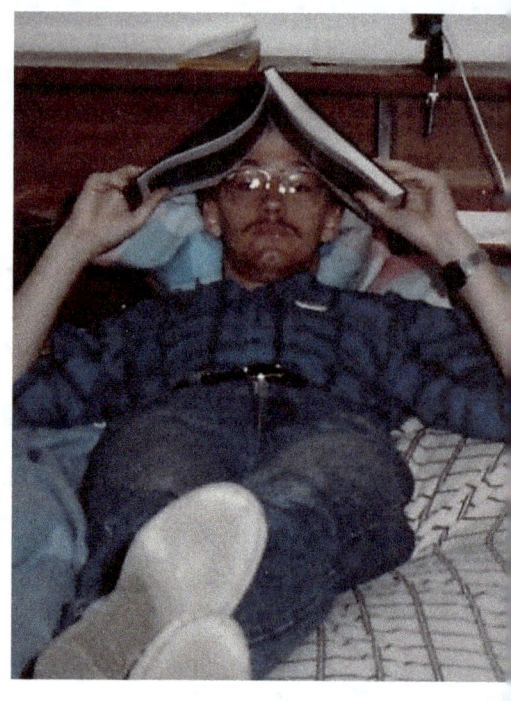

Unsuspected at the time, my queen-size bed would, in just two quarters, meet a fine female form not once, not twice, but thrice – a feat topped only by the bed I would buy in 1989.

One night while Guido was out of town, Fred came over to catch up. (And maybe gloat at his success in "converting" me?) We drank two bottles of wine with (vegetarian) pizza. It was the first time I had been pleasantly drunk, countering the other, unpleasant time I had been drunk. (Yes I had started drinking in college. Yes I am a cliché. But in my defense, I had finally discovered something other than Bud Light.)

This was also when I met Mary.

I was now the photo editor for the school yearbook, as well as a writer for the school newspaper. Guido was also a photographer for the yearbook, a new skill we were learning together.

Early in the term, he and I were part of a recruitment event for the yearbook. There, I became infatuated with Mary at first sight. As Guido and I left to photograph a basketball game, he said something like, "She seems like your type." "Oh yes," I panted. "I'm in lust."

Mary stopped by the basketball game and Guido kindly cleared out. She and I went out for calzones and then sat in my Chevy for well over an hour talking about all sorts of things.

The next time, she came over to my place and I cooked a vegetarian meal. Hers is the first first kiss I really remember. Then we ended up rolling off the couch and all around until Guido was due back. The next time, we skipped food and headed straight to her king-size bed where she taught me that there was much more to life than Tab A / Slot B.

(She lived at home and had the big house's big Master Bedroom. Her dad had a five-car garage and collected Cadillacs, one of which Mary drove.)

At Homecoming, I let her go up in the helicopter to photograph the football game from above, after which she rewarded me with a show of just how enthusiastic and insatiable and loud a woman could be.

Some days, I was *exceedingly* happy.

So it was fortunate for me that I got a job just up the road in Dayton Ohio, engineering for Booz Allen Hamilton right next to Wright-Patterson Air Force Base. It was an anticipation-filled hour down to Cincinnati to see Mary, a drive I was ever eager to make.

In addition to photography, my proficiency with math served me well. I was able to tutor her through one class, even though I was continually, desperately distracted. "You're really good at this," she said after another concept clicked. "You should be a teacher."

But that wasn't what I was going for.

One very late night, when I was driving back to my Dayton apartment, I woke up trying to turn somewhere where there was no place to turn. My conscious brain had somehow fallen asleep, but I had still driven the correct route for at least a few minutes, safely turning one street too soon for my apartment complex. I woke up only when the sensory signals did not meet what the functioning brain expected.

Zombie World!

At Booz Allen, I wasn't given any orientation or any specific class to bring me up to speed. When I arrived for my first day, I was given a few hours training on the current project, and then I was doing the exact same work as my office partner. It was pretty thrilling, despite the fact that I was earning less than a quarter what he was.

In preparation for the job, I had gotten a security clearance so I could work on classified projects. I had to sign so many documents that my signature degraded from childish into scribble. Two years later, when I submitted an invoice while working at Pratt & Whitney, the person wouldn't accept it because it didn't look like anything but a scrawl. Now, when necessary, I revert to my first-grade-style handwriting. (*Foreshadowing!*)

There was quite a bit of interesting work at Booz Allen. For one project, we worked with the Air Force to shoot portions of American F-16 fighter planes (one of the three military airplanes always swooping around Tucson) with captured Soviet anti-aircraft munitions. I could tell you more, but then I'd have to kill you.

As the home to the Museum of the Air Force, Wright-Patterson Air Force Base has a number of amazing airplanes. The star is the B-70 Valkyrie (vid, and below) an *incredible* piece of engineering. There is only one of this strange, white, cobra-like plane left in the entire world – the other one crashed along with four other planes during a photo op. (I'd say "Oops," but that's just terrible.) The cost of developing the B-70 was more than the weight of the remaining plane in gold: The whole program cost over $8 billion in today's dollars, so the plane cost over $31,500/pound, while gold is just over $22,000/pound. I still love looking at it. If I am ever forced to go back to Ohio, I hope to go back to visit.

(This is when Anne nods and smiles. "Mmm-hmm" while actually planning her next reorganization of ... something.)

Over the course of that school year, my relationship with Mary ran hot and cold, up and down. She wasn't attractive in a pinup, swimsuit magazine type way, but she was popular with many guys. We never talked about whether our relationship was exclusive because I was too afraid to ask. We didn't last long; by mid-spring 1988, our time together had sputtered out haltingly and frustratingly but not rancorously. It was probably because she was with someone else. Ignorance may or may not be *bliss*, but on good days, it was definitely better than knowing.

Photo from Georgia O'Keeffe Museum

Day 6's Wild and Crazy Ending

And in the end
the love you take

Is equal to the love
you make.

–Paul McCartney / The Beatles

But that *wasn't* quite the end.

I just happened to run into Mary on December 31 1991 – the day before I moved to Urbana Illinois. I was driving past her parents' house – they lived on a major road – when I saw her car out of the corner of my eye. I went to the door, but she wasn't there. I left my number – her mom recognized me from three years before – and Mary came over shortly thereafter. Even though we hadn't seen each other in years, we were in bed pretty quickly. (OK, fine: the famous futon first, then bed.)

When dinner time rolled around, we untangled and went out for Chinese food, where she told me about her photography and her different suitors. She seemed genuinely shocked that one of them had written her a poem. Back at the apartment, we went at it again. In my dresser was one last lonely condom from my time with Diane (*foreshadowing*) and it called to me with its siren's song. But, still smarting from Diane, I stuck to my silly "no Tab A / Slot B until marriage." (Marriage-ish, it turned out. Wedded – that'll count!) Mary came back the next morning for a last entanglement in my empty apartment before I got in my Nissan Sentra and drove West.

Still not over.

Something like three months later, Phil, who had moved to Illinois with me (which is why I was living in a two-bedroom shithole instead of an efficiency shithole) woke me up after midnight. (Phil would be my best male friend for several years after Guido graduated and left Cincy in June 1991. One of my aerospace cohort, Phil was as tall as me, raised Catholic [is everyone? Yeesh], very smart, and not very social. I was Casanova compared to most in my engineering cohort.)

Back to the middle of the night: Mary was on the phone, and Phil knew I'd want to take the call. *Yup.*

I hadn't had any contact with Mary since the morning of January 1, so I was bewildered by her call. She made chit-chat in her low-for-a-woman voice while I was cold and confused as to what was going on. After maybe five minutes, she said in the most offhand way, "Oh, and I'm getting married." One of the men she had told me about on Dec. 31 had proposed. I, um, had nothing to say to that.

Almost done:

She called *again* me something like a month after that to say one of her *other* suitors had convinced her to break off the engagement.

And *that* was the end of that wild and crazy story.

Sex Is Gross

Don't say "Fuck" anymore
'Cause "Fuck" is the worst word that you can say
We shouldn't say "Fuck"
No, we shouldn't say "Fuck," *Fuck no!*

–South Park: Bigger, Longer, Uncut, *"It's Easy, m'kay"*

Although not the biggest *South Park* fan, I have never laughed so hard at a movie. Anne laughed just watching me laugh. The humor is juvenile, but the point they are making – that many people care more about bad words (or books about having two dads, or teachers mentioning slavery) than actual violence (45,000 gun deaths in the U.S. in 2021, the regular slaughter of school children) – is at least as relevant today as then. And Matt and Trey did *Book of Mormon*, which is genuine genius.

Anne and nearly everyone I have ever met was raised Catholic. But I was raised in Ardyth-world, so it was drilled even deeper into me that sex is dirty and sinful and evil.

But really, if you just think about it on a theoretical level – which is the only way priests are *supposed* to experience sex – *they kinda have a point.*

The type of sexual intercourse I've experienced involves one person who starts with this weird fleshy tube in the middle of his body that is used to excrete waste. He has no control over it, unlike his limbs, fingers, tongue, or even eyelids. By any objective measure, the penis is *uhhh-gleeee*, both when small from shrinkage and erect from the idea of transferring gametes.

The other person starts with a hole right between the solid-waste-removal hole and the liquid-waste-removal hole. Again, no control there, either.

Tab A is inserted into Slot B, and then one person repeatedly slams into the other, hopefully trading off. (To repeat – this interfacing isn't with our heads, where we think, see, hear, and smell. Or with our hands, where we do most of our physical interaction with the world. No, this is down in Waste Management land.) If Tab A has lasted through Slot B's slammin' time, Tab A finishes up hammering into Slot B, often with great, frenzied violence.

I can attest to that. Once, I was so suddenly overcome with lust that the next thing I knew, Anne's back was being slammed into the wooden futon armrest. Part of my brain said I should care about hurting the woman I loved, but that part was *overruled*. Luckily, it was over very quickly. And all we had been doing the minute before was quietly reading!

Digression: That memory reminds me of when writer and comedian David Rakoff was on *The Daily Show with Jon Stewart*, discussing his interview with Robert Knight, director of the anti-gay right-wing (redundant) Culture and Family Institute:

> His view of what he kept calling the homosexual agenda was literally ... it's a written agenda. Things to do: Recruit children. Have sex with them. Spread AIDS.

I finally said, "You know, HIV is transmittable by good old-fashioned, red-blooded, hetero-normative, married sex." And he says, into my telephone, knowing that it's being recorded, "Yeah, but not as much. The vagina can take a lot of punishment."

Don't get me wrong! *Sex is literally fucking awesome!* I love it! Marital Relations are, without doubt, the best thing in my life. In dark times, like after my broken neck and subsequent disability, it was the only thing that made life worth living, if only for a few awkward moments every few days.

If I could go back to my younger self, I would tell him to get over Catholicism and have safe sex at *every single opportunity*. (Including masturbation. Get to it young man! You end up going blind anyway!) And I would console him that yes, sex with an *actual woman* will be possible! [OMG!] *Multiple women!* [OMG!] No, I'm not lying! (But over time, not multiple at once.)

Young Matt might not believe the soulmate part. But maybe I could convince him to not take breakups as the end of the world. No, Young Matt, relationships don't have to be "hard work." They don't have to suck a large part of the time.

And for many of us, sex is not just awesome, but also an integral part of existence. For men like me, it is *the* central part of existence for many years. The Catholic Church has done great evil by teaching untold millions that our inherent genetic programming is dirty and shameful and damnable. (Imagine teaching children that eating is evil.) (Of course, the Church has done far more evil by forbidding contraception. *Fuckers.*)

Yeah, I get it – the Catholic Church and others have made many of us very uncomfortable talking about sex. I was never one of those locker-room guys bragging about their supposed conquests. (OK, that was mostly because I had nothing to say. But even after I did the Slot B Slam, I only told one person and only a week later.)

But for most of us, sex is a thing, often *the* thing. (And not just Tab A / Slot B – there's *a whole universe* of possible ecstasy that natural selection has left us able to explore.) It may technically be gross if you analyze it, but it is *not* dirty, evil, or wrong. It is *not* embarrassing. It should *not* be denied. It should *not* be suppressed. It should be celebrated!

There would be far less anxiety in the world, and *much* more joy, if we talked about sex more openly, honestly, and respectfully, without shame, without giggles, without machismo. Our questions, concerns, fears, failings, as well as new discoveries, positions, and locations. (Desks and counters and hillsides and forests and graveyards at night. Get a good chair! Pools are as close as most of us will get to zero-g.) For those of us who are sexual beings and willing to get over our cultural baggage, sex can and should be *fucking fantastic*.

He said some things are really best left unspoken
But I prefer it all to be out in the open
Sexuality, don't threaten me with misery
Sexuality, we can be what we want to be

–Billy Bragg

"Don't Threaten Us"

There are times when you get suckered in
by drugs and alcohol and sex with women, m'kay…

–South Park: Bigger, Longer, Uncut, *"It's Easy, m'kay"*

I can't leave that topic without this exchange:

Actual elected United States Representative Marjorie Taylor Greene, reading from her script: "They just want you to think that all of a sudden the entire population is steadily turning gay or turning trans. Just generation, generation … probably in about four or five generations no-one will be straight any more."

Jon Lovett, former Hillary and Obama speechwriter, reacting on Pod Save America: "Marge, Marge, don't threaten us with a good time."

PS: Bonus Jon Lovett: "I wouldn't wish being a woman on my worst enemy. My God, the idea of dating a straight person. I don't know how any of you do it."

PPS: I first heard the term *SportsBall!* from Lovett, to indicate his lack of knowledge about and interest in sports.

Cologne (Köln) Germany

Day 7: The Bullet Is Fired

I said: "Lady,
step inside my Hyundai."

–Beck, "Debra"

My near-marriage experience started at the very end of spring term 1988, right before I went back to work at Booz Allen for the summer.

Quick interlude: Early that spring, I had a relationship with a senior who had never been in a real relationship before. (My time with her overlapped with an unexpected "darkroom session" with Mary, the only time anything non-monogamous has happened to me.) I don't even remember this senior's name. She was cute and smart, shy and insecure. I once left a rose on her windshield (Guido and I did stuff like that all the time) and she said it was the nicest thing anyone had ever done for her. How sad is that? I don't think she wanted to be a virgin any longer – a desire I would almost but not *completely* fulfill <sigh> – but her mom wanted her to stay her little girl. For graduation, knowing she and I would be off together after the party, her mom bought her a jumpsuit. Which only slowed us down a bit. Sorry mom.

Re: names: It isn't her, it's me. I'm truly terrible with names. It is like face blindness, but for names. I'm sorry – please don't take it personally.

I might not remember her name, but I remember her car: A super-cool Honda Prelude, which she sadly totaled while we were dating. She wasn't hurt, just shaken up. I comforted her but was upset about the car.

But back to the story at hand. I was in the computer lab and the young woman next to me leaned over to ask for help. In my memory, Diane subtly pushed up against me, but when we talked about it a year later, she denied that she was coming on to me.

Yeah, sure, whatever.

I probably knew about a hundred engineering students in some way or another, and *maybe* three of them were women. I hadn't seen Diane before. She had a degree in math and had tried teaching high school, but it was severely stressful and took a real toll on her mind and body. She left after a year, having applied to and been accepted by UC's aerospace graduate program.

When she was finished in the computer lab, I walked her out and set up a date. For that, I went over to her parents' house (I'm just realizing that everyone I had dated to this point lived at home – Gretchen, Mary, Nameless 1, and Diane) to watch a movie, which we … didn't watch. Next I had her over to my place when Guido was out, so only the neighbors had to hear us. (Sorry.) We were on our way.

We had problems from the beginning, and more as time went along. At first she thought I was too young. (She was three years older than me. *Pshaw.*) This came up several times early on, including one long conversation in my car in the rain. She said that she was close to needing to settle down and get married, while I was just getting started. I don't know what convinced her otherwise. Probably my general study-ness. Especially relative to our classmates. Score one for relativity.

I was also in my prudish phase where I told her that I wouldn't risk pregnancy unless we were prepared to deal with it. This was a serious point of contention for about a year of our three together.

What led me to get over myself was Ardyth dying. (I know this sounds like a ham-handed plot twist, but I swear I'm not making this up.) Diane was visiting me – after Booz Allen, I worked at Pratt & Whitney's Florida lab – when Grandma Anderson died after a long, horrible battle with cancer.

God is such a bastard.

I flew to Ohio for the funeral, leaving Diane in my West Palm Beach apartment to get hit on at the pool, including by a doctor. While in Ohio, I went to the family planning section of the pharmacy for supplies. When I got back to Florida, I was all in, much to Diane's delight. After that, we assumed we would get married. We even took a pseudo-honeymoon in the Florida Keys after my first night back.

Falkenhaus, Würzburg, Germany

Day 7 Continued:
"We're here, we're queer, we don't like the government"

Roam, if you want to.

–The B-52s

After joining the Animal Rights Community of Greater Cincinnati in late 1988, Phil and I went to various protests. Mike, an egomaniac, would direct the rest of us with theatrical sighs to show how far beneath him we were. "Do me a favor...."

That is where we met Judas, a recent college grad living, of course, at home. Phil, Judas, and I figured one or two biggish protests (~ten people) weren't going to have any impact on people wearing fur. We decided to be at every cultural event that winter, two of us holding an anti-fur banner and the third handing out anti-fur fliers. If people *knew* we were going to be there, they might be less inclined to wear fur. (Our thinking was clearly not utilitarian – no cost/benefit calculations, just action.)

It was cold. Always cold. We would listen to the B-52s' "Roam" before every protest. It took me a bit to realize Fred Schneider (another vegetarian Fred!) doesn't sing at all on that track. (I'm listening to it now, much softer, on a cool but not cold morning. When it finishes, I'll go back to listening to the early birds.) (Update while editing: The B-52s are retiring. <sniff>)

Not a B-52 – a B-36.

In January 1991, the three of us went to DC to be part of the first Iraq war protest. It was, of course, freezing. After walking around the periphery of the crowd, Judas joined the anarchists, his bright knit cap a lantern amidst a sea of bouncing black. All their chants were great, but the best is this chapter's title. (Anne and I still use it in various contexts, e.g., "I'm here, not queer, and need more beer." That was funnier before Brett Kavanaugh.) Phil and I stayed within sight until the roiling, angry mob started picking up debris from a construction site to hurl at government buildings. Then we bid the anarchists *adieu*.

I don't remember much else except that Phil and I ate expensive pasta and sauce in the beautiful Old Post Office building. Back in Cincy, Diane was waiting in my apartment. I cranked the radiators full blast, but still came down with a horrible cold.

Oh – and we had zero impact on the war. So it goes.

The previous June, Diane and I had gone to DC for 1990's big March for Animals. We stayed with her cousin, who horrified me when we were talking about dinner. Diane expressed concern about the cost, and he said, "Just put it on your card." When we protested that we would have to pay for it next month, he exclaimed, "Just don't pay it!"

An estimated twenty-five thousand people marched, by far the largest animal advocacy event I've ever been a part of. I would table at the next national event (where Uncle Carl was scheduled to give a keynote but was too sick to attend).

I would be a regular speaker at subsequent conferences. My schtick: "I hear everyone saying, 'Oh, it's so great to see you!' But while I love you all, I don't want to see you. At least not here. Seeing you here means we have not been successful. Let's put this conference out of business."

I would speak to the entire assembled conference several times, including in 2004 when I accepted induction to their self-congratulatory "Hall of Fame" on behalf of ... let's call him Benedict. And again when Judas and I were inducted the next year. That time, in front of hundreds of people, I almost broke down when crediting Anne, who was, as always, unseen in the back.

Then, for the crime of quoting a celebrity, I would be excommunicated and banned from this impotent, insecure, and incestuous club. So it goes.

Ball

Day 7 Continued:
Inevitably, the cops came.

But we were never being boring.
–Pet Shop Boys

In 1990, we used the last of Phil's National Merit Scholarship money to print a one-page booklet called "Vegetarianism." Phil's National Merit money came from Procter & Gamble (P&G) the local Cincinnati behemoth we were targeting for their animal testing.

We had tried to get media attention for our campaign, holding protests with ever-sillier stunts. But P&G's advertising kept the local media afloat, so the press stayed silent on our efforts. We had to do something more.

That was why, in spring 1991, Phil, Judas, the egomaniac, an anarchist, and I were trying to get into P&G's shareholder meeting. (Actual shareholders had given us proxies, so we did have a legal right to be there.) We got through one set of doors, but were stopped in the vestibule before the next. There, we sat down, pulled out our banner and signs, and waited.

Inevitably, the cops came.

They took us away. We didn't resist. We didn't go limp. We just walked out. The cop who was handcuffing me asked, "Do you have any weapons?" I replied, "I have an umbrella and it is spring loaded."

We were carted off to jail and sat in a clean cell. Unbeknownst to us, we *had* been successful in getting media attention. A national group was claiming us as their own. Jayne, who hadn't been arrested, talked to reporters as though she had been.

(Jayne – *who had watched me being arrested protesting animal testing* – would later go on a jihad trying to have me excommunicated from the animal advocacy movement for being "pro-vivisection." Why? I had written an essay questioning the allocation of animal advocacy attention and resources, given that farmed animals are more than 95% of the animals abused in the United States. She was not the first to want me out of their church, and she was not the last.)

Despite my jocularity with the cop, I was nervous, as was Phil. We still had to graduate in a few months. Eventually, we were bailed out, after which we walked to the nearby Subway restaurant. There, my first meal as a free man consisted of bread, iceberg lettuce, pickles, and mustard. (Having picked and cleaned thousands on Virgil's truck farm, I just don't like tomatoes.)

Getting back to campus that evening, Phil and I went to the environmental club's meeting, already in progress. We opened the door to darkness. Then the lights came on and the group broke out in applause – they had been watching the local news coverage of our arrest. In my memory, it was a standing ovation, but I realize I'm biased. (I'm actually choking up a bit remembering this.) What I am sure of is that there was an overwhelming outbreak of approval that was shocking and very touching.

Counterpoint! Our aerospace cohort was appalled, especially with Phil, who had been one of theirs. Two months later, when Phil was slacking off on a project in our final quarter, Ken berated him: "I understand *Matt.* He only wants to have fun and … uh …

quote Thoreau."

That's me! Mr. Funtime!

Diane spent the night after the arrest. She was ... hard to read. In
retrospect, this was just another moment where she and I had
grown apart.

The next day at the courthouse, I was waiting in my funeral
suit. Then I saw this strange apparition moving across the
courtyard. It was ... hmmm. Ever since, I've tried and failed to
describe this with words. Like an oversized child had raided his
parents' and siblings' closets? A teenager had picked through the
discards of a second-hand store? A scarecrow had come to life?

It was the anarchist. He had begged and borrowed whatever
shoes, pants, shirt, tie, and jacket his collective could find. I know
you're not laughing, but it was absolutely hysterical to see.

Phil and I pleaded "No contest." The national group's lawyer
explained our situation, to which the judge replied, "It sounds like
you were in the right here." (We *had* been unlawfully prohibited
from attending a public meeting.) "Are you sure you want to plead
'no contest'?" We did, and he fined us one dollar. And that was my
great adventure in civil disobedience. Gandhi-esque, no?

Oh, and we had no impact on P&G. So it goes.

Another picture that would be better bigger

Day 7 Concluded:
The Bullet Is Dodged

She captured both rock and bird
Tied one to the leg of the other
Kept them as prisoner
Till they knew who was master
Then she threw them to the sky
Bird with unbarred wings disappeared
Rock with weighted heart returned
And rock became her anchor
And bird became her dream

–Cowboy Junkies

No birds were harmed in the production of this chapter. And sorry for the gun metaphor.

At Booz Allen, I worked with a fascinating older guy. He wasn't an engineer, had a PhD, and was almost a caricature of the Absent-Minded Professor. One time, Diane and I were hanging out at his place – he had the best stereo system I've ever encountered – and he played Cowboy Junkies' *The Caution Horses*. Diane commented on liking the album. Sometime later, Cowboy Junkies were coming to Cincinnati, so I got tickets. I just told Diane I had a surprise, so she didn't know until she saw the marquee. She didn't remember anything about hearing or liking them, and she didn't enjoy the concert. Sorry.

Hiccups aside, we now had our plans – when asked, we would confirm we were going to get married. Yet Diane and I had some very different ideas.

For example, we argued about an engagement ring. I asked what was wrong with a man-made diamond, since they're exactly the same. But she wouldn't have it. (Phil rightly mocked the very idea of an engagement ring. Later, Anne agreed with Phil.)

I thought it was offensive – *viscerally offensive* – to have a father "give away" his daughter. *How does this not perpetuate the idea that a woman is property?* Diane wanted to take my name, which again is symbolic of a property exchange. (We couldn't hyphenate, trust me.) She wanted a big wedding, which I thought was ridiculous when we were utterly broke; she was at home and I was living in a slumlord's basement where Guido had a waterbed.

(These years – ~1987-93 – were probably the top of my intellectual abilities. I always had two tracks running in consciousness; at random times, Guido, Phil, or Diane would quiz me about what the two tracks were thinking. Externally-prompted mindfulness! I could work with music on; I can't now – this book is being written almost entirely in silence.)

Diane also wanted kids, full stop. I was leery. *Very* leery. I asked many questions, including things like "Why mess with a good thing?" I noted that we were just being driven by our evolutionary programming (yes, I *was* that romantic, I'll wait while you swoon) but we didn't *have to give in*. (More on this later.)

The kids thing was probably enough to doom us.

Yet I kept with it. What I had learned growing up was that marriage mostly sucked but it was what you did. (Just as I assumed that all kids grew to hate their parents and rebel.

Remember: I was Peak Lead. Also: My parents *definitely* should not have married, nor my siblings or I been born.)

And, of course, sex. I would put up with a lot for that.

There is one night that stands out vividly. We had fought – about what, I don't remember – and she dropped me off at the (awesome) two-bedroom apartment Guido and I shared for the last two years of college. In the U-shaped courtyard, I looked up at the sky and internally screamed, "I can't marry her!"

Don't get me wrong. I truly loved Diane, far deeper and more completely than anyone prior. She was great: smart, mathy, funny, goofy but serious when needed. (A trait I lack; Anne often has to say, "Can you be serious for just a *minute?*" No, no I can't.) Diane came from a background very similar to mine. She was also a former Catholic and was a near-vegetarian when I met her. She stopped eating meat entirely, and then dairy and eggs as I did.

In good times, we seemed like the perfect couple, especially to all our male engineering colleagues. Sometimes even to ourselves. After Ardyth's death (both physical and metaphorical) we would hand-write loads of love letters when apart. Diane was living with her sister when I was working at Pratt & Whitney, and one week I had sent her a letter a day. In her first letter the next week, she wrote, "Chrissie [her sister] said, 'He must really love you.' 'Oh yes, yes he does.' But not as much as I love you!"

Driving back to Diane, I got a ticket (in a *Chevy Citation*) from a Tennessee cop. After, I was speeding *again*. The cop beeped his siren at me. I slowed down a bit, but my genes were driving.

The straw that eventually broke the proverbial camel's back was that Diane felt she didn't fit in with Phil and the animal advocacy friends I made during that time. *Especially* Judas. After I graduated and had no plans (I didn't hear about the Department of Energy Global Change Fellowship until later) I spent more and more time doing advocacy.

Diane and I would fight, then make up. Multiple times, we had crazed, frantic, animalistic makeup sessions with tears still on our faces. This is what I thought relationships were, that they couldn't be different. Hell, fifty percent of couples don't even stay married. "It is what it is."

The key moment that saved us from probable divorce (probably with kids) was when Guido was leaving town following graduation. I asked Diane if she wanted to move in with me. (By this time, she had moved to Cincinnati in a place two blocks east.) She said "no." (We were in a trough at the time.) So I asked Phil if he wanted the Guido's room and he agreed, moving out of his parents' house. A week later, Diane changed her mind: it *was* time for us to live together. But that ship had sailed, thanks be to the FSM (Flying Spaghetti Monster, for those of you who aren't yet enlightened pastafarians.)

Touched by His Noodly Appendage

In the fall of 1991, after about three-and-a-half years together, things completely collapsed. I went to Iowa to visit Judas, who was living with an undergrad back at his alma mater. When I got back, I put roses outside Diane's apartment door. The next morning they were still there. I knew she was with this guy in her lab who had pined for her for years. We had talked about him several

times. Once, she said, "He'd be a great friend if he was a woman."
"Or gay," I replied.

Later in the day I confronted her. She denied vehemently. I
kept at it. Sobbing, she confessed. Five minutes later, we
maniacally made up, tears still on our faces. The next day, we sat
in her car and she insisted it couldn't work. "I'll never be accepted
by your circle." I would have been willing to drive off with her
right then and start over.

Ah, the power of genes.

I planned a romantic night out, going to a restaurant we had
visited early in our time together. We dressed up – she wore a
skirt and I wore a tie – and I drove. It wasn't good. We went back
to my place and went right to bed. (Despite everything else, our
animalistic attraction was unabated.) After finishing, she climbed
off, got dressed, and left.

And that was that.

I fell apart.

I literally went to pieces. (One of the official definitions of
"literally" is now "figuratively.") I saw the shrink who put me on
Prozac, which made me worse. (If it wasn't a lifetime ago, this
would have been one of the Worsts.) I thought I was going to die.
Literally. Not figuratively.

I was sure – *absolutely positive* – I would never meet another
woman so similar to me. Judas told me, in his blunt and often
crude way: "I promise you, your balls will ache again."

He was right. I was wrong.

During all this, I got the Global Change Fellowship from the
Department of Energy – full tuition and fourteen hundred dollars
a month. An amazing bounty – more than twice what I had been
living on since graduation, being paid under the table to use toxic

solvent to strip paint in a house in Over the Rhine (not the band) while listening to Pet Shop Boys on repeat:

> I bought you drinks, I brought you flowers
> I read you books and talked for hours
> Every day, so many drinks
> Such pretty flowers, so tell me
> What have I, what have I,
> What have I done to deserve this?

But I wasn't in any shape to move. I deferred until spring '92 and tried to pull myself together. I found a two-bedroom apartment in Urbana (a shithole, but not as bad as the waterbed basement) that would take cats. Phil (seen here – aren't we so tough?) wanted to come along, to get out of Cincinnati for the first time in his life, to see what life was like without his parents and their lifetime of expectations. He was bringing his rescued cat, TS (for TS Eliot).

Then the day before we left, I ran into Mary and we had our brief, bizarre, intense fling. Driving west, I had a *different* woman on my mind, and in a completely different way! It was wonderful. It was the perfect break.

Then I didn't see the sun again for thirteen long January days.

OK, not so perfect.

Phil and I joined Students for Animal Rights and became enamored with the same undergrad. She chose Phil – another bullet dodged – who moved in with her. (He would ultimately marry the founder of Pangea: The Vegan Store in the most elaborate wedding I've ever attended. At the conclusion of his best-man toast, Dolf said, "To Phil, who will clean up the world before he cleans up his house." It's funny 'cuz it's true.)

I then had a fun and rejuvenating fling – that ended on good terms! – with Nameless 2, a 20-year-old undergrad. (That was the only time I was really with a younger woman; Gretchen, my first "older woman," was the only teenager.)

The stage was set.

Day 8: Soulmate.
Literally. Not Figuratively.

We knew a love like ours would always save the day
And that we'd always be ok
Tell me everything I want to hear
Like that was your favorite year

–The Chicks (formerly The Dixie Chicks)

Here we go!

Literally! We're about to embark on our first trip together in over three years. Almost *exactly* two years later, we're doing the European expedition we had planned for May 2020, with my hyper-planning started in October 2019.

Back to our story:

In the summer of 1992, I went to the Seattle area for a week, including Mt. Rainier and whale watching around the San Juan Islands. (Orca family of three below – *foreshadowing!*)

Little did I know that Anne Green, a PhD candidate in Germanic Languages and Literatures at the University of Illinois, was also in Seattle. That summer, she gave up dairy coffee creamer, the last animal product she consumed. I like to think it was the influence of my karmic aura.

When she got back to Urbana (where she shared a *nice* apartment with a guy who wanted to be her boyfriend but … eh, no thanks) fate intervened yet again.

Anne called the Student Union and asked for the contact info for the campus environmental group. Nothing was on file. She asked about the vegetarian group. Same answer. With resignation and a little trepidation, she asked for the contact info for her last choice, the animal rights group, and her destiny was sealed.

Obviously I'm joking about destiny and karmic aura. But it amazes me at all the tiny things that could have happened that would have kept us apart. Judas's comment that my meeting Anne is a good argument for a benevolent god is … OK, a joke, but … hmmm.

However, as will become clear, I am not fucking around with the term "soulmate."

After the previous spring semester ended, literally everyone in Students for Animal Rights left except me. (And Phil, who wasn't a student.) I won't go into everything I tried to do to get someone else to take over the group, but I failed.

So Anne, who lived about four blocks north of me, dialed my number. After that call, she turned to her roommate-not-boyfriend and said, "That's an interesting guy. I'm going to get to know him."

Indeed.

I remember that call in the fall of 1992, standing next to my desk, talking into the beige corded phone. I remember an odd sensation ripple through my aura when I hung up.

I wish that I could remember the first moment that we met

If I knew then that I
Would spend the rest of my life with you
I imagine I would have held your gaze a little longer
When first our eyes met

–Billy Bragg (so old!), "The Fourteenth of February"

Day 8 Concluded: Stone Cold

I don't get many things right the first time
Now I know all the wrong turns, the stumbles and falls
Brought me here

–Ben Folds, "The Luckiest"

Not only am I now at the best part of the story, we're also in Germany! We were first in Würzburg in 2018 and later we're going back to VeggieBros. First, though, we're also going to walk through the big winery overlooking the town.

I know most people are insecure about themselves. Many of us, especially in the Midwest, are taught to be humble and self-deprecating. But consider a picture I have taped to my monitor. It was taken in 2000, when our kid was six and my parents paid for the whole family to go on a cruise. Getting out of Pittsburgh in the winter made it worth it. We even mostly had a good time.

A roving ship's photographer snapped a picture of Anne and me, which we, criminal masterminds, stole at the end of the cruise by slipping into a book. *Ocean's Two.*

In the photo, I'm on the left, in a shirt and tie, with a goofy "I can't believe this! *Can you effing believe this?*" look on my face.

Anne is on the right, looking like a stone-cold fox.

Absolutely no one disagrees with that assessment. Not even Anne, who is, *by far*, her own worst critic. Looking at this picture, she admits she is truly model-level hot. I have become better looking – more confident – the longer I spent with her. But in this picture, you can see just how far out of my league she was, even eight years and one child after we got together.

Or, as Fatboy Slim sings:

> Girl I want it
> You got it
> Your body's like a narcotic

And now I'm spending days with just her, traipsing across Europe. Amazing. God*damn* am I a lucky sunnabitch. Maybe the Flying Spaghetti Monster *is* real?

Update: it occurs to me that some people might think that pointing to a picture from 22 years ago is not representative. But just to the right of that picture is a 2018 picture of Anne at kAffé dAdA in Regensburg Germany, a restaurant we will revisit on this trip.

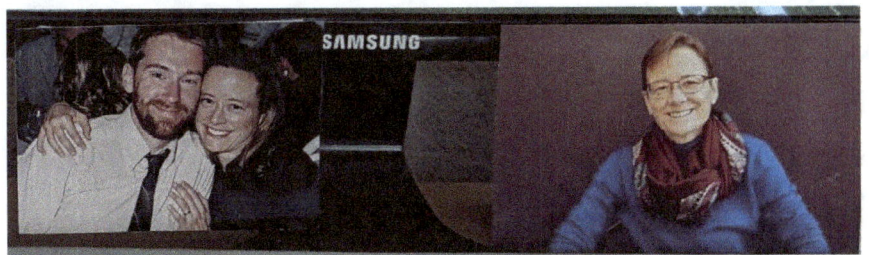

On my monitor: Cruise 2000 and Regensburg Germany 2018.

Even though she looks different – short hair, wearing glasses, and, admittedly, older – she is still a total babe. Not that looks are everything. She also exudes joy and kindness in the picture, even more so than the 2000 photo. She looks like someone that you would be lucky to know. Truth in advertising.

And no, snoogums, I won't cut this.

Day 9: The (Two Hour) Courtship of EK's Mother

The truth, with love,
is that the heart knows straightaway

–Hervé Le Tellier, The Anomaly
(translated by Adriana Hunter)

Ain't no use wastin' no time
Gettin' to know each other

–Beck, "Debra"

The chapter title is a play on *The Courtship of Eddie's Father*, a sweet comedy that ran from 1969-72. It starred Bill Bixby, who went on to much greater fame as Bruce Banner in *The Incredible Hulk*. I watched a lot of *Courtship* in 1985-86 as I was doing piecework while home sick with mono and depression.

That fall of 1992, I was very nervous about the first meeting of Students for Animal Rights. I wrote out the speech, ran it by Phil for edits, read it over the phone to Judas, and practiced it in the room ahead of time. We had a full house that evening, and in a testimony to my ability to win friends and influence people, almost none of them would still be there in a few months.

But *one* person kept coming.

After the meeting ended, Anne came up to volunteer to be Outreach Coordinator. I said "Great!" (*hubba hubba*) "We should set up a time to meet to discuss outreach plans."

"*Outreach.*"

In the meantime, she would drop by outreach tables I was running in the vestibule of the Student Union. Luckily, I had started to grow my winter beard – she likes beards. (I was also wearing a pink triangle "Ally" button. This makes EK's origin story the perfect liberal fairy tale.)

That vestibule table was also where I started ruining Joe's life.

As he tells it, he was coming into the Union to get a soda and some cash when he heard a commotion. He walked over to witness a dairy farmer screaming at some tall but composed stud sporting a drop-dead sexy beard. Based only on that (my calmness in the face of the farmer's anger, not the beard) Joe signed up for Students for Animal Rights. Then he would stop eating animals, eggs, and dairy.

After graduation, he didn't use his biology degree, but became a social worker in a methadone clinic. He did stunts for PETA, and then went on to hand (pro-vegetarian) booklets to more people than any other volunteer in history. After the shocking inevitability, he would co-found One Step for Animals with Anne and me (with help from Cathy, Mandy, Dan, Ginny, and Peter Singer).

> Don't look back, a new day's breakin'
> Today is the day.
>
> *–Tom Scholz / Boston*

Because of weird scheduling issues – e.g., I was out of town a lot for an ecology class, and she was busy teaching and looking for jobs – Anne and I didn't meet to "discuss outreach" until a Friday in mid-October. She came over to my place, which despite my efforts at cleaning and improving, was a poor-man's bachelor pad that smelled of cat pee.

Maybe I cooked something, but neither of us remember. What I do remember is that we didn't talk much about animals. We got right down to "outreach." At one point, I leaned back and asked, "What do you want to do now?" She replied, "I'd like to give you a backrub." "Oh," I gushed. "Will you marry me?"

Let the record show that she just giggled. Several hours later, Anne said, "Well, I guess I should head back." I didn't want to ruin things by being pushy (although I was tempted, and she seemed potentially open to persuasion – after all, she had initiated the removal of clothing) so the evening ended.

This might be as good a spot as any to list some of the things we have in common:

From a redneck, small-minded, cow-forsaken cowtown; easily high school valedictorian; raised Catholic (goes without saying by this point) and Catholic schools; male and female siblings; father a pharmacist, mother worked in the school system.

(Another set of coincidences, this time between me and Barack Obama: 6' 2", 160 lbs; wed the love of his life in October 1992 in Illinois (!); first child born in July; a self-described nerd; Leader of the Free World.)

(Another funny bit – Nick Offerman – Ron Swanson in *Parks & Recreation* – was an undergrad at the University of Illinois when Anne and I met there. Sadly, he never came to any of my Students for Animal Rights meetings. <sniff> I was going to title this book

The Greatest Love Story Ever Told, but Nick beat me to it. [Pic here of me doing my best Offerman imitation.])

Anne is also an athlete. She ran cross-country & track in high school and into college, and has also run a full marathon. Before I met her, she did a lot of cycling, including one tour up the whole west coast of Michigan. She is muscular and strong yet lean.

She is also brave, going off to live in Germany with very little background. But she had already established her bravery while still a little kid by recognizing and accepting she couldn't count on adults.

Our nature and nurture have left us very similar. We are both introverts who prefer a book to a party. We have few good friends. We like being outdoors, especially in the sunshine, but we aren't *crazy* – we love not camping.

We like physical activity and walk at the same pace (brisk) although I slow her down to take photos. (*Sooo* many photos. But they *are* truly awesome photos.) By the time we met, we were both rationalists, materialists (philosophically, not in terms of purchases), skeptics, freethinkers, and had both slowly stopped eating meat, eggs, and dairy, although *she* had never liked meat except sausage.

And we both realized there *ain't no use wastin' no time*....

She is – *by far* – the least stereotypically female woman I've ever known at least moderately well. She has no interest in gifts, romance (we've replaced our $35 wedding bands with $0.90 fidget rings) (edit: we no longer wear rings at all), foreplay, or much smooching (generally, although there have been a few exceptions that involve external forces and wine).

My wife is quite a dish.

We don't celebrate birthdays or holidays, a mistake I made as an overreaction to the stress and impossible expectations of "important" days when I was a kid. (We have a running joke that my birthday is The High Holy Day, which we count down via BirthdayEve^X – e.g., a week before is Birthday Eve Eve Eve Eve Eve Eve. Today is BirthdayEve^217.)

Our differences include the fact that she is left-handed and an absolute champion sleeper. (So jealous!) I think about Marital Relations far more. She reads much faster, likes cauliflower, and has *way* less patience. She has a bias for action; mine is cogitation. I'm taller and have a beard. (Early on, I shaved several times, which she *did not like*.)

They say you shouldn't marry yourself. (Or a foxier, more-mature version of yourself.) But it worked out *damn* well for me.

Day 9 Continued:
The Road to Perdition (and Prague)
The Giddy-Up Courtship becomes
Time the First

In your face, Springfield!

–Homer Simpson when Marge agrees to marry him

Sitting in a hotel in Regensburg, Bavaria, one of our favorite towns in the world as well as one of the places Anne lived before we met. The Roman fortress Castra Regina – the northernmost Roman fort in Europe – was built here in 179 AD. The stone bridge was built in the 12th Century. Last night, walking along the river to kAffé dAdA, we saw graffiti that says (translated) "Animals have rights, too." Soon, we're

boarding the train to Prague. That will be the first time we've been to a country where Anne doesn't speak the language.

Our "Outreach" meeting was on Friday, October 16, 1992. By this time, we were exchanging emails. (Again: 1992) This included sending her poems which no one should ever see. (Uh-oh. She dug them up. Holy shit! Now I want to divorce me.) Anne, however, was incredibly kind; she even said she used one for her morning meditation. *That's* how much she wanted to get with me. Why, I'm not sure. But using all my life's luck for that was worth it.

Sunday, October 18, Anne went out for a run and stopped by my place. As she told me later, she was doubting that things could really have been what they seemed to be. (Before we met, she had decided she was never going to marry and made peace with it.) By the time she left to continue her run, she was certain she was falling in love. (As was I! *Wheeeeeeeee!*)

The next Students for Animal Rights meeting was Wednesday the 21st. She came over before, and on the famous futon, we were sorely tempted to ... just skip the meeting. But we pulled back. On our way to campus, the subject of condoms *just happened* to come up. "Someone once told me it is like petting a cat with gloves on." "Yeah," I replied. "A cat you really, *really* want to pet."

That was the first night we spent together, but without said condoms. The next day, I urgently rushed to CVS, looking all over for the condoms. Being half-blind (my blood was elsewhere) I couldn't find them, so I asked an older woman working there. I must have had lust written all over my face because she looked at me with utter disdain and *disgust* before pointing me to the display under the pharmacy.

I sent Anne an email of my adventure and then found that she had already written saying we *needed* to get condoms. (In a clever and sexy way that I can't repeat here.) That Thursday night, October 22 1992, was the last night we willingly spent apart.

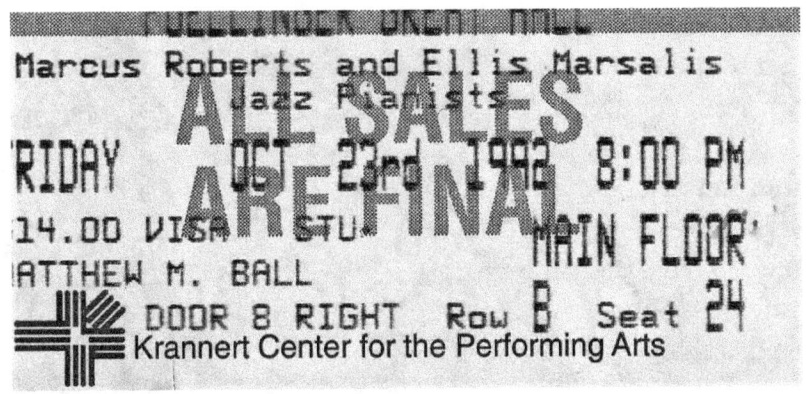

ALL SALES ARE FINAL

KELLINGER BRENT HALL

Marcus Roberts and Ellis Marsalis
Jazz Pianists

FRIDAY OCT 23rd 1992 8:00 PM

14.00 VISA STU MAIN FLOOR

MATTHEW M. BALL

DOOR 8 RIGHT Row B Seat 24

Krannert Center for the Performing Arts

We were scheduled to go to a concert by Ellis Marsalis and Marcus Roberts on Friday the 23rd. Again on the famous futon, again terribly tempted to skip, but again we went, left early, and rushed back. That night is when we declared we were wed. And we began our life of sin.

("Wed" being the commitment, "marriage" being a formal legal contract. I didn't know this distinction until writing this book. We didn't care about words; we just knew. October 23 is the primary date we celebrate, inasmuch as we celebrate anything. Except the High Holy Day of course.)

They say youth is wasted on the young. But yee-*haw* – for the next year, we took *full advantage* of our youth and vigor. It was Time the First: The first time my life was truly and completely *wunderbar* and I recognized and appreciated it as so.

Having hardly slept following the concert (from excitement – get your mind out of the gutter) (well, maybe a little in the gutter) (OK, fine) we got in my little Sentra and drove to Hillsdale Michigan, where my parents were wrapping up a visit to their cottage on Lake Wilson. The four of us went to Pizza Hut where Anne and I ate pizza without cheese. (Yum.)

When Anne left to go to the bathroom, I told my folks, "She's *The One*."

They didn't know what to think. I had been with Diane for over three years, bringing her to Tiffin and to family events. Now here was Anne – almost the same name! – who they had just heard of.

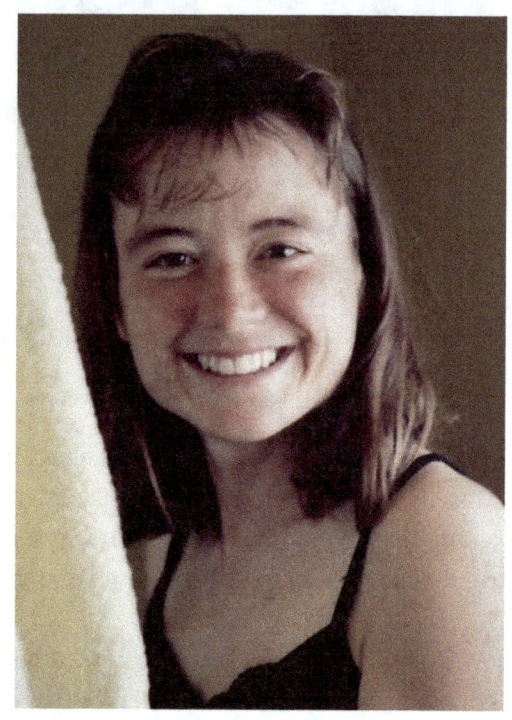

In short: they were dubious.

After they left for Tiffin, Anne and I were alone at my childhood's favorite place. The next day, I took her out in the canoe to the middle of the lake. It was a beautiful clear autumn day, a bit past peak color. I got down on one knee, careful not to capsize, and again asked her to marry me. This time, in addition to giggling, she said "Yes." It was all great fun.

On the drive back to Urbana, we continued to make delightfully detailed but doomed plans for a spring wedding (technically: marriage ceremony).

It was an autumn of glorious sights, sounds, and ... other senses. Anne and I held hands as we walked to campus in the lovely autumn weather while every love song I knew played in my head. We biked through the Illinois countryside amidst rustling corn awaiting the combine. We visited her friends Shelley and Katherine a half hour south in Charleston.

(Katherine, who was vegan when Anne met her, had come to Urbana for that fateful first Students for Animal Rights meeting, after which she hypothesized, "I bet Matt is gay. Phil moved here with him. Why else would he do that?" Ha-*ha*!)

Later that fall, Anne had a second interview at Carnegie Mellon University in Pittsburgh. At the small Urbana airport, I watched her get on a little dual-prop Beechcraft. This was the first time that we spent a night apart since October 22nd, and would be the last until her parents wouldn't let us sleep together during the holidays. (Booo!) But I would sneakily visit her. (Yay!)

Anne was picked up at the Pittsburgh airport in a normal car, but was driven back to the airport in a limousine. This meshed with her opinion that the interview and teaching had gone very well. She found out later that while she was doing her teaching demo, one CMU professor leaned over to another and whispered, "Can we just offer her the job now?"

While she was gone, I bought a small live Christmas tree, which we would later plant in Shelley's yard. I wrapped it with a string of blue lights. Anne had made many improvements to the now somewhat-less-shitty apartment; the tree and lights were my contribution to our first holiday season together.

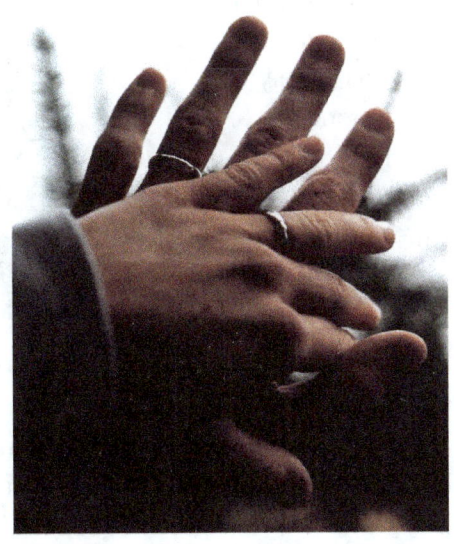

We had already gone to a catalog store at the mall to buy the least expensive wedding bands we could find. (Our friend JL would top me later. He and Jhini would have rings they bought at a hardware store. Wearing that ring, Jhini would save my life years later.)

(Given how bad my hands have been since breaking my neck, I can't get that 1992 ring on or off most days, which is why I don't wear a ring.)

Anne and I would wear the wedding rings around the apartment but not yet out in public. We have a picture of our ringed hands intertwined over our little holiday tree. It was a pretty amazing feeling. It was my first jewelry since my Cub Scout ring in second grade. The nun took it from me one day because I was fiddling with it. I never saw the ring again.

It was the best winter up north ever. The best winter ever. Easily. Much of it was simply Perfection.

Importantly, *I knew it.* We were in Tiffin on Christmas, sitting with my family in front of the fireplace. I had my head on Anne's lap when mom asked everyone for their favorite Christmas memory. When it got to me, I said simply, "This."

In a shocking twist, I was now the one who wanted kids. *Psych!* We talked about it that season, sitting by the fire. I waxed philosophical, asking, "Isn't it something we should experience?" Anne took my former position: Why mess with a perfect thing?

She also had very specific concerns: What if the kid was abused? What if the kid was abducted? (We were children of the '70s: *Stranger Danger!*) What if they were severely handicapped or severely depressed?

Of course, I was following my genetic programming, the programming that had successfully led to an unbroken line of a billion fruitful couplings since Phylum Chordata first appeared.

This manifest in the feeling of being madly, thrillingly, *overwhelmingly* in love.

I am *still* madly in love. Being in Europe, where I basically interact only with Anne all day every day, makes it all the more intense.

Now we're on the train to Prague. I'm re-reading Kurt Vonnegut's *Slaughterhouse Five* in preparation for our later visit to Dresden. If you haven't read *Slaughterhouse Five*, it is basically a fictionalized version of the Vonnegut's time in World War II, including living through the firebombing of Dresden.

(Which, unlike what Vonnegut says, killed fewer people than the atom bomb over Hiroshima. The firebombing of Tokyo was the deadliest attack in human history. However, reading *Last to Die: A Defeated Empire, a Forgotten Mission, and the Last American Killed in World War II* convinced me that in terms of lives saved, at least the first atomic bomb (Little Boy) was probably justified. Check out *Last to Die* if you think otherwise.)

In *Slaughterhouse Five*, Billy, the main character, bounces around in time, so his pre- and post-war stories are interspersed throughout the main narrative. I was not thinking of that structure when I started writing *Losing My Religions*. (And good sweet Jeebus knows I'm not comparing myself to Vonnegut.)

It is amazing to be *in* this thrilling time of my life while *revisiting* the *most* thrilling time of my life. But enough of the past. I'm going to log off and live this day.

Day 9's Surprise Conclusion!

So we go inside and we gravely read the stones
All those people, all those lives
Where are they now?
With loves, and hates
And passions just like mine

–The Smiths, "Cemetery Gates"

One day when I was probably about twenty years old, I took a random exit off of Interstate 75 somewhere in Ohio. I'm not sure why, but I'm sure it had something to do with my general expansiveness and inquisitiveness of mind at the time. I thought it profound that I was driving past houses in which so many lives were being lived with no connection to my own. That moment – looking at them through the window – would be my only interaction with them. There are literally billions of past, present, and future lives like that – lives that haven't and never will intersect with my consciousness.

Since October 2019, when we started planning to visit Prague, I have been watching videos from the YouTube channel "Honest Guide." Janek, on camera, and Honza, behind camera, have over a hundred videos about Prague. (And other places they visit, but mostly Prague.) Anne would sometimes stop in my office while I was watching these videos during physical therapy, so she's also seen a lot of Janek.

Now watch in amazement *again* as I connect those two seemingly-random paragraphs to our story!

Once we got into Prague this past Thursday, after the great and glorious germ-filled train ride from Regensburg, we dropped off our stuff at the Airbnb and headed out. After a good meal at one of the many of Prague's plant-powered places, we went across the Charles Bridge and up to the castle, where we could get in free (it was after five). There, we wandered the grounds with *many* fewer people than throng the place during the day.

After this, walking briskly (the only way Anne walks) on a side street at twilight, I suddenly, without thinking or even conscious recognition, blurted to the empty sidewalk, "Are you the Honest Guide?"

Janek was already past us, but he stopped and came back, submitting to a selfie.

It was pretty freaking incredible! He had been out filming and just happened to be on that random side street. Anne quickly processed how amazing this was – we know of only *two people* in all of Czechia and we ran into one of them. Anne kept saying, "Oh my god! How cool was that? Why aren't you more excited?" I was mostly just stunned. It didn't seem real. But we have the picture, and I messaged him on Facebook and heard back, so I guess it really happened.

At least so far, the trip has been amazing. Not "make up for three-plus years of not traveling" amazing, but quite a bit better than could be reasonably expected. Prague is everything Janek promised. The architecture is just incredible. So many great restaurants! Easy to get around without knowing the language. (I'm hesitant to use the few words I've learned.)

Anne once got a fortune that says, "Among the lucky, you are the chosen one." (She still has that slip of paper.) That has come to mind several times on this trip.

Ball

Why Reason Is Needed

Morality doesn't mean "following divine commandments."
It means "reducing suffering."
Therefore in order to act morally,
you don't need to believe in any myth or story.

You just need to develop a deep appreciation of suffering.

–*Yuval Noah Harari,* 21 Lessons for the 21st Century

In 1986, my first year at the University of Cincinnati, Fred and I became friends with Bill, with whom no one wanted to room. Bill was the first person I knew personally who was openly gay. One of the few times I ever went to a bar, he, Fred, and I sat at a table and drank beer. After a few glasses, I was bemoaning my lack of female companionship. "Maybe I'm just not attractive." Bill leaned over the table and said, "Believe me, you are *very* attractive."

Four years later I met Carl in Illinois at Students for Animal Rights. He was my age and very thoughtful, and we started hanging out, talking big topics. (We still get a card from him at Christmas.) Years later, Anne and I were staying with Carl and his boyfriend in Boulder Colorado. As Anne was walking away up the stairs, I said jokingly, "How can you not want *that*?" "Ugh! Her butt's so *big*!" Anne stopped dead and we all laughed uproariously.

I remembered those events when Anne and I were touring the fortress overlooking Würzburg. Most of the spires have crucifixes topping them, but one has a statue of a beautiful naked woman, approximately Anne's height and shape. I noted to Anne how so very deeply and lustfully that shape moved me, and how I found it basically impossible to imagine otherwise.

This is why reason is so necessary. My emotional, visceral reaction to the idea of one type of attraction versus another should have absolutely no bearing on how others should be allowed to live. Reason allows for the recognition that others are enough like us to deserve basic respect and freedoms. This is codified as rights, protecting everyone from the inherent prejudices and biases we all have.

This is probably self-evident to you. But in the scope of human history, rights are a recent invention. (And a joke.)

This morning, I woke up to the expected but still shocking news that the United States is about to strip half the population of the right to bodily autonomy. A right women won only fifty years ago – within my lifetime. All because much of the population is unable to reason, but instead want to impose their religious views

– their prejudices – on the rest of us, legally equating a single, microscopic, fertilized egg with a fully-realized human being.

As Peter Singer has noted, reason is a ladder that can lead us to unexpected places. Beyond overriding my anti-choice indoctrination, reason has led me to recognize that many other animals are enough like me in fundamental ways as to deserve basic respect and freedoms. The famous quote is from Bentham: "The question is not, Can they reason? Nor Can they talk? but, Can they suffer?"

When I give talks about animal issues, I often get the question, "Wouldn't you sacrifice a rabbit to save your kid?" I pull out a cute baby picture of our kid and reply, "I sure would. Actually, I would sacrifice *you* to save my kid. I would sacrifice *all of you* to save my kid. This is why we don't make laws based on our personal feelings."

Except when we do, like the religious fanatics on the current Supreme Court.

Martin Luther King, Jr. famously quoted another preacher: "The arc of history is long but bends towards justice." I hope so. It isn't always obvious. It certainly isn't obvious today.

One of the many peacocks wandering Prague's parks

Day 10: "Not comin' all that way just to eat *vegetables*."

And I have no compass.
And I have no religion.
Don't worry baby, it's gonna be alright.
Uncertainty can be a guiding light.

–U2, "Zooropa" (released in 1993)

When you hear the term "crazy in love" (or "madly in love") it isn't a metaphor. We were. Crazed. Literally, not figuratively. We had lost our critical faculties. We were so happy that we couldn't imagine others not being happy for us.

Ha-*ha!*

We continued to plan the doomed ceremony and celebration. The former was to be just immediate family (parents and siblings) and our best woman and man. As far as we could tell, this was the only way we could keep it small. Everyone would be invited to the reception, but we wanted an intimate ceremony.

Of course, this did not go over well. Anne's parents were outraged at the suggestion that her never-married aunt wouldn't be included. Then, when told there would be no animal meat at the reception, her dad said, "I'm not comin' all that way just to eat vegetables." "All that way" was 227 miles. For the first of his children to get married. And it would be *just one meal* after the ceremony. And there would be hardly *any* vegetables!

Their reaction was quite enough, thank you very much. We weren't *that* crazy. We sobered up enough to pseudo-elope. We picked the weekend of February 20 because that was when my pal Mark could come down from Madison. Jerry and Ursula, friends of Anne's who had also eloped, told us the local Protestant minister served as the *de facto* Justice of the Peace. So technically, we *did* get married in a church. My folks and my sister came, as they hadn't been jerks about our original plans. *Those* confrontations were in the future, although my sister has always been cool about everything.

After Mark got in Friday, the three of us went to see The Kronos Quartet. (Check out their Adagio.) Saturday, we got up, put on decentish clothes (*not* the funeral suit) and went to the church.

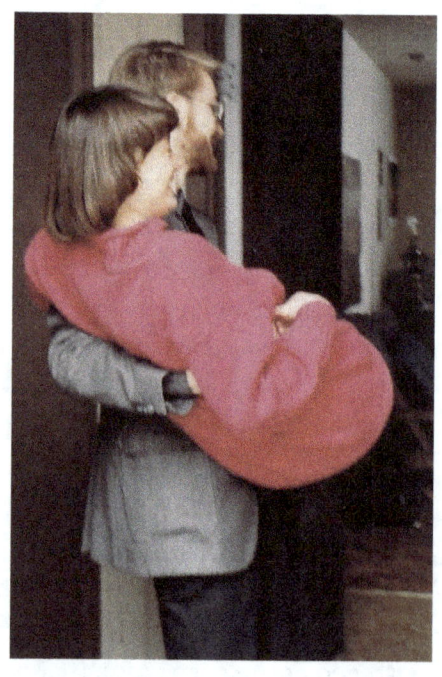

After the ceremony (as short as we could convince the minister to do, which he joked about during the ceremony) I carried Anne over the threshold of our apartment. (No lie. There is photographic proof.) Then we all drove the thirty minutes to Shelley's house where she had baked a cake that had risen unevenly, but was at least covered with frosting. It was topped by wedding trolls, which we still break out every February.

I had made soup the day before, and overnight it went from spicy to inedible. (Mark ate it, though, sweat dripping down his forehead like Ed before him.)

It had been spitting snow (and rice) when we left the church, and was *really* snowing when Mark, Anne, and I were driving back to Urbana that night. They were chatting happily when, about two hundred yards ahead of me, I watched a car skid and then slide off the road. I asked Anne and Mark to please stop talking so I could concentrate – neither had seen the accident – so the rest of the trip was in sober silence. The drive was so stressful that there wasn't a standard wedding night to bookend that morning's sin, but the following evening made up for it.

The following dawn revealed a heavy cover of snow blanketing Illinois under crystal clear skies. If you're going to have cold, snowy weather to start your legal marriage, it may as well be brilliantly beautiful. The three of us drove to Chicago so Mark could catch the evening bus home. First, though, we went to the Art Institute, where we split up. Talking after, Anne and Mark had the same favorite painting – Renoir's *Two Sisters (on the Terrace)*. Mine was Van Gogh's 1887 self-portrait.

If I could say

If I could give perspective,
we would all know that all
that can ever be expected
from the outside world
are two: beauty
and the caring
warmth and love
of a good friend
to hold moments
into the future...

The cover of our self-designed and printed official announcement.

After that, we went to Star of Siam, a Thai restaurant on Illinois Street. As his wedding present, Mark said we could order anything and everything we wanted. This was a real treat – easily the best gift we got – since we were broke and always scrimping. Soon, we had a table chock full of appetizers and entrees. At one point, Mark said with deep appreciation and satisfaction, "This is *chow!*" We still use this saying when the meal is excellent and plentiful. We ate every last morsel.

That evening was something new to me, which happens with Anne more than I would have ever imagined.

When Anne told her family we had eloped, her never-married aunt said: "That's a strange way to get married." *Feel the love.*

Her father's reaction to the first of four children getting married was, "Well, I like your living arrangements now." And he was the nice one.

He'll be dead soon.

Travelog Erfurt

In the vastness of space and the immensity of time,
it is my joy to share a planet and an epoch with Annie.

–Carl Sagan … and me, removing the second-to-last letter, "i".

Greetings from Erfurt, Germany. This is the most beautiful town that I've ever been in that has basically no American tourists. Or, as Rick Steves puts it: Unspoiled Germany.

Prague was incredibly beautiful. Just amazing architecture. Definitely worth a visit. But it was overrun with tourists, especially from the U.S. If we were to ever go again, we would avoid the weekends. Last Saturday, mobs of loud, drunken men roamed the streets.

Erfurt, however, is almost your quintessentially beautiful small-town Germany. It is not in Bavaria, which is the part of Germany Americans think of as Germany. (Most Americans stationed here after the war were in southern Germany, which is why Bavaria became our stereotype.) But there are enough half-timbered houses in Erfurt to be recognizably German.

Yet there are no Americans here! Lots of tourists – German tourists. We walked all over town yesterday, in all the most touristy places, and didn't hear a word of English. Just German.

We are also staying at an absolutely amazing Airbnb. (Thanks, Lothar!) For years, I resisted the idea of Airbnbs, worried about getting a bad one. I figured hotels would be more consistent. In 2018, we stayed in an Airbnb for the first time, in Würzburg. It was very nice, better than a hotel room. (Although the slog across town after our international flight over to Germany, via Atlanta and Paris, was quite miserable. It was one of those things that makes you say, "I will never travel again." But then, of course, you wake up the next day refreshed and in *an entirely new country*.)

Before Erfurt, we stayed in a seventh floor Airbnb apartment in Dresden. It was the very top floor, on the corner, with the roof cutting into the apartment and the windows all basically skylights. There were lots of plants too, making it seem like we were living in a greenhouse. It was absolutely beautiful; we could look out over Old Town and see the spires of Dresden's most famous churches.

We saw hot air balloons the first evening (one shaped like a heart) which just added to the romance.

But this Airbnb in Erfurt is probably the nicest place Anne and I have ever stayed. It has two bedrooms – more than we need, but it was the best deal available. The second bedroom is huge, with perhaps the biggest TV I've ever seen, and an entire living area separate from the bed. That is where I am now, a little before five a.m., talking into my phone while Anne sleeps.

There is a lovely garden out back, which our bedroom and the kitchen overlook. The right-hand side of the garden contains part of the original city wall.

Today we are going to walk to the EGA Park, a huge botanical garden. It was built in the 1950s to showcase Communism (we're still in the former east Germany) and has been expanded and improved since reunification. It should be yet another lovely day. (Plant-based chicken shown here.)

I know you didn't pick up this book to read an advertisement for Airbnb, or the city of Erfurt, or the country of Germany. But I wanted to give you a flavor of where I am writing this, how amazingly lucky I am right now.

(In case you're wondering, the rest of this book is *not* like this.
Although *bits* are.)

Day 11: Remembering Perfection while Flying Coach

We've come a long, long way together
Through the hard times and the good
I have to celebrate you, baby
I have to praise you like I should

–Fatboy Slim

I realize I didn't say much about Dresden. It exceeded expectations!

Dresden largely escaped damage during WWII until the last few months. It was a known "open city" with no military significance. This is why many prisoners of war were housed there, including Kurt Vonnegut. But then, in mid-February 1945, less than three months before the end of the war in Europe, Allied bombers destroyed the main part of the city in one of the most intense bombings in human history.

As noted, it was not the worst firebombing – that would be Tokyo – but it was pretty freakin' horrific. Dresden spent the next 55 years basically under Soviet rule. So while visiting, we had to keep in mind that just about everything we saw were reconstructions, mostly in the past two decades since reunification!

Not counting vacations like this, there have been three times when my life was, for all intents and purposes, Perfect. And, maybe more importantly, I *recognized* life as Perfect at the time. Our narrative is now in the first of these – from our first date until the first wave of morning sickness – about thirteen incredible months.

Being so desperately desirous and yet so seemingly repulsive to the opposite sex from age 13 through 17 seems to have marked me, at some deep level, as undesirable and unworthy. This Time the First in 1992-93 left me feeling great gratitude but also wonder and even bewilderment that Anne wanted to get with me.

I *still* feel that, thirty years on. I have had that feeling a number of times on this trip. Even to this day, after 30 *years* together, I get this brief but stunning realization that this smart, sexy, sane babe wants to be with me. I regularly have dreams where we meet in some situation, and I am flabbergasted that she's interested. "Wait. What? Who, *me*?"

Yes, I know this isn't rational. I mean, she is not the first person who's wanted to get with me. Not a literal ton of other people have, but more than a quarter ton!

(Honestly, I think this is driving Republicans, especially in red states: Men who were sexually frustrated for years developed a subconscious hatred of women. Any woman having sex must be punished. This gets couched in religious language, but deliberately citing rape-justifying Matthew Hale gives away the game.

What about the women, you ask? If you raise children in an angry, repressive, hell-threatening patriarchy, many if not most will adopt that worldview. Many unlikely factors must come together for children to get out of their parents' cult. It is deeply sad and truly tragic.)

Back to our for-now glorious story:

There in Illinois, even though we were broke, living in a shithole with a fetid feline (sorry TS) it was the best of times, it was the best of times, it was the age when all our programming's desires were fulfilled.

So *many* jigsaw pieces had to have fallen into place for this to happen. Another example: the year before we met, Anne had been one of the top candidates for a job in Minot North Dakota. *North freakin' Dakota.* How incredibly fortunate that they chose the other teacher. The cold must have addled their brains.

My *eternal* thanks to them.

As mentioned, Anne interviewed for a job at Carnegie Mellon (CMU) in the fall of 1992. They were doubling the size of their Modern Language Department, hiring on two tracks: research and teaching. Her first interview was at a conference in Chicago a month after we wed. It was a nice hotel room, and we weren't paying for the heat, so I had the room quite hot. After she got back from the

interview, it got hotter. All over the room.

Before we went out that evening, I took a picture of us in the mirror – something I would do regularly. This one is the best, since my face is mostly blocked.

After a very nice Italian dinner, we went to a comedy club. As we stood to leave early – the hotel room wasn't gonna heat itself – one of the comics yelled at me: "Where the fuck are you going?" I should have replied: "Exactly."

Shortly after Anne took the limo back to the Pittsburgh airport and flew home to me and our tree, I was looking for her in the University's foreign languages building. My memory is that she came out of her advisor's office, saw me, and yelled down the hall, "I got the job!" When she got back to the apartment that evening, I met her at the door and pinned her to it as soon as it closed.

Sweet Lord Jeebus, We. Were. So. *Young*. I was 24. She was 28. Our kid is about to turn 28 and they're *just a kid!*

And now, in the fall 1993, Anne would start a real job – a job, she was told, that was to do what she loved: teach. Her salary would be $30k, which in retrospect is pretty insultingly low, even for '93. (She would soon meet high school German teachers in the area making over $70k.) But after years of living well below the poverty line, it felt like finding a pot of gold.

The rest of the school year in Urbana went by way too fast. We flew to Pittsburgh to look for an apartment, finding one that was quite nice – pure luxury compared to our Illinois place. I finished my first Masters (not the golf tournament) in Forest Ecology focusing on carbon sequestration, after some drama:

Back in '90, I had applied to grad schools doing interesting and (I thought) important work. The Environmental Engineering professor I originally started with at the University of Illinois was a self-professed progressive. We would quickly fall out over my refusal to electrofish: i.e., *killing every living thing* in a certain area of a body of water. That allowed researchers to "sample" the "life" (now dead) and extrapolate to the whole ecosystem. (The technique has evolved to be relatively non-lethal these days.)

I was in a class he taught, and one day he went off against animal rights activists, for no reason other than to attack me publicly. He said "animal fanatics" really cared only for cute mammals, even though *he knew* I didn't eat chickens, eggs, or fish, and *specifically refused to kill any fish.* To keep myself from saying anything, I put my head down on my desk as he talked and bolted from the class as soon as it ended.

Good times. Literally. OMG literally.

Shortly after that, I shifted to another professor, a bigshot in her field. She was not a liberal and didn't give a shit about my politics or my diet. We got along great. This pattern would repeat, almost exactly, as farce at Carnegie Mellon a few years later.

Day 11 Concluded: Won't go naked, but open to party.

All of us in society are supposed to believe
that cruelty to animals is wrong
and that it is a good thing to prevent needless suffering.

–Ingrid Newkirk

As the head of Students for Animal Rights (SAR) I was in charge of bringing in a speaker for the year.

Previously, the group had bought in Dr Ned Buyukmihci, the head of the Association of Veterinarians for Animal Rights. He was a sweet guy who gave a really nice talk open to the public. I don't remember exactly, but not a lot of people came, and it didn't create much excitement on campus. Ned, Tom, and I went to a bar on Green Street, where I had Guinness for the first time. (I thought that Becks was the height of sophistication in the beer world. Oy.)

In 1992, SAR's insightful and inspiring outreach coordinator (Anne) thought we should bring in Ingrid Newkirk, the founder and head of People for the Ethical Treatment of Animals. PETA was and is the most famous – and infamous – animal rights group in the country, if not the world. They were known for many different stunts, including going naked to protest whatever they wanted the media to cover. PETA knew that as a relatively small group, they would not be able to sway public opinion with just their own advertising budget. Instead, they decided they had to leverage the media's reach. That would allow PETA to bring animal issues to the general public as well as policymakers and companies. As such, there was no such thing as bad press.

There are many examples of their controversial actions, but they had limits. One story I heard was a proposed billboard featuring singer Kurt Cobain, with the text "I need fur like I need a hole in my head." This was just after Cobain had committed suicide by shooting himself in the head. One of their department heads at the time nixed this idea.

Although Anne and I had used command-line email in our week-long courtship, not a lot of groups were using email for anything yet. (Despite my urging, PETA would fall behind in the digital realm for a few years. In 1995, they lost PETA.org to People Eating Tasty Animals. It took until 2001 for PETA's lawsuit to win the domain.) After a number of expensive long-distance phone calls (yes, phone calls used to cost money) PETA eventually agreed to have Ingrid come at a discounted rate, since SAR did not have much of a budget from the university.

The condition was that we had to get Ingrid a bunch of media.

Anne and I set up several radio appearances and two talks on campus. The first was a lunch lecture that, if I am remembering correctly, was about feminism and animal rights.

The main evening event was to be in a big lecture hall and open to the general public. We put up flyers around campus, screaming in big letters her quote "A rat is a pig is a dog is a boy." (Even then, chickens were left out. <sniff>) We thought that that would be the most provocative way to get attention for the event, as this quote from Ingrid had often been pulled out of context. But we were going for controversy, not accuracy or fairness. We wanted to get butts in the seats. The rest was up to her.

Ingrid had just published *Free the Animals: The Story of the Animal Liberation Front* (ALF). ALF would research what laboratories were doing the most egregious animal testing, often by finding sympathetic people on the inside. Then they would break in, vandalize the lab, and rescue some of the animals – hopefully the most sympathetic and photogenic. (In terms of PR, a rat ≠ a dog.)

Taken in isolation, the logic is pretty compelling: If you knew that someone was being tortured for no reason other than to test a new shampoo formulation, wouldn't you have a moral obligation to break in and rescue them? Or, alternatively, if *you* were being held in prison and tortured for the sake of a new line of mascara, wouldn't you want someone to ignore whatever unjust laws allowed your imprisonment?

When Ingrid got into town, Anne and I picked her up at the airport. The next day, we drove her to her first radio appearance. Later, when I was driving Ingrid to the lunch event, I asked her obliquely if she thought that I should do something other than pursuing a degree in forest ecology while doing animal advocacy on the side. But she didn't give much of an answer.

From my memory, the first talk went well. I don't remember much from it. Anne introduced her, and I think all of the discussion was generally friendly.

When I was driving Ingrid to her next radio interview, she thought she might have seen an injured bird, but we had gone by too quickly to get a good look. She asked me if we should go back. That would mean missing the radio interview, where she would reach thousands of people, so I stammered something about needing to make the appointment. I kept driving, and she kept looking behind us.

(This is an example of the main difference between Anne & me and many other animal advocates. We are not "animal people." We don't tear up at a specific case of animal abuse, and we aren't "recharged" by going to an animal sanctuary. Although Anne does like cats, that wasn't what led her to co-found and fund Animal Liberation Action and One Step for Animals. It was one of the things we had in common with Judas, who once took a sharpie to a shirt that said, "Love animals: don't eat them." He crossed out "Love" and wrote in "Respect.")

(But, as you'll see, I also have plenty of differences with the more calculating utilitarians.)

Attendance for Ingrid's evening talk was very good. She showed two video clips, one about animal testing and the about the abuse of pigs by animal agriculture. (Mingling in the crowd afterward, I heard one student say, "I'm not going vegetarian, but I'm sure not eating hot dogs ever again.")

There were some inquiries in good faith during the Q&A session, but the ag department – which is huge at the University of Illinois – had sent a large contingent to try to rattle Ingrid. But she was too much of a pro to take any of the bait they offered. The one question I remember specifically was about research on goldfish that the person claimed would be useful to understanding the function of nerves, with that knowledge helping children suffering from brain disorders. It was much better than "a dog or your daughter," because there's no sympathy for goldfish. I don't remember exactly what Ingrid said, but it seemed to me like a reasonable position rather than the rantings of a fanatic.

Ingrid was staying at fellow SAR member Jackie's apartment. Some of us met over there after the talk and constructed a human pyramid. (Why? I don't remember.) Ingrid is kneeling on top with one arm raised in victory. (Anne is on the bottom instead of me because my back was out.) The picture cracks me up every time.

Ingrid also wanted the apartment to be very hot, because she, like me, was cold all the time. Ingrid ended up moving PETA from

Washington DC down to Virginia in part so she could be a little bit warmer.

I can identify!

On the drive to the airport, I came right out and told her that I thought that I should be "throwing parties" instead of going to school. ("Throwing parties" is the euphemism the Animal Liberation Front used to talk about their raids.) Ingrid was unequivocal in her response: She said I should definitely continue doing what I was doing rather than throwing parties.

We had also talked about Carl Sagan and Ann Druyan's previously-mentioned book, *Shadows of Forgotten Ancestors*, which had also just come out in '92 and which Ingrid hadn't yet read. It is full of insightful quotes, such as:

> Humans – who enslave, castrate, experiment on, and fillet other animals – have had an understandable penchant for pretending animals do not feel pain. A sharp distinction between humans and "animals" is essential if we are to bend them to our will, make

them work for us, wear them, eat them – without any disquieting tinges of guilt or regret. It is unseemly of us, who often behave so unfeelingly toward other animals, to contend that only humans can suffer. The behavior of other animals renders such pretensions specious. They are just too much like us.

I bought and sent Ingrid a copy after she left (no Amazon at the time – it would be founded the same month our offspring was born) and we've been in intermittent touch ever since. She wrote the introduction to one of my previous books.

However, the most important thing that came out of this event was her eventual introduction to Benedict, whom she would hire in 1996 in part because he was the kind of person willing to streak the Queen with "GoVeg.com" written on his backside. Despite his extroversion, he would become one of my closest friends, having me accept his induction into the Animal Rights Hall of Fame on his behalf. After Judas, he is the person with whom I am closely associated within the animal rights community. And he would become the person who, fifteen years later, would leave me lying in bed, in agony and suicidal, during Pandemic Summer 2021.

Brains! *BRAINS!*
(There *is* a self! But no free will.)

Man can do what he wants
but he cannot will what he wills.

–Arthur Schopenhauer

On the train to Dresden, Anne brought up that we are each other's karass, for those who have read Vonnegut's *Cat's Cradle*. If you haven't read that, you definitely should.

A bit before five a.m. on our last day in Dresden, I woke up from a bad dream that put me in a bad mood. Instead of immediately meditating to let go of the strange scene my brain had concocted (fighting a guy with a box cutter) I stopped to look at what I was feeling, which led me down this path:

Brains are effing incredible. I didn't really realize at the time, but I had a hint early on. I was probably about ten, lying in bed upstairs at the Toledo house. The evening was about as perfect as you can get – a slowly fading twilight, windows open, temperature in the mid-seventies, no one else around, no noise from the street.

For some reason, the thought appeared in my still-unformed brain: "What if there was nothing?" Not "What if the lights went out?" or "What if I hadn't been born?" or "What if Grandpa Anderson had been killed in the Pacific?" But more, "What if there hadn't been a Big Bang?"

I kept exploring that thought, focusing on it more to the exclusion of everything else. (Something I'd never done before and haven't really been able to replicate since.) After a while, a funny feeling came over me. It was like I became that nothingness. I existed but I didn't. It wasn't pleasant, it wasn't unpleasant. It didn't last long or short. It was nothing. But the *memory* of it has always been thrilling for how deeply unusual it was. I stopped trying to explain what I had experienced after two failed tries.

(There was also a time when the color yellow looked different to me but no one believed me. Anne won't have a problem believing, given how messed-up my color vision is. Her: "What color is that?" Me, meekly: "Blue?" Her: "*It could not be more pink.*")

What color *is* this?

Yes, I know I have rewritten the "nothing" memory by recalling it dozens of times since it happened, including now. As Lisa Feldman Barrett writes in *Seven and a Half Lessons about The Brain*, "A brain doesn't store memories like files in a computer – it reconstructs them on demand with electricity and swirling chemicals. We call this process remembering but it's really assembling."

But the memory I have today of that moment forty-four years ago is that it made a deep impression when it happened. It has stuck with me as one of the most profound experiences of my life; it was, I think, the most singular.

While that anecdote may *seem* spiritual, one last week is yet another example that I'm just a six-foot-two bad of chemicals.

We had had an absolutely lovely day in Prague, a city largely spared bombing in World War II. (One thing that *was* bombed by allied bombers who thought they were over Dresden: Vinohrady Synagogue, Prague's largest. If there is a god, It has a sick sense of humor, to paraphrase Depeche Mode's "Blasphemous Rumors.")

That Prague day is what happiness experts mean when they say to buy experiences (memories) instead of things. We walked for miles, up and down hills, seeing some of the most memorable sights in all of Europe. We held hands or went arm-in-arm. (We probably looked like a stock photo of a white couple in Europe, if stock photography ever used older people.) I felt about as close to Anne as ever.

After we were back at the Airbnb for a bit, my mood started to go south. I got increasingly both sad and kinda angry. When I finally stopped to examine my feelings, I could come up with no explanation. No nausea, no headache, no unrecognized ache or pain; my hands were not troubling me more than normal. My blackening spirit entirely contradicted my situation.

I kept thinking about it, because the disconnect was so disturbing. I finally realized that at lunch, I had only taken the nerve pain capsule but not the antidepressant. I popped one right away.

Yes, I realize that drugs like Wellbutrin are not supposed to act on the order of a day. But if it was all in my mind, so what? *What is the goal if not to impact my mind?*

Our mind – our consciousness – is all we have! So why do people knock what might be the placebo effect? As Feldman Barrett writes:

> [T]hink of the last time you were thirsty and drank a glass of water. Within seconds after draining the last drops, you probably felt less thirsty. This event might seem ordinary, but water actually takes about twenty minutes to reach your bloodstream. Water can't possibly quench your thirst in a few seconds. So what relieved your thirst? Prediction. As your brain plans and executes the actions that allow you to drink and swallow, it simultaneously anticipates the sensory consequences of gulping water, causing you to feel less thirsty long before the water has any direct effect on your blood. ...

> [Y]our brain issues predictions and checks them
> against the sense data coming from the world and
> your body. What happens next still astounds me,
> even as a neuroscientist. If your brain has predicted
> well, then your neurons are already firing in a pattern
> that matches the incoming sense data. That means
> this sense data itself has no further use beyond
> confirming your brain's predictions. What you see,
> hear, smell, and taste in the world and feel in your
> body in that moment are completely constructed in
> your head. By prediction, your brain has efficiently
> prepared you to act.

By the next morning, I was feeling sober, neither happy nor sad. I took another antidepressant and we went out exploring again. Before lunch, I was back to feeling nearly giddy, appreciative of the beauty around us and grateful to be healthy and well-off and lucky enough to experience it with Anne.

(This trip again seems to show Anne is the "Chosen One" – when we had looked at the forecast for the trip a week before we flew out, it was supposed to be cold and rainy. It has turned out to be simply wonderful weather.)

I'm not so sure my experience above was the placebo effect. For one, I was not aware I had forgotten to take the pill. For another, I have had very mixed results with antidepressants; as mentioned, Prozac made me worse. If it was just the power of suggestion, wouldn't they have all worked?

Who is the "real" Matt? The unhappy and upset person without the mood-altering drug still in his system? The sober evaluator the next morning? The not-quite-manic-but-within-spitting-distance Matt who sat with eyes closed appreciating the amazing sensations of a walnut strudel in the midst of a wondrous day spent with his soulmate?

The Catholics (and others) would obviously vote for the no-drug person. If we suffer, God wants us to suffer. Don't mess with God's ways.

But of course there can be no single way, no "real" Matt. When we eat anything, we alter our chemistry. When we experience anything, we alter our consciousness. When we fast, when we exercise, when we drink, when we realize our jaw is wired shut, when we lie *au naturel* beneath our eight-and-a-half-months pregnant wife in Hartwood Acres Park, when we slowly come to in a pool of blood and realize we can't feel our legs as the firefighters take the door off to get to our face-shattered and neck-broken body – *everything* alters who we are.

The Buddhist idea that the self is an illusion comes in here. (Instead of plugging *Why Buddhism Is True* again, here's a podcast.) It is an extraordinarily difficult concept to even begin to consider. Take the examples earlier in this chapter – exactly *who* is examining feelings and exploring his thoughts, if not my self?

But even though it totally *feels* like there is someone running the show, no one is in *control*. "Control" is the important point, not that there is no "self." While there *is* someone who *experiences* the contents of consciousness – my "self" – there is no one *in control* of consciousness. The self exists – the one reading this, the one focusing on their breath, the one examining their thoughts, the one tasting the strudel – but no one is running the show.

Neuroscience backs this up. *Seven and a Half Lessons about the Brain* again:

> Now here's the final nail in the coffin of common sense: All this predicting happens backward from the way we experience it. You and I seem to sense first and act second. But in your brain, sensing actually comes second. Your brain is wired to prepare for action first....

Yes, your brain is wired to initiate your actions before you're aware of them. That is kind of a big deal. After all, in everyday life, you do many things by choice, right? At least it seems that way. For example, you chose to open this book and read these words. But the brain is a predicting organ. It launches your next set of actions based on your past experience and current situation, and it does so outside of your awareness. In other words, your actions are under the control of your memory and your environment. Does this mean you have no free will? Who's responsible for your actions?

I don't mean to say that we should *act* like we don't have free will. What could that even mean? Natural selection has built a thorough and compelling illusion of control / free will that gets us through the day.

But just as being aware of all our cognitive biases can help us be happier, it is also useful to realize that everyone around us is just following their programming. Each one of us is literally the embodiment of our internal chemical reactions. (Here I'll plug Danny Kahneman's *Thinking, Fast and Slow* here. But be warned, reading it is quite a commitment. And some of the studies he references in the book have fallen victim to the great replication crisis. Michael Lewis' *The Undoing Project* – the story of Kahneman and Tversky – is an easier read that covers much of the same territory.)

This is not to say that everyone should be allowed to run about higgledy-piggledy. To have a chance at good outcomes – to give people the chance to thrive – we need laws and social norms. But like the Texas tower sniper who left a note asking to have his brain examined – and he *did* have a tumor pressing down on his amygdala, a part of the brain involved in anxiety and the "fight-or-flight" response – criminals are just doing what their genetics and environment hath wrought. The spouse who cheats, the thief who robs, the asshole who cuts you off on the freeway, the best pal who cuts out your heart for all to see – all just following their programming.

I'm not saying we have to understand, and I'm definitely not saying we have to forgive. (Aww *hells* no.) But we would have less suffering if we could realize more often that the person who is smoke-smoke-smoking, or talking loudly in the quiet car, or asking you to read his egomaniacal memoir – that person is just a bag of chemicals following programming developed for the African savannah and not the security line at Frankfurt Airport.

My Brain Flaps, Again

Ultimately, happiness comes down to choosing between the discomfort of becoming aware of your mental afflictions and the discomfort of being ruled by them.

–Robert Wright, Why Buddhism is True:

One way to think about the purpose of meditation is to make your mind "unflappable."

I've achieved something like this a few times. Surprisingly, one was my journey in January 2020, the last trip I took before this one. When it got to the point where the alternative would have been worse, I agreed to go to my parents' house in Texas. For several weeks beforehand, I was filled with dread, especially since I would be traveling without Anne – who wasn't invited. I will willingly, if not gladly, suffer more to spare her.

But once I arrived, I somehow successfully entered into "Leave your body, Homer" mode. The results were striking, even to me. My dad and sister razzed me about it, but after I left, dad wrote an email to Anne referencing how well I had it together. He now refers to me as "really laid back."

There was one moment when my brain flapped, though: When my sister unwisely mixed an edible with alcohol and subsequently lost it with mom. Yelling and crying and "I can't answer that" took me over the edge for the rest of the evening.

At the end of our last full day of this Germany / Prague trip, my brain flapped again.

It is suggested that couples should travel together before getting married because the stresses of travel will show just how strong your relationship is. Anne and I have generally traveled just about perfectly. I had even specifically commented this past Wednesday how Anne is the ideal travel companion.

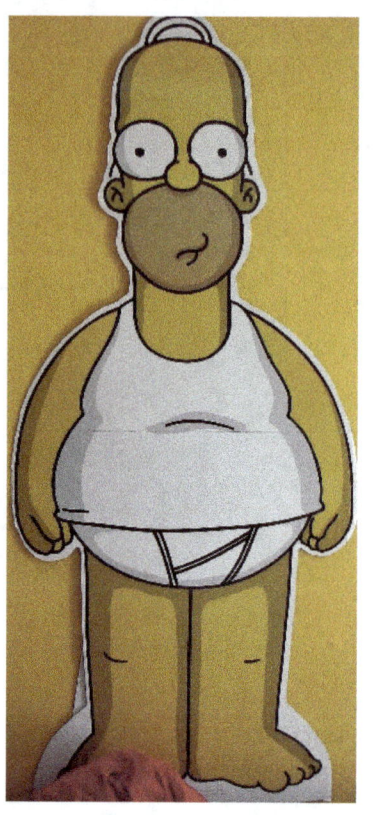

On the day in question, we had a lovely morning walk to and through the Erfurt castle, then took the train into Frankfurt. There, we had a wonderful Ethiopian lunch (oddly with rice; see below) sitting outside with no one else around.

Then it went south. Using my phone, I bought tickets for the train from the main station to the airport. (OMG, how did we travel before these? Phone, camera, maps, email, texts, purchases, research – holy chicken!!) As I had numerous times before on the trip, I showed the QR code to the agent. But this time, I had bought only *one* ticket. DOH! That agent called the senior guy, who took us off the train at the next stop and walked us to an ATM to get cash for the (non-negligible) fine.

OK, it's just money. When we're about to ride our tandem bike over the cliff, I won't look back and bemoan that withdrawal. I felt stupid, but not too much – people goof up, especially on a website in a language they don't speak. But things kept going wrong after that for the next few hours, ending with us backtracking in the blazing-for-Germany sun after yet another wrong turn trying to walk to the hotel. And the entire time we were slogging with our backpacks and carry-ons, Anne was thinking that we're going to

have to do it all again in the morning to get to our flight. At the hotel, they mentioned a shuttle that runs in the morning (which I knew about) but Anne heard "forty euro a person" instead of "four."

Sorry.

I am well aware of the "peak / end" effect of memories: That you judge an event based on its peak emotional moment as well as its end, rather than its average emotional valence or the overall balance of good vs bad. But luckily, during nearly every moment of this entire trip, I *knew* I was having a magical experience, and I know the memories of the trip will be a regular source of joy going forward. (I know that even while in pretty significant pain right now, crammed into this cattle-car seat on the 777 flying back to America.)

(PS: Things would be sub-optimal at the Dallas airport, too. Two lessons: One, if you get a boarding pass with SSSS on it, be prepared to go into "Leave your body, Homer" mode. Two, always check the menu's prices, even if you've been there before. Lunch ≠ Dinner.)

777 loading up for flight back to the United States.

Day 12: Hot for Teacher

You know that I love you girl.
You're my way out of hell.

–Tears for Fears, "No Small Thing"

I'd like to watch him eat a pie.

–Abbey Bartlet, The West Wing, *Season 6 Episode 10*

The first four seasons of *The West Wing* are the best television ever, but too much of a liberal fantasy to watch these days – just so painful.

Writing this book has, of course, brought to mind many memories, some of which I've been discussing with Anne.

Today I learned that in addition to the University of Illinois (where we met) Anne was also accepted into the graduate program at Northwestern, a more prestigious school. They were also going to pay her as a research assistant, rather than a teaching assistant, giving her more time to work on her dissertation.

Not to keep you in suspense: She turned Northwestern down for UI. Not because she knew she was going to meet her skinny soulmate in Urbana years later, but because she wanted to teach. Yet another flap of a butterfly's wing.

Her teaching ability was on display when she presented to Students for Animal Rights in the fall of 1992. She became this different person – a more serious demeanor, different emphases, and a calmer, slower voice. She even looked older. Because she spoke softly, people had to lean in to hear what she was saying. Everyone was paying close attention. (She was much more animated when teaching German.)

Shortly after starting at Carnegie Mellon, Anne would become widely known for using the still-new "internet" to augment language instruction. This was back when hosting things on a school's local, closed network was the cutting edge. She became even better known for using German children's and youth literature – not translations – to teach German.

That was one of the things she did when in Germany, Switzerland, and Austria: look for new books aimed at children and young adults that she could use in her classes. Then, she would put her lesson plans online, letting other teachers around the world understand how to use these materials.

The Computer Aided Language Instruction Consortium recognized Anne's work with a prestigious national award. She was elected Vice President and then President of the American Association of Teachers of German.

She was also well known at the Goethe Institut, working with them to improve Carnegie Mellon's study abroad program. Because of all her fame (if not fortune) she traveled a *lot*. EK and I had a running agreement that we would have Tater Tots and pie when Anne was gone. Not establishing healthy habits. One of my many, many mistakes. Sorry.

Anne also won the college's top teaching award. That came with $1,000, part of which we used to take friends out to a "This is chow!" feast at a local Thai restaurant.

Of course, the male colleague who wrote obscure books earned more, was treated better, and given more respect. And received many more sabbaticals to write papers like "Weimar sexual cynicism." Then there were all the departmental machinations and petty jealousies. Anne loved the teaching, even though the course load was too much, but she hated all the politics. There is a joke that goes something like, "Why are professors so vicious to each other? Because the stakes are so very low."

When she eventually told the next department head that she was leaving in 2007, he didn't try to convince her to stay or be magnanimous *at all*. Instead he told Anne: "You will *never* work in academia again!" Such class. She still has nightmares about Carnegie Mellon, 15 years later.

After word got around that she was quitting, the Dean offered to make Anne a Dean if she stayed. His offer reminded me of when another university was trying to poach Anne. Only then did CMU see fit to give her a computer to use at home. She was using that computer to work on a big, national teaching program during her *only* semester sabbatical the entire 14 years she was there.

Death Valley

Day 12 Concluded:
I Used to be Smart ... and Dumb(er)

This idea that a book can either be about
character and feeling, or about politics and idea,
is just a false binary.

Ideas are an expression of the feelings
and the intense emotions we hold about the world.

–Richard Powers
Quoted in John Freeman's How to Read a Novelist

Writing about formerly being smart while foggy with jetlag.
Ha-*ha!*

When Anne and I met in 1992, I was probably just a bit down from
the height of my intellectual powers. Today, that summit of smarts
is no longer within view.

(Side note, and this is entirely true: Growing up, whenever I
thought about what constituted being an "adult," I always pegged
it at age 24. I met Anne when I was 24. Our kid was born when I
was 26 – the same age my dad was when I was born.)

In 2018-19, Richard Powers' *The Overstory* was The Thing with the educated environmentalist class. Anne and I both read it, as well as a number of our friends and colleagues.

I had previously read his book *The Time of Our Singing*, which I just picked up from the library today to re-read. He is a magnificent writer – sumptuous sentences that are experiences in and of themselves. It can take me many minutes to finish one page, as I read over and over, soaking in the amazing structure and wonderful word choices.

You realized long ago that this book is not like that. No Pulitzer or Obama's Summer Reading in my future. But I want this to be an easy read and more about plot and ideas than language. If you don't find the story and topics interesting, there's no number of immaculately-constructed sentences that would make this worth your time. Life is too short to read something as an intellectual exercise.

(Powers' *Bewilderment* is a less-sumptuous read, but punchier. You read for the heartbreaking plot and well-drawn characters more than the brilliant writing.)

In the time leading up to when I met Anne, I could read "fine literature." I read Herman Hesse's overwrought *Siddhartha* and loved it. I read Salman Rushdie's *The Satanic Verses* and thought it was Nobel-level brilliant. I could quickly understand concepts like the Monty Hall problem in a way I can't now.

Even at the time I met Anne, I was still sharp in many ways. I would get things right on tests – especially statistics tests – that the professor had wrong. But neither humility nor interpersonal relations were my métier. <sigh>

It was shortly after meeting Anne that my animal advocacy took a turn. Still operating under the idea that getting media attention was the way to help animals, Judas and I organized the "Fast for Farmed Animals" outside a slaughterhouse in Cincinnati.

And we did get one bit of coverage – a quite amazing piece, actually. The TV segment started with the anchor turning to the camera and saying, "You can hear the screams of the animals outside the gates of the Hillshire Farms' processing plant. So says a group of animal rights activists...." Cut to the reporter talking over footage of pasta going into boiling water as we're interviewed about our Last Supper before the public three-day fast. (Three days because that was how long many pigs went without eating before slaughter. That time is shorter in most cases today.)

Starting the morning after that pasta, a group of us – including Mark, my "This is chow!" Best Man – sat along the street outside the slaughterhouse, holding our red-on-yellow "Stop Eating Animals" banner.

Given how hungry I was, it was even harder than normal to sleep the first night. And it sucked to be away from Anne, who was fasting in solidarity back in Urbana. (Gawd, we were so foolish.) It was especially hard to be separated during our first year together, the time of our singing.

The second day was even worse. That day, I didn't think much about Anne. I thought about food. Every single minute, all day long. You might think that vegan food isn't tasty, but that idea is mistaken. Vegan or not, however, try fasting for two days. Just about anything will elicit fantasies and drool.

Oddly, the third day wasn't as bad, hunger-wise. At that point we realized that it wasn't much good being outside a slaughterhouse – which is, as you might guess, not in a high-visibility part of town. (One worker passed by us and said, "We got to eat something." Another, more sympathetic worker said, "A man's gotta work.") So some of us left to take the banner to streets around my first alma mater, the University of Cincinnati.

That evening, the strawberries were the sweetest I ever tasted.

After the fast, we officially formed the organization Animal Liberation Action. Judas, Mark, Anne, and I were the Board.

Relatively soon after, Mark wrote us a personal letter (on paper! In the actual mail! Email still wasn't a thing for most people) that mentioned in passing that his partner had handed him a piece of pizza. Judas and I fretted that this meant Mark had eaten cheese pizza, which led to Mark being off the Board. (Gawd, we were such twits. It makes me sad to this day.) Turns out the pizza *was* vegan and in retrospect, Mark's removal probably led to Day 22 and my second deepest, most uncontrolled sobbing as an adult.

Very Little *Really* Matters

When shit brings you down, just say "fuck it"
and eat yourself some motherfucking candy.

–*David Sedaris,* Me Talk Pretty One Day

As humans, we are wired for action. This leads us to have a
reaction to many things we see and hear. Responding to nearly
everything made sense when we were living in a small band and
anything we could see or hear directly impacted us. But now, with
the 24/7 availability of news, we see and hear much more than
people did 25 years ago, let alone 100,000 years ago.

In the end, however, *very little* of this news actually impacts us
as individuals. (And vice versa.) Thus a negative reaction to bad
news serves no purpose. (However, feel free to have all the
positive reactions you want! Those flowers really *are* beautiful!
These curried chickpeas really *are* delicious! I really *am* lucky to
have met my partner! I'm *super fortunate* to live in a time of clean
water, indoor plumbing, modern sewage systems, and HVAC
systems! This book really *is* amazing: funny, touching, compelling,
and helpful! It also has perfect use of the serial comma!)

Mindfulness and meditation can help. Although difficult, we
can use the insights of others to train ourselves to not react to
events that aren't relevant to us and/or that we don't have any

power over. For example, things will be grating (a loud car revving past) annoying (how expensive food is in an airport) frustrating (my computer froze and needed to be restarted) or just silly ("Secret Location" and "Let It All Evolve" didn't make Tears for Fears new album. Boo! Luckily, you can find them on YouTube. Yay! Be sure to use AdBlock).

But we don't have to hold on to our reactions. We can just release those annoyances with a few deep breaths and memories of pleasant things.

I'm not saying ignorance is bliss. I am sure you know plenty of bad things that motivate you to want to make the world a better place. But you don't have to watch every video of animal cruelty forwarded to you. You don't have to read every report about climate change. You don't have to watch every "issue" movie.

If you take on every bit of information available to us today, it is hard, if not impossible, to live a happy life. It is even harder to help make things better, as there is always another report to read, documentary to watch, podcast to stream.

One of the very few times I've ever been in a bar, I was sitting next to Tom, who I had met at Students for Animal Rights. (He is in the Ingrid Newkirk pyramid.) Phil and I were hypothesizing that maybe depressed people are more likely to be animal advocates. Tom growled, "We're depressed because we know what is done to animals."

Today, it is easy to know what is done to many and various individuals. We are bombarded with reports of poverty, war, mass shootings, abuse of animals, attacks on LGBTQ people, subjugation of women. It is difficult to *avoid* cruelty. And then, social media is the perfectly-optimized tool to program us with anxiety and depression.

But taking in horror after horror doesn't make you a good person. Making a difference makes you a good person.

Choose where you can make a difference. You don't need to know everything. You don't need to read or watch everything. As

Nobel Laureate (and one of Anne's colleagues at Carnegie Mellon) Herb Simon said: "[A] wealth of information creates a poverty of attention." (Quoted in our fellow Illini Nick Offerman's *Gumption*.)

Relatedly, as Matthew Yglesias said, "One shouldn't be complacent about the problems in the world, but one should avoid frustration about them." (Offered even though you should never trust anyone named Matt.)

You don't need to be depressed. You don't *deserve* to be depressed. You can be happy and still make a difference. Indeed, I would contend that being happy makes it *easier* to make a difference over the long haul – both in your ability to work constructively and in the example you set for others.

Day 13: The Puritans were Assholes

You have to make your own happiness, wherever you are.
Your job isn't going to make you happy,
your spouse isn't going to make you happy,
the weather isn't going to make you happy.

–From a newsletter that arrived while writing this chapter

Sorry newsletter, but you are as wrong as you can be. All those things – job, spouse, weather – *can* make you happy or unhappy. *Especially* your spouse! I will also add drugs to the list. *Viva drugs!*

Many "make your own happiness" people buy into the bullshit Puritanical idea that happiness comes down to our own hard work. "Pull yourself up by your bootstraps" is a *joke*, a physical impossibility!

Good lawd. Along with their horrible anti-pleasure stance, the Puritans sure fucked up a lot.

With that said, let's hop back to 1992,

when, because of my spouse, I was so happy it was scary.

Anne had gotten the job at CMU. The University of Illinois had approved her dissertation with revisions, which she wrote in the fifteen-foot U-Haul I drove east, towing our two-door Sentra.

We're sure Illinois only gave Anne the PhD because she had a job and had been there so long. Anne hated that dissertation. Gawd how she loathed it. Before we met, she was on one of her multi-day bicycling tours, complaining about the absurdity and futility of what was expected with regards to research. One of her companions suggested she change from "Women in the Novellas of Clemens Brentano" to "Pre-Popeye-esque Configurations in the Novellas of Clemens Brentano." Anne laughed so hard she almost crashed her bike.

Anne was only in it for the teaching, to open minds in the special way that learning a new language can. By recognizing we think in the finite words of a certain language, we gain *all sorts* of insights into consciousness and our own mental processes.

Anyway, we drove from our Illinois shithole – TS had gone back to Phil – to our very nice third-floor Hobart/Wightman apartment, just east of Pittsburgh's lovely Schenley Park. Walking to Carnegie Mellon, where my Department of Energy Fellowship transferred, we would stroll along a road through the Schenley Golf Course, where golfers tried to hit their drives from a hill on one side to a hill on the other side. (We were never struck by a stray ball, luckily.)

Anne was thrown right into the deep end, teaching four classes. Carnegie Mellon had hired a number of new people, including Bonnie, a big-personality extrovert with whom Anne shared an office. This room assignment would significantly impact our lives – the two of them would progress professionally together over the next fourteen years, and our families would go through a hell of a lot together. Other than Anne, I have shared more profound life experiences with Bonnie and her husband Tom than anyone else.

We were really self-righteous vegan jerks that fall. (OK OK, it was me.) For example: there was to be a social gathering for Anne's department, and my memory is that I made a stink about not wanting to be around "dead animals." (You know, to make a good first impression.) At the party, Bonnie, in what we would come to know as her normal fashion, told Anne, "You and I are going to have to learn to get along. I'm not going to stop eating meat, *no way*." Her entire family would soon stop eating meat.

Yay us?

Having taken a Masters in Forest Ecology, I started working on a PhD in Engineering and Public Policy. As at the University of Illinois, I started with one of the department's most superficially-liberal professors as my advisor. (In my defense, I chose him because of the work, not his alleged politics.) Once, I came into his office while he was eating a burger, and he blurted out, "You always make me feel guilty." As you have already surmised, this would end badly for me. After he stabbed me in the back, I learned that a number of his previous grad students had had similar experiences. (Not regarding meat, but being undermined.)

As at the University of Illinois, the classes were relatively easy, and my fellow students were not, on average, the top one percent. It took me until EPP, my third grad department, to realize that my aerospace cohort at the University of Cincinnati had been *extraordinary*. There, I was just middle of the pack, even though I had gotten straight-As in all my non-engineering classes. Steve, one of our aerospace classmates (the only one who said anything nice to me and Phil after we were arrested) had taken one course with the class behind us, and that professor went on and on about the Class of '91, how exceptional we were. (And by "we," I mean the top ten – all boys – who *were* truly brilliant. Like top-of-MIT brilliant.)

At Carnegie Mellon, I impressed Mitch, who would eventually be my fourth and final advisor. In his advanced statistics class (where I once took an exam standing up because my back was so bad) I would sometimes get problems right that he had done wrong. For the last exam, he left the room after we started. Twenty minutes later, he came back and exclaimed, with what seemed like sincere surprise, "Matt's still here?"

It was also at this time when I took a class from a French professor. (From France, that is, not a teacher of French. Although as it turned out, he may as well have been speaking French.) There were about ten of us in the class, and we had no idea what he was talking about. Really. We got together to review, and none of us had *any* clue. Our grade would be based on a presentation, so we went back to the course description to try to figure out what we could do. I read James Gleick's very fine *Chaos* and talked about that. I got an A but learned nothing from the class except what I picked up from *Chaos* and a few of the presentations.

During that class, one of my fellow confused students pulled me aside in the hallway to tell me he was gay. Remember, this was the mid '90s, the time of Don't Ask Don't Tell, before putting anti-gay initiatives on state ballots won Ohio, and thus re-election, for the war criminal George W. Bush. I note this to try to reassure myself that although things are bad in 2022, they were bad back then, too.

Or:

The easy way to go is to say, "It's all gone to shit"
When the great moral of the story is that
It's always been shit.

–Conan O'Brien, quoted in Nick Offerman's Gumption

A "lighter" hallway exchange followed a particularly difficult class on Bayesian reasoning. One classmate moaned, "That was brutal." Another said, "I've got it figured out. Either it happens or it doesn't. Fifty-fifty." She won the day.

Taking classes in Social and Decision Sciences exposed me to the work of Kahneman and Tversky. Googling them now, the first hit is a *New Yorker* article entitled, *The Two Friends Who Changed How We Think About How We Think*. Now *that's* a good headline.

Wikipedia's entry for Danny starts:

> Daniel Kahneman is an Israeli-American psychologist and economist notable for his work on the psychology of judgment and decision-making, as well as behavioral economics, for which he was awarded the 2002 Nobel Memorial Prize in Economic Sciences.

(Danny is also married to an Anne. Smart!)

In addition to making my first advisor feel guilty and vengeful by simply not eating animals, I would also piss off Social and Decision Sciences Professor D, but in a more active way. In his class, we would read papers – mostly Kahneman and Tversky – and write papers applying the concepts. One day toward the end of term, Prof D told the entire class, "Don't just write every paper about how it's wrong to eat meat."

Guess who he was talking to?

In my defense, every paper I wrote *was* a legitimate application of the topic at hand. Kahneman and Tversky's work revealed the mechanisms by which we manage the psychological disconnect that allows good people to eat animals. But I sure didn't get an A in *that* class.

While things had not yet gone south for me, they did sour pretty quickly for Anne. It was only midway through the first semester – remember: she had *four* classes and her job was supposed to be about teaching not fame – when the department head decreed, "You have to get your name out there."

<sigh>

Walking home through the golf course shortly after that edict, one of us said, "Let's just run away." But things were about to take a bigger turn than that.

Day 13 Concluded: Freezing, Snuggling, and Wine Undrunk

Humans think in stories
rather than in facts, numbers, or equations,
and the simpler the story, the better.

–*Yuval Noah Harari,* 21 Lessons for the 21st Century

Earlier today, we left the Georgia O'Keeffe Museum in Santa Fe, New Mexico. (Yes, I've spared you details of Chiricahua National Monument and White Sands National Park.) (Edit: OK, I didn't spare you; see "Travelog for Introverts.") In keeping with how glorious this month has been, the sun was brilliant. As I tried to attach my clip-on shades (I am just *that* cool) the right lens fell out of my glasses.

Now I'm quite nearsighted. (And yet also somewhat farsighted – intelligent design!) My right-eye script is -14. So it was *really bad* not to have glasses! And Anne certainly wouldn't want to drive in an unfamiliar city. Using the phone (thanks again, Google!) we found an optical shop a few blocks away. Anne carefully led me there, around people and obstacles and cars.

That event happened exactly as written, May 2022.
But it is, of course, also a metaphor.

In 1993, a year after we wed, we were *both* blind. Love-blind. Only fate was leading.

That October, we took a trip we called our belated honeymoon. Unbeknownst to us, and completely without our planning or intention, this long weekend would set in motion not one, but *two* major changes down the road.

After Anne finished teaching that warm and sunny Friday, I picked her up at Baker Hall and we headed to a (cheap, of course) motel in Erie PA. That night, a cold front went through. (Remember, this was before you could check out the forecast at weather.com.) The next day, when we drove on to Farm Sanctuary in upstate New York, it was cold, even some snow flurries!

This was the last weekend Farm Sanctuary's brand-new cabins would be open. When I say "cabin," I mean a room about fifteen by fifteen, with two double beds, a small space heater, and a hundred yard walk outside to the shared bathroom.

Romantic!

Given that the room was *so very cold*, and there was no TV (and no Netflix or YouTube or wifi) there was little to do other than snuggle, to cite Marge Simpson. This may have been what caused the first major change.

While we weren't in the cabin setting up a sharp turn in our future trajectory, we were out sightseeing. Ithaca is a beautiful little town, with gorgeous gorges. They also had a shop where we bought winter coats! (My upstate coat is hanging in the closet for when it falls below fifty. This was the trip that started our saying, "It's not a vacation unless we're freezing our asses off.")

We also visited many of the small- and medium-sized wineries that dot the hills surrounding the Finger Lakes. Whenever we had a sample from one we liked, we would buy a bottle or two. Because of our snuggling, we would end up giving away the sixteen or so bottles we brought back to Pittsburgh.

In addition to the consequence of my booking us a primitive, freezing "honeymoon," this trip obliquely set in motion the other life-altering event, although that one wouldn't play out until the fall of 1996.

In their list of local food options (e.g., "This place offers a salad you can make vegan by asking them to remove the egg, cheese, bacon bits, and dressing.") Farm Sanctuary also mentioned a small vegan store attached to a nearby motel. We stopped by and saw a "book," *The Most Noble Diet*, which was just some bound letter-sized pages of dot-matrix printouts.

There was no one around, so we took a copy and left some money. Back in Pittsburgh, we contacted the author, George Eisman, and offered to typeset his book. (I knew the page-layout program QuarkXPress from my time working at the school newspaper back in Cincinnati, and I would soon replace my original, *much*-modified nine-inch screen Macintosh SE – seen here with Anne in the super-cool hat – with a sleek new PowerMac 6100.) He replied enthusiastically, also asking for our feedback and edits. Eventually, we ended up with an actual, professionally-printed paperback, and George insisted we also put our names on it.

George will be back in a few years, seemingly as a hero.

How to Be a Stud: Relationship Advice

*Lasting love is something a person
has to decide to experience.*

–Robert Wright, The Moral Animal

I have a simple definition of love: The happiness of a person I love is more important than my own. I currently truly love two people, although I care deeply about the happiness of many others.

If you adopt my definition, then reacting to situations becomes simple: Do whatever makes the person you love happy. (Unless you are pretty darn confident they are making a mistake that would have significant bad consequences.) If adopting this approach makes you feel taken advantage of, it is time to re-evaluate your relationship.

Not Sharing is Caring

It is sometimes good to keep things from your partner.

Now I'm not advising that you keep your *feelings* to yourself in stereotypical male fashion. To truly love someone, it is generally necessary to know how they're feeling.

But there are some things that your partner can't do anything about, and knowing will just make them feel worse.

A prime example: My sister and I often have dealings with our mother that I keep from Anne.

Also, when we lived in Pittsburgh, something went down between Anne and a family we were friends with for a while. I don't know what – Anne dealt with it by talking with another friend and keeping me out of it. (I'll bet he came on to her. Hard to blame him – Anne is irresistible.) The dude involved was a multiple-level black-belt in Taekwondo, so I'm sure not telling me was the right decision.

There are also various pain examples. For Lung II, I didn't tell her how bad it was until I was safely back home. (She still doesn't *really* know how bad it was, but she will once she gets to Day 30. Sorry sweetums.)

And we've never talked about my ambulance trip and hospital stay after my accident last year. (She wasn't allowed to visit due to covid.) Unfortunately, she did have to hear me out of my mind following surgery on my broken neck. It seems that the amnesia-inducing drug didn't wear off before the anesthesia. Thus, when I woke up, I had no recollection of the accident or the hospital. I kept falling into a *very* realistic dream where I was in my office and the blurry fragments of the hospital were the dream. (I didn't have my glasses, so things were just vague shapes.) Seems I was so agitated that instead of waiting for things to right themselves, they called Anne. She then had to convince me I really was in the hospital. How terrible is that?

Sorry.

Never expect change.

One thing we hammered into EK was: Don't *ever* think you can change someone, or even *hope* that they will change.

People will change over time, of course. Partners will get older – saggier and flabbier and less energetic. Successes and failures will come and go. Smells will worsen.

But how people change often doesn't make relationships *easier*. It is a well-known fact, but yet the fading of passion's flame *still* surprises couples, leading to disillusionment and the pursuit of greener grass elsewhere. This is why the average marriage in the United States lasts *only eight years*.

If you are caught up with an "opposites attract" partner, enjoy! But don't think that magnetic attraction will sustain you when there are screaming, needy kids. Or when all your quirks and foibles have become familiar to each other, but the lust and excitement have receded.

Better times. Yes, Niagara Falls, but on a work trip.

You can never say "thank you" too much.

And the idea that "Love means you never have to say 'I'm sorry'"? *Total crap.*

Don't holler from the other room.

Just don't do it. Get up and go to them. You've been sitting too much as it is.

Also: Set and strictly follow the rule: You can't answer a question with a question.

Also: Take everything your loved one says to you in the best possible way. If they really love you, they are probably saying it because they want you to be happy.

Just forget anything said in a moment of passion.

Also in moments of anger, stress, and intimacy.

Jonathan Franzen (whose best book, *The Corrections*, is brilliant but quite painful) said it well in 2011:

> Trying to be perfectly likable is incompatible with loving relationships. Sooner or later, for example, you're going to find yourself in a hideous, screaming fight, and you'll hear coming out of your mouth things that you yourself don't like at all, things that shatter your self-image as a fair, kind, cool, attractive, in-control, funny, likable person.

I've never read a good explanation of why, but our minds don't always function clearly in times of strong emotion. It is *not* the case that we are saying what we *really* feel, that emotion removes the filter behind which people hide their true selves. So many *strange* things have been said when people were really emotional. Things that just came out of *nowhere*.

You have two choices:

Trust when the other person says, "I have no idea where that came from. I don't really think that." Then just forget it; it isn't as though we haven't said things along these lines.

End the relationship.

But don't stay around and dwell on it. Fear is the mind-killer; if you live in the fear that what they said was true, you will never have a healthy, affirming relationship.

Your body will fail and embarrass you.

It doesn't mean you don't love each other. Bodies are gross. We weren't designed [sic] to get old, but nowadays we generally do. As the great Billy Bragg sings in "Sexuality":

> I'm sure that everybody knows
> how much my body hates me.
>
> It lets me down most every time
> and makes me rash and hasty.
>
> I feel a total jerk
> before your naked body of work.

Corollary: You will fart. They will too.

A comedian once did a bit on how he would always leave the room or go over to the window when he was first dating his future wife. But inevitably, the farts came. They were in bed and he let one, leading her to exclaim: "Oh *God!* Did you let the *dog* in?"

It is fine to be alone!

This doesn't necessarily apply to extroverts. I don't know what it is like to be an extrovert.

But for introverts, I think we need to be aware of society's expectation that we pair bond.

(And I do think that most of us will be better people if we are able to be by ourselves without being lonely. Or wanting to shock ourselves.)

I know. Just as it is ridiculous for a memoirist to offer the advice "ask people about themselves," it is absurd for someone who has been with his soulmate for three decades to talk about being alone.

After I'd been married a while, Judas and I were walking with a younger new activist and the conversation turned to relationships. The kid asked, "But don't you have to love yourself before you can love someone else?" Judas and I burst out laughing.

I very much did *not* love myself when Anne and I met. For as calm and composed and complete as she seemed – she had decided she would be alone the rest of her life – she didn't love herself, either. But she would have been fine – she wasn't needy and unstable like me.

And yet, we became each other's entire karass – the people (or person) to whom you are connected at the deepest level. After EK had been away at college for several years, Anne came across one of those "life checklists." One of the items was "live alone for some time." Anne's immediate reaction was, "Yeah, it's great that we live alone."

I lived solo several terms while working at Booz Allen but would regularly go down to Cincinnati to "socialize." My last term working at Pratt & Whitney in Florida was when I was most on my own. I wasn't a part of the co-op group. (Although I did meet a kid from Georgia Tech whose mother had married someone younger than him. In case that isn't clear: This kid was twenty-one and his "stepfather" was twenty. *Holy shit.*) After leaving work on Friday, I often wouldn't say a single word to anyone until Sunday night when I made the (expensive) long-distance call to talk dirty with Diane.

(Praise be to the Flying Spaghetti Monster, Anne and I have never been apart for weeks – except the horrific weeks of Lung II – let alone months, so we've never had to hone *that* skill.)

Sorry. This has lapsed back into story instead of advice. But one last observation: kids these days seem to be making different choices than my generation. They're marrying less often and later, and having fewer unplanned babies. (Yay for no lead and free contraception!) EK is about to turn twenty-eight, and none of their college pals have gotten married or had a kid.

No one has it figured out.

Another thing we drilled into EK: *Everyone* is just a person. Everyone has a monkey mind. Everyone has doubts. Everyone makes mistakes. Everyone has regrets.

While at Pomona College, EK and some pals were going to hear a guest speaker. One of them said to E, "Hurry up! He's a Nobel Laureate!" E replied, "He's just a person."

I still beam when I remember that.

(When EK was four, my mom asked them what values they had learned. I honestly didn't know what E would answer. They thought for a moment and then said, "Safety and kindness." Score one for us.)

Distance friendships are hard.

Particularly those that have almost always been remote.

At my last place of employment, I thought I had built a number of good friendships. I did spend *some* time IRL with all of them (and many other great colleagues) at several different events.

For example, I shared a room with Zak at a conference, and the first night we stayed up till two talking philosophy. The last night, while everyone else was at the after-parties, fellow introvert Rose and I ate Taco Bell bean burritos and drank ginger ale and Trader Joe's whiskey. As people came back to the hotel, a number of them congregated in our room. At midnight, Annie, a raucously-fun fireplug with an eight-foot-tall personality, said, "OK, at twelve-thirty, we have to call it a night." Next thing we knew, it was two a.m. again.

But that isn't the point. (My father and sister tease me that I always have a story, no matter what the topic.) The point is that I have many doubts as to how to think about my six main virtual friendships. (Five of whom are with women, I'm just now realizing.)

Anne and I are staying with one of them this summer, so I'm guessing that we're on good terms. But for four of them, a pattern has repeated: After sending several emails and getting no reply, I have the thought, "OK, it was great, but I guess they've moved on." (For one of them – someone who read a draft of this book when it was only a few dozen pages, and with whom I've talked and chatted and laughed more than anyone else – that is a sad thought.) But each time, within a week of my "moved on" thought, I have heard from each of them. (Edit: it happened again this week.)

Another side story: Since I was abruptly terminated during 2021's Pandemic Summer, one person I *thought* was a good friend has not replied to a single text, email, or Facebook message. I thought we shared a deep yearning to help animals and a joyful love of science, but everything I've sent her has been met with stony silence. Yet she still "likes" things I put on Facebook. She did it twice again just this week, nearly a year after we last had contact. It is so strange. I can't help but think: *What is going on?*

So I don't know. And I have it easy – I don't care anymore what people think of me. One Step's main donors have long believed in our reasoning and vision, even as we've been ostracized, attacked, and betrayed. And I think at least some of my friends will be my friends regardless. But who knows. I've been totally – and, the second time, bewilderingly – wrong about that before.

Rats. Again, I've fallen into the trap of talking about myself when I meant for this chapter to be straight advice for you. Sorry. At this point in my life, I only want to be helpful:

> It's more important to try to help people than to know that you did.
> More important that someone else's life gets better than for you to feel good about yourself.
>
> –*Naomi Nagata,* The Expanse

PS: Get a good, sturdy snuggling chair. Why didn't someone tell me this when I was 17?

PPS: You will never be younger than you are now.

(In case it wasn't obvious, the first five words of the title of the chapter are a joke.)

A *very* tolerant wife.

Day 14: Prelude to
The End of Happiness

I don't resent being pregnant.
I resent everyone who hasn't been honest.

I resent the culture of how much women
have to suck it the fuck up
and act like everything is fine.
I really resent that.

–Amy Schumer

One day late in that first semester at CMU, Bonnie asked Anne how she was doing. "Tired. Nauseous. Bloated." Bonnie jokingly replied, "Sounds like you're pregnant."

Silence.

Then: "NO! Really?" *Squeel!*

(Driving in New Mexico a few days ago, we listened to an episodes of the podcast No *Stupid Questions* where psychologist Angela Duckworth [*Grit*] and Stephen Dubner [*Freakonomics*] noted that women in our society are judged first on their looks, and second on having kids. Men are judged for what they do.

Anne and I are lucky that we got out of our cowtowns and are generally around a liberal, highly-educated, progressive crowd – there is less pressure to breed. There is even a *very* loud, *very* judgy anti-child faction of vegans – another fine example of *How to Win Friends and Influence People*.)

But yeah, there we were, late 1993, standing in the bathroom looking at the peed-on stick with a mix of disbelief, shock, excitement, and terror. We hadn't made any decisions in this realm, leaving it sit while we were busy finishing up in Illinois, moving, and starting new positions. Yet in retrospect, we should have done the math. If a form of contraception is effective 99% of the time, four hundred times later....

The nausea came pretty soon after the pee stick, with the barfing on its heels. As you might expect, it made the stress of a new job / four classes / "get your name out there" worse. (Except for Bonnie, who figured it out, we told no one those first months, given that god is the greatest abortionist. If anything at all had happened, loads of people would have blamed not eating animal products.)

When she *could* eat, Anne went through the stereotypical jags. Luckily, when the Chinese food phase hit, there was a good place only a few blocks away. (They had the best spicy green beans, and I don't like green beans!) But when she turned to Taco Bell bean burritos (not any burritos I could make) the nearest one was a good distance away. (Taco Bell is way underrated. They offer inexpensive, tasty, not-terrible-for-you animal-friendly fast food at more places than anywhere else.)

In one of our many "it seemed like a good idea at the time" decisions, we went with Birthplace, a midwife center. That choice would lead to the first of my three Worst experiences. (I've shattered my face, broken my neck, and had my lung drilled twice without anesthesia, and none of *those* specific horrors make the top three Worsts.) Now when we're talking to people who are pregnant or even thinking about it, our advice is: "Bring on the epidural!"

Remember, this was 1993. Veganism wasn't a thing, not even a negative thing. It was a no-thing. The midwives made Anne keep a food diary to prove that she was getting the right nutrients. And once people found out Anne was pregnant, *everyone* turned into an obnoxious nutrition expert.

Ah, Pittsburgh

That winter was the snowiest we will ever experience together. (In fifteen years, it has snowed thrice here in Tucson. And I bitch every time.) Of course, El Cheapo here didn't spring for an indoor parking spot, so I spent a lot of time digging the little two-door Sentra out of the snowbank left by the plows. (Value your time *and* safety!)

(I would wise up about parking after the baby was born. One day, we went down to the garage and a chunk of the ceiling had fallen onto the new four-door Nissan Altima we bought in the spring of 1994. That was the start of falling being a thing for me. The worst of the items falling on *me* came about ten years later, when the heavy, '50s-era thick-glass light fixture in my office fell, without warning, right on my head. I took a picture of the pieces and labeled it, "God fails to smite me.")

Both of us had strong feelings that Anne was carrying a girl. When we had dreams about the baby, they were always about a girl. Ultimately, ultrasound backed us up. But before you read too much into our premonition, we ultimately turned out to be wrong.

Gender led to an awkward situation that Christmas. While we were trimming the tree in Tiffin, my dad said, "Let's hope it's a boy to carry on the Ball name." (This was really a *big* thing with him, one that would ultimately disappoint him, with EK being his only grandchild.) Anne, whom I had failed to brief on this topic, replied, "Oh, we've decided the baby will have my name." I mean, c'mon, this is obvious – Green is *vastly* superior to Ball. Why would anyone saddle a kid with "Ball" when "Green" is *right there*?!

The surname was continually a big deal. In yet another example of how men are considered owners, women would ask, "How will people know who the father is?" *That* one caught me by surprise. Women's willingness to allow themselves to be "given away" from father to husband, with the surname changing to reflect the change in ownership, is utterly repulsive. Everyone who thinks that women have it easy should imagine being so indoctrinated that you go along with it.

But the biggest deal, *by far*, was birthday cake. I'm *serious.* Once they knew Anne was pregnant and vegan, about half the women would ask in horror, "*But what about birthday parties?*" I know this seems like a joke, but I am totally serious. It was as though childhood was only sleep, school, and eating birthday cake. And using the last name to track down the unknown father.

This particular insanity continued all through EK's childhood. We got it from vegans, too. Carolyn the Second was *infuriated* that I had said in an interview that I wouldn't police what our kid ate before they were old enough to understand why we didn't eat eggs or dairy. Carolyn justified her fury by saying it would send "mixed messages" if a four-year-old ate a piece of non-vetted cake. I replied that I never knew anyone who said, "Oh, I *would* have stopped eating animals, but then I saw this preschooler having cake!"

(I am happy to say that this Carolyn and I are now friends, and she regrets how things went years ago. [Just as I regret many things, like helping to force Mark off the board of Animal Liberation Action. Again: <sigh>] Carolyn proves the vegan fever *can* break! But she was replaced by the next group, and then the next, and then the group that would excommunicate me. At that point, I was more than happy to go.)

OK, enough cake. To get out of going to the insanity of Christmas in Michigan, we mailed Anne's parents a bottle of the New York wine with a baby bib. That was our way of saying Anne was pregnant. (Weren't we cute?) Anything to avoid spending time with a person, to this day, disdains me. (Not her dad, though. He's long dead. Anne is now older than her dad was when he died.)

At a birth class that winter, the other couples proved you don't need to really know one another to breed. We played a version of 1966's *The Newlywed Game*, where the men left the room and the women were asked a series of questions – "What is your husband's favorite meal? ("Partner" was not the word used in those days.) "Where were you when you found out you were pregnant?" (And *please* stop with "We're pregnant." *Only one person is pregnant,* having her body completely transformed while building *an entirely new person.* Who will then exit through a *tiny* opening!) The women wrote their answers on cards, then the men came back in and were asked to guess what answers their partner had given. Then for the next round, the women left.

Keep in mind, Anne and I had only met a bit over a year before. We easily got every question right except one. I didn't know what her greatest fear was: Not being able to do it. (The birth, that is; she was obviously able to "do it.") But none of the other couples got even fifty percent right! I was shocked.

We stopped going after the second class. Being told to "breathe" is bullshit. We didn't know *just* how absurd it was, but we knew it wasn't helpful.

Also that snowy winter, we bought a used window-mount air conditioner. Our west-facing apartment got hot, and Anne was due in July. In retrospect, carrying it over icy hills of snow was not a good idea, but we would be glad we had it come summer.

The spring was nice. No more morning sickness, and Anne actually didn't mind when *total strangers* asked to touch her belly. Anne cut her hair short, and one day in Baker Hall, a woman Anne had never met suddenly squealed (so much squealing!) and exclaimed, "Oh *my gaaaaahd!* I didn't even know you were pregnant! When are you due?"

It turns out Anne had a short-haired Doppelgänger at CMU. The two of them never ran into each other, but people regularly asked Anne: "Why didn't you wave at me on (some day Anne wasn't on campus) when I called out to you?"

Fight the Power Part 1:
"To breed or not to breed"

Natural selection didn't design your mind
to see the world clearly;

it designed your mind to have perceptions and beliefs
that would help take care of your genes.

–*Robert Wright,* Why Buddhism Is True

tl;dr: your genes and society don't have your best interests at heart.

We human beings are obviously wired to bond and breed. (Not to be a broken record, but please read Bob Wright's *The Moral Animal* for more.) If your millions of direct ancestors hadn't followed the drive to breed, you wouldn't be here. And our society is set up for marriage and kids to be the norm. Many people don't like anything outside the norm (kinda the very definition of "conservative") especially anything that makes them question their choices.

Those whose genetic line depends on your actions – parents and grandparents – may be especially motivated to pressure you to bond and breed. Both genetically and socially, we've been indoctrinated to love and honor our elders, so their pressure can be especially powerful and insidious.

Also, some people breed because they think their kids will love them and make them happy. This is often *not* the case, especially in the unhealthy situation of a needy parent. If you have kids, it should be to bring a (hopefully) happy person into existence, not to assuage your unhappiness / emptiness.

Please be aware of all these pressures and evaluate your decisions accordingly.

Not to denigrate family, but it is often not all it is cracked up to be. About half of all marriages end in divorce, which messes up *many* kids. (I'm not saying that only divorced couples mess up their kids. To this day, into her eighties, my mom is still broken that "pro-life" Ardyth once told her "I wish you had never been born!" News flash: Many parents have had that thought about a child, at least fleetingly.)

Of the people you know well, how many were provided a happy, healthy, balanced, lie-free, totally-loved childhood? (Religion counts as a lie.)

And many parents are far less happy than you would think (or than they will let on). As is probably obvious, parents feel internal and external pressure to sing the praises of their children. But simply Google "Are single people happier?" or "Are childfree couples happier?" and you will find seemingly endless studies showing that having kids is definitely *not* the key to happiness. Doing this search while I write this, the top results say, "the data suggest single people are happier and more satisfied with their lives than commonly believed," and "Couples without children have happier marriages, according to one of the biggest studies ever of relationships in Britain. Childless men and women are more satisfied with their relationships and more likely to feel valued by their partner." And this happiness is in *spite* of our genetic and familial and social pressures to breed.

If you think your life would be empty without a child, your life has bigger problems than a child could or should fill. If you think your life won't be full without a child, are you sure you want to fill it with pain, screams, worry, regret, poop, worry, anguish, apprehension, guilt, and then a topping of worry?

This *isn't* to say a child or children aren't worth it. Loads of people love their kids! I just want us to recognize that although our genes want us to breed and our families want us to breed and society wants us to breed, none of that means we *should* breed. We *should* do what is best for our actual happiness, not to just go along with the program.

Also: Please don't buy all the anti-only-child propaganda breeders put out there. It's hooey. Studies have shown that only children do at least as well as children with siblings. Throughout their life and unsolicited, EK has thanked us for not having more kids. Furthermore, I know I ruined my younger siblings' lives. I'm not saying they shouldn't have been born; I'm saying my parents shouldn't have married or reproduced *at all*. As you've seen, it was against all odds that Anne and I met. If anything had deviated, I'd almost certainly have killed myself or ended up in a Diane-esque unhappy marriage with unhappy children.

I truly think that there would be a lot more happiness if fewer people got married and many fewer people had kids. Even before the pandemic, this seemed to be happening with folks currently in their twenties and thirties. So maybe more kids these days are breaking free of the pressures and doing what's right for their own life satisfaction.

Want something to fill your life? Give to organizations that educate and provide contraception to girls and women. Want a fascinating take currently outside the Overton window? Google "The Case for Not Being Born."

PS: Editing this chapter, I was reminded of the first person Phil and I met who didn't eat animal products. Jake, as I'll call him, felt *hugely* guilty about being a third child and using more resources than "deserved." He basically starved himself. (He was also the first person with whom I talked about how people changing their diet in the *direction* of vegetarianism could hurt more animals.)

Some years later, Jake married someone I'll call Ocean, and they started a sanctuary for cuddly mammals. When Anne and I visited, it was obvious Ocean was sublimating her desire for a (human) baby. Shortly after, she punched a hole in her diaphragm and got pregnant. Jake, the *very last* guy I thought would breed, went on to have a second child. That was when I really realized just how much the urge to pair bond and breed could overcome. After that, I wasn't all *that* surprised when this happened with others.

Day 14 Concluded:
Worst the First

Not the kind of congress that contained Paul Tsongas.

–*Homer Simpson, "Catch 'Em if You Can"*

I will luxuriate in retelling our first year together, only avoiding various stories – like the two days it took us to watch *The Unbearable Lightness of Being* – in order to minimize what will cause great discomfort and pushback when Anne reads this draft. ("I'm telling you: *No one wants to read about your sex life!*" Sorry.)

But I will race through the events following our final maximally-curvy congress. That July 15 1994, I was able to get to sleep after, but Anne wasn't – congress' contractions had induced birthing contractions. She was past her due date and naïvely "ready to get on with it." (On the other hand, what was the alternative?) She woke me up at midnight, and the next seven hours were the first Worst of my life.

Two lessons for anyone pregnant:

Please please *please*, don't do "natural" childbirth. You wouldn't let nature run its course if you had cancer, so just don't do it.

Have a supportive team that you know and trust so you can force your partner out of the room.

See, a partner who has no control over their love will have such empathy that they will experience your pain. But here's the kicker: *the partner* will have no rush of endorphins after. While Anne was holding the baby, she was blissed out, even as things were being done to her – *without anesthesia* – that would normally cause screaming. (I scream internally just remembering. AHHHHHH!!) Anne's peak/end memory of events are mostly just those first bonding moments.

My memory, however – seared into my brain with a branding iron – was of the Worst torture I had ever witnessed. For over a year, I wouldn't even let anyone mention the events of the first seven hours of July 16, 1994 within my earshot.

"La-la-la-la, I can't hear you!"

More Unpopular Opinions

If we were all on trial for our thoughts,
we would all be hanged.

–Margaret Atwood, Alias Grace

One of the hardest things to do
is differ with some of the people
you agree with on most issues.

And people need to learn that's not a betrayal.

–Barney Frank, quoted in Nick Offerman's Gumption

Opposition to physician-assisted suicide is immoral.

Why oh why do we think we can tell *anyone* that they can't end their life in as painless a way possible? *Who do we think we are?* We let "any butt-reaming asshole" bring any number of new lives into existence, regardless of circumstance, regardless of how much the child will suffer. Yet we deny those same people the right to end *their own life?* Crazy.

Not that there aren't issues. But we should deal with how we treat the elderly rather than denying individuals the ability to control their own life.

Let's hope Switzerland's death pods become a thing.

Killing is fine. Suffering is not.

A commenter is appalled that I'm so "right" about animal issues but so "wrong" about abortion ("killing babies"). But there is no *inherent* moral problem with *actually* killing babies, just as there is no inherent moral problem with killing animals. There is no *inherent* moral problem with Anne killing me.

Ethics come into play when there is suffering. (And pleasure, but primarily suffering.)

It is often sad, but there are times when killing is the ethical choice. The obvious example is an animal who is terminally ill. One of our family's saddest days was when we had Sunny, the guinea pig EK grew up with, euthanized. But it was the ethical thing to do.

This is one of the areas where we sometimes treat some non-human animals better than human animals. We don't make our companion animals suffer more at the end of their life.

So yes, taking two pills to (kill a baby) expel a small clump of cells is more ethical than bringing yet another unwanted child into the world. (U.S. families adopted more than 7,000 children, yet over 100k children await adoption from the American foster care system.) It is also ethical to kill an actual newborn baby if the alternative is for them to suffer and then die.

Eating organic can be immoral.

Don't tell me that conventional agriculture uses "chemicals." *Everything* is "chemicals"! Oxygen? A chemical! Sucrose? A chemical!

And pesticides? "Organic" farmers use pesticides. Also, from *New Scientist*:

> All fruit and vegetables contain large numbers of naturally occurring pesticides. These are the result of an arms race with insect herbivores.
>
> If we tested for these, we would find that they are just as nasty as synthetic pesticides, but present in food in higher amounts. However, they don't affect us when we consume them because their concentration is only effective against insects, not anything large.
>
> The real problem with organic farming is low yield. You need much more land to obtain similar yields to other forms of farming. I think we should be returning farmland to nature, not increasing its area.

And because of their low yields, advocating organic agriculture means there will be less food grown – advocating for organic means more hunger.

Or, as Robert L. Paarlberg says in *Resetting the Table: Straight Talk About the Food We Grow and Eat*:

> My research experience tells me not to yearn for an organic, local, or slow food system, since that would mean abandoning a century's worth of modern science. It would force farmers to accept more toil and less income, consumers would be given fewer nutritious food choices, and greater destruction would be done to the natural environment...
>
> I want a food solution that works for all, including people who live on a budget and those without a lot of spare time. Dinners at Chez Panisse may be wonderful, but start at over a hundred dollars.

Assembling healthy meals from fresh, unprocessed ingredients is a joy for many, but the time required for shopping, preparation, and clean up may be too much for a single parent with school-age kids.

PS: While editing this, Vox's great Kenny Torrella wrote an issue of their great Future Perfect newsletter which documented how Sri Lanka's banning of synthetic fertilizer and pesticide imports "proved disastrous." Now the country is in free-fall. Google "Sri Lanka's organic farming disaster, explained" for more.

PPS: Of course, in terms of efficient use of land and other resources, growing crops and feeding them to animals instead of people is *far* worse than organic plant-based food.

Plastics are awesome and trash is fine, except food waste.

Example: a recent study by the Swiss Federal Laboratories for Materials Science and Technology ("To wrap or to not wrap cucumbers?") found that plastic wrapping was responsible for only 1% of the cuke's environmental footprint. On the other hand, each cucumber thrown away has the footprint of 93 wraps. The conclusion? By extending shelf life, wrapping had a net environmental benefit 4.9 times higher than not wrapping.

As reported in *New Scientist*: "Plastic food packaging gets a bad rap, but does it always deserve it?"

> The upsides of plastic packaging don't stop with shelf life, but can retain the nutritional value of the crops too. Broccoli is a good example. It can lose up to 80 per cent of its glucosinolates, a group of phytochemicals thought to be responsible for some of the crop's key health benefits, when loose on

supermarket shelves, versus the shrink-wrapped version in the chiller. Such effects have been found in a wide range of crops, which is one of the key reasons retailers go to the extra expense of using wrapping in the first place.

What about all the plastic in the ocean?

Do you want to know how that plastic got there? Are you *sure*? Not because you threw a straw away, but because you put a Dasani bottle in the recycling bin. That bottle, and much else, was sloppily shipped to Asia. If it didn't fall off the "recycling" ship, it was dumped. (Also: fishing nets. Lots of fishing nets.) (More: Want to save the oceans? Stop recycling plastic.)

But when you throw plastic away, you know what happens? As told to me by someone in the industry:

> All that carbon bound up in the plastic just sits there, sequestered in the landfill and not contributing to greenhouse gasses. In a sense the carbon has gone full circle, being pumped out of the ground to form plastic, and then returning to the ground in a landfill.

Compare that to "organic" waste:

> The decomposition of food and other material quickly uses up the oxygen in the landfill, so most of the food decomposes anaerobically, producing methane. Methane, of course, is a major greenhouse gas.

Passion, love, and/or dedication *are not enough.*

When you commit yourself entirely to the pursuit of something, that produces excellence, and that is intoxicating for people who want to be close to excellence.

–*Jane Friedman*, The Business of Being a Writer

Sorry, Jane, this is simply not true.

Same for Steve Jobs' (in)famous 2005 commencement speech at Stanford: "Don't let the noise of others' opinions drown out your own inner voice. And most important, have the courage to follow your heart and intuition. They somehow already know what you truly want to become."

Blargle.

OK, fine, you got me – this is probably not horrible advice for *graduates of Stanford.* They not only have a Stanford degree, but to even get in, they must have had both a privileged life with connections in addition to their vastly above-average talents.

But for *the vast majority* of the tens of millions of people who watched the speech on YouTube, following "your heart and intuition" is a path to disappointment and/or your mother's basement. For every Steve Jobs or Serena Williams or David Sedaris or RBG there are countless – Hundreds? Thousands? – of people who passionately dedicated themselves to something *and failed.*

Yet this shit advice is *so common.* It feels like everyone who succeeds thinks it is just because they wanted it more. Fish-man Michael Phelps was on Colbert saying anyone can be anything they want. Sorry, but no one without once-in-a-generation physical skills will ever out-swim Phelps. And there was no way *he* could have then turned himself into a Tiger-beating golfer, or a Nobel-winning physicist, or a brilliant and insightful memoirist.

My life is a testament to this. In seventh, eighth, and ninth grades, I *lived* basketball. I ran, I lifted, I practiced before and after school. But as soon as other kids got close to my height, I wasn't even good enough to play for a shitty school with a graduating class of 69.

And my passion to change the world, to reduce suffering? This book is testament to that failure as well.

I *did* meet my soulmate, but as is clear in this book, that was a lucky, unlikely accident, *not* as the result of passion or dedication.

Chihuly.

Opposition to mosquito eradication is immoral and incredibly arrogant.

Mosquitoes are the deadliest animals on earth. Every single year, they kill between 700,000 and 1,000,000 people – mostly poor people of color in the global south. Humans only directly kill about 400,000 other humans every year.

In addition to the people they kill, mosquitoes sicken hundreds of millions each year, with many facing long-term health consequences. Mosquito-borne diseases have kept any number of countries from being able to develop, trapping their people in poverty.

We now have the technology to wipe out these horrible monsters. Yet wealthy white whiners wail about "ecosystems" and "unintended consequences." (And create idiotic straw men about "all mosquitos" when the target is obviously only disease-carrying species.) Excuse me, but *we already know* the consequences of inaction. Just because this havoc isn't being wreaked upon them or their children shouldn't make a difference. Every day that passes that we aren't going full-bore into eradicating *Aedes aegypti* and *Aedes albopictus* is another day of terrible and unnecessary suffering. A lot of us prissy, self-centered "liberals" are directly to blame for this disease and death.

In general, all those who oppose GMOs should go down as some of humanity's worst monsters. People are suffering and dying every single day while the "No GMOs!" crowd drive their Teslas to Whole Foods. It is simple: our world will continue to be far worse than it needs to be because of them.

If you doubt any of this, check out MarkLynas.org and read the regret of a former anti-GMO activist.

Fuck Nature & Make America Great

Back to Worst the First: A younger friend went through almost exactly the same torture watching his partner give birth in 2021. Before talking with him, I had not personally known anyone who admitted to having such a terrible, scarring time witnessing their child being born. It is pretty dang depressing that we don't talk about what dads go through, just as it sucks that we don't take postpartum depression seriously enough.

Ezra Klein talked about another problem on one of his podcasts after Annie Lowrey had their first child. (Here is a thread on his second child, and Annie's story. *Please* read the latter before you decide to have kids.) In the Bay Area, Ezra and Annie felt a lot of pressure to have "natural" pregnancy and childbirth. But Annie had many complications, and it was only modern medicine that allowed her and her child to survive and thrive.

Contrary to what we liberals say, "natural" is often very *very* bad. And people who promote "natural" as "good" are very often *wrong wrong wrong.*

Childbirth is just one example. "Natural" selection discovered it was worth killing off bunches and bunches of women during childbirth in order to get individuals with bigger brains.

And only about a hundred years ago, being pregnant was about as bad *as having breast cancer today.* Not back in the Stone Age – in the early 1900s, as documented in Steven Pinker's *Enlightenment Now.*

Isn't that f****** unbelievable? (My phone won't transcribe "fucking.")

And then let's consider that, well into the 21st century, the infant mortality rate in the United States is *terrible.* Of all the OECD countries, only Turkey and Mexico are worse. The rate at which infants die here is more than *three times* that in Japan.

Maternal mortality is *even worse* – even Turkey is better than the U.S. in caring for mothers. Many countries have a rate of *zero* maternal deaths, including Ireland (Catholic, although abortion access is better there than here), Estonia, Slovenia, and the Slovak Republic.

The United States isn't only far from "Number One!" – we are utterly shameful – we should literally be *ashamed.* In this regard, we really *do* need to make America great again – we should lead the world in these categories.

Let's be truly "pro-life" and keep *actual people* from dying unnecessarily. If we can have people rich enough to build themselves private space penises, we're rich enough to protect women and babies at least as well as Iceland does.

F the Founding Fathers.

I understand wanting to feel special about your country. In the Bicentennial year of 1976, I celebrated as much as anyone.

But I have an excuse: I was eight.

We're adults, not children. We must stop worshiping the "Founding Fathers." What they and their contemporaries "intended" is simply irrelevant to the 21st Century.

More than that: *Their intentions were actively immoral.* They intended for people to be enslaved. They intended all the native people to be pushed aside. (At best.) They intended for women to be *de facto* property with zero voice in government. ("It's 1800. Ladies: Tell your husbands Vote for Burr!") They intended a shitty form of government that protected only white land-owning and slave-owning men.

Or as Elie Mystal puts it in his *absolutely magnificent Allow Me to Retort:*

> Our Constitution is not good. It is a document designed to create a society of enduring white male dominance, hastily edited in the margins to allow for what basic political rights white men could be convinced to share. Conservatives are out here acting like the Constitution was etched by divine flame upon stone tablets, when in reality it was scrawled out over a sweaty summer by people making deals with actual monsters who were trying to protect their rights to rape the humans they held in bondage.

Or, as George Carlin summarized: "This country was founded by a bunch of slave owners who told us 'all men are created equal." That is what's known as being stunningly full of shit."

Or a meme online: "Rather than trying to read the minds of white, slave-owning men who have been dead for two centuries, maybe we should just do the right thing for the people alive today."

Ya think?

You know what the Founding Fathers *didn't* intend? That the country be a Christian theocracy. Google "The founding fathers were not Christians." Washington was a theist, not a Christian. During John Adam's administration, the Senate, filled with Founding Fathers, ratified the Treaty of Peace and Friendship, which states "the government of the United States of America is not in any sense founded on the Christian Religion." Jefferson, the author of the Declaration of Independence, was a Freethinker.

But regardless of what they thought, *fuck them*. "Originalism" is just another word for sexism, racism, and intellectual cowardice. If you're a bigot, don't blame the Founding Fathers. Time to grow the eff up and think for ourselves.

Mmmmm ... prickly

Day 15: A Lot of What?

You're only as happy as your least happy child.

Jumping ahead for a second: When we decided to buy a house in 1997, we looked in Pittsburgh's best school district and bought the cheapest place without common walls we could find. (We did the same here in Tucson.) One time in first grade, Elaina, one of EK's friends, came over and asked, "Where's the rest of your house?" To us, our house was huge! JL was able to live in the finished part of the basement and we wouldn't see or hear him. But Elaina and her very nice family lived a few doors down from Bill Cowher, the revered coach of the Steelers, and was used to a house five times the square footage of ours. (And a vacation house *just as big*.)

I bring this up because Anne, who is reading the local news right now, just asked me if I'd like to buy an eight-million-dollar lot. "A lot of what?"

Back to 1994: The baby who would become EK was extraordinarily unhappy. (I say it that way because I don't connect that baby with the person we know today.) There were a number of times I gave up and drove the baby to school so Anne could nurse and comfort them. We eventually hired a nice older woman to come in for parts of the day to relieve us both. (Anne had to remind me of this, as I had forgotten. Trying to blot out that entire year!)

Also, we eventually wised up to the fact that disposable diapers were invented for a reason: Cloth diapers suck! Another example of us trying to be "natural" that led to unnecessary unhappiness.

Probably our main memory from the end of '94 and early '95 is walking up and down all the halls of our apartment building, trying to get the baby, writhing and screaming in the sling, to fall asleep.

Our poor neighbors. I'm so sorry. We did go to every floor to try to spread out the pain. But again: Sorry.

At one point, Anne and I were wrestling with the screaming baby, trying to change the diaper. We looked at each other, both of us in tears, and said, "This was a mistake."

As mentioned, many parents have that thought at some point or another, but few share it. Again, this is a situation where more openness and honesty would lead to less suffering. Obviously, feeling like you've made a mistake *at one point* isn't a judgment on the person the baby will become, so we shouldn't have to worry about sparing our kids' feelings. They should know the reality of parenthood so they can make informed decisions.

When the philosopher Peter Singer was staying with us just after we moved to Tucson in 2007, he commented on how well adjusted EK was. (E was very confident and happy from maybe age three to fourteen or so.) I said, "I can't really take credit, or else I have to take the blame for how unhappy they were that first year.

Fight the Power Part 2: Family Feud

It is not easy
The war within us
But it gets easier
The more we learn

–Pet Shop Boys, "Happiness is an option"

As Robert Wright documents in his books *The Moral Animal* and *Why Buddhism Is True*, your genes are not there to make you happy. Indeed, except in the case of simple survival, your genes' interests are markedly *not* your interests, assuming you're interested in being happy and content.

If we want to be happy by any measure(s), we have to overrule our genetic programming. In addition to our genes' desires to make us breed, we face an uphill battle when it comes to family. (When I say "family" in this chapter, I mean "biological family" – parents, siblings – not "chosen family" – spouse and even closest friends, if either or both of these are for you. As you'll see, closest friends clearly didn't work out for me.)

We are programed by our genes to care about our families far above that of anyone else. The prominent biologist J. B. S. Haldane reportedly said he would give up his life for two brothers or eight cousins. Genetic humor!

Most, if not all, cultures have taken this instinct and codified it into norms and even laws. It is hard for me to believe, but we have it easy in the United States compared to many other countries.

This is *not* to say that family is *always* bad, just as believing in god(s) is not *always* bad. There are people who take great comfort in family and/or god (and don't do bad shit by forcing their beliefs on others).

(And of course there are those who *really* combine religion and family. EK was friends with several Mormons in grades 8-12. E asked one of them about the South Park episode "All About Mormons." In it, Trey Parker and Matt Stone expose how crazy the Mormons' faith is ["dum dum dum dum dum"] but are very kind to the actual Mormon characters. [They expanded on these ideas in "The Book of Mormon." If you can't see that show, listen to the soundtrack.] EK's friend was put off by the South Park episode, but couldn't *quite* say what they got wrong.)

But of course, just as with god(s), the worship of family can lead to much suffering. "Family" is used to stifle individuality and persecute anyone different. Expectations placed upon children and enforced by "family" can stunt their development and do significant harm. (As noted in the first Fight the Power chapter, some people have kids and want those children to be happy. Others have children and want the kids to make *them* happy.)

(Also, there is the old sawhorse: "Oh, you should have kids! Who will take care of you in your old age?" Speaking as a kid: *Not freaking me!* I'm not your nurse! I didn't sign up for any "I raised you, so you owe me" contract! In addition to "Ewww," this is another reason EK can't ever see this book – they exist only to make us happy and take care of us in our dotage.)

Family issues have played out in different ways for Anne and me. In 2012, after EK had gone off to school and my brother was staying with us at a motel in Flagstaff, he had a freak-out that led Anne and me to feel physically unsafe. (He threw knives and books at me when we were growing up. He once sent me into such a killing rage that I put my right fist through the bathroom door. The hole stayed there for months as a testament to our brotherly love.) He had to move to another room in the motel, as we didn't want him near us while we slept. When we were leaving the motel, he flew into another rage, jumped out of the car, and slammed the door. I just drove off. I had had it. And that was the last contact we've had with him.

Less dramatic: Starting as a little kid, it was a steady drip with Anne and her mom. For example, she wanted Anne to get a "real" man, telling her to put on makeup and go down to the bar in their redneck Michigan cowtown. Anne was also supposed to be a "real" doctor. Her mom *still* wanted both of these things after Anne and I were married and Anne had her PhD.

Following her mom's visited here in Tucson, Anne just stopped returning her phone calls. She had had it. Her dad was long dead and she had already lost contact with her brothers. Her mom still calls and leaves messages, sometimes including the comment, "Haven't talked to you in years." It is lousy, but a Pareto equilibrium – no one could be made happier without increasing another's unhappiness.

It is difficult to take a hard look at any relationship that isn't emotionally healthy. But you don't owe your parents *anything* for things they did for you after they brought you into the world. (This is one point my brother got right long before I did.) You don't owe siblings anything because they share half your genes. You are your own person and deserve your own life.

It is not easy, and many of us don't currently have other strong relationships in our lives. But I believe the ultimate goal should be to build a "found family" – people with whom you have things in common that aren't genes and forced history. We should spend our time with people who love us for who we are, rather than expecting our love because they sired or birthed us or grew up with us.

But it can be difficult to even *try* to evaluate relationships without the bias family entails. What Anne and I have done is to ask ourselves: if this person weren't family, would we have anything to do with them?

If the answer for you is "Yes," congrats! That's awesome! I have regular contact with my sister – we just had a great time together in Santa Fe.

But if the answer is "No," don't let them continue to stand in the way of healthy relationships and greater happiness.

Sorry to sound like a self-help book. It isn't as though I have it all figured out. Not all of my relationships are free of baggage and unfulfillable need. But I do hope that I see the bad relationships with greater clarity than in the past, and that I'm making the choices that maximize my chosen family's happiness.

Good luck to us all!

Day 16: "Who eats animals?"

*I haven't the slightest idea how to change people,
but still I keep a long list of prospective candidates
just in case I should ever figure it out.*

–*David Sedaris,* Naked

In that eventful fall of 1993, our nonprofit, Animal Liberation
Action (ALA) tried to organize activists around the country to
stand at busy intersections with our "Stop Eating Animals"
banners. We also organized another Fast for Farmed Animals,
which served no purpose. At least it was less miserable because I
was with Anne and didn't spend all day sitting in front of a
slaughterhouse.

While fasting, Anne and I held our banner in Pittsburgh's cold
autumn rain. At one point, a mom and daughter walked by. "Who
eats animals?" the mom asked, incredulous. The daughter grabbed
her arm and pulled her past: "Shhh! We do."

Right as my academic career was about to come off the rails,
ALA decided to shift from holding banners to developing, printing,
and distributing booklets. I did the design in QuarkXPress. As you
might guess, my design was ... utilitarian, to put it kindly. Later,

the great designer Lauren volunteered to redo the booklets. We were lucky to be able to hire her eventually.

It was somewhat around this time when we changed Animal Liberation Action's name. We rightly realized that a focus solely on farmed animals was key to helping the most animals, but we wrongly thought putting the word "vegan" in our group's name and titling our booklet *Why Vegan?* would help animals. Of course, these booklets mostly just helped vegans feel superior.

It turns out that you can be popular with vegans, or you can reach new people with a message that might actually help animals. I didn't realize that at the time. Once this started to dawn on me, I thought I could be the exception. I was wrong.

We scrounged around for cheap printers. One said that if we printed on yellow paper, we could get full color with only two print colors. I got the samples right before I drove Anne to her last sonogram. I still remember the crushing disappointment when I opened the envelope.

Not that these booklets were *entirely* worthless, especially after Anne and I developed ones without the word "vegan." For example: Anne kept a stack of those booklets in a holder on her office door in Baker Hall. One day, another PhD student in Environmental Engineering happened to take one. After reading it, Ross and his wife Tonya went vegan and contacted us.

In addition to being an engineering grad student, Ross was also tall, blond, and outclassed by his partner. And a meat lover. After I had Tofurky deli slices for the first time (Hickory Smoked are the best) I immediately emailed him: "Stop whatever you're doing. Go to the co-op *right now* and get Tofurky deli slices. They're in the refrigerated section." He emailed back within the hour: "HOW DO THEY DO THAT?" I still eat Hickory Smoked slices – they're even better today – and am friends with Seth, the founder.

Ross and I would remain friends up until the second Iraq war, when he did not take kindly to my anti-war and anti-W emails. I just couldn't shut up. Sorry.

In the summer of '95, I had to work at a Department of Energy facility as part of my fellowship. We chose the National Center for Atmospheric Research (NCAR) in Boulder.

NCAR, an I.M. Pei design, small in front of the Boulder Flatirons.

An older woman let us rent her beautiful home near Chautauqua Park; she and her cat went to her summer place in the mountains.

Those months were one catastrophe after another. The baby was *not happy* being strapped in a car seat. Then in Colorado, Anne had ever-increasing breathing issues. Everyone kept saying it was the altitude, but one night she was literally gasping for air. I called the one friend we had in town to come over to watch the baby and took Anne to the hospital. (*Almost* in the middle of the night.) Turns out Anne was having an allergic reaction to the woman's cat's fur, which was resolved by an inhaler and a professional steam cleaning of everything. This is one of the changes that happened to Anne during pregnancy, as she had grown up with cats and had never been allergic to them or anything else. (Another change: Anne can no longer eat super-spicy foods.)

What I *thought* was the final tragedy of the summer happened when Anne's father died while on a fishing trip in Canada. He had been the long-time pharmacist in Shepherd, a two-stoplight Michigan cowtown, so his funeral and associated events were a big deal. Our trip to Michigan was the second time we had flown with EK. The first had been our San Francisco trip earlier in the spring. That time, Anne's parents went with us to the airport. It was the last time we saw her dad alive.

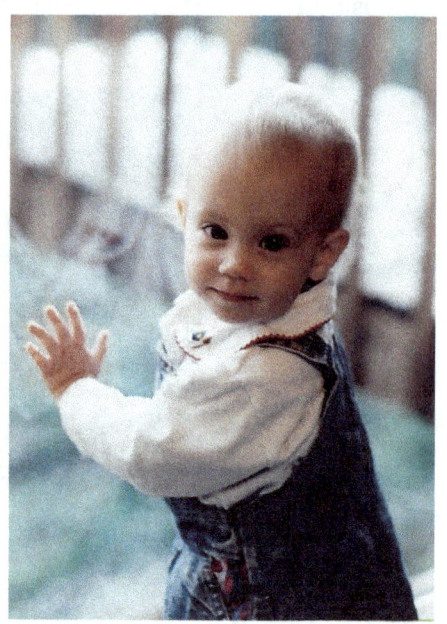

The End of Veganism

I'm a level-five vegan.
I don't eat anything that casts a shadow.

–Jesse Grass to Lisa Simpson,
mocking her mere vegetarianism

Nothing in this chapter applies to you.

Following 2021's horrors, one of my few remaining close friends told me I should write a book about why advocates should not focus exclusively on "longtermism." (That chapter comes later in the book.) I had blogged about this topic in the past, beginning with a post titled, "Where I part ways with the smartest person I know."

That smartest person, JL, lived in our Pittsburgh basement during the summer of 2001. During those months, he became hugely popular by playing "Bear" in his t-shirt and Goodwill pants and wingtips, roaring at our laughing six-year-old and the other squealing neighborhood kids. EK soon adopted JL as her big brother. At the moment of this writing (May 2022) JL led White House policy on technology and national security at the National Security Council and the Office of Science and Technology Policy.

But I just found out he has been named ██████████████. His wife Jhini saved my life six years ago. (More on that later, too.) She is currently ███████████████████████████████████ ████████████████████████ NASA ████████████████████ ██████████████████████████. The ultimate power couple!

But the anti-longtermist idea was only an article at most, and these ideas have already been articulated by Alexander Berger – whom I quote a lot in my blog and do again in the longtermism chapter – and Phil Torres.

After Paul's prompting, two people got me to actually sit down and write this book: Anne and Natalia. Whenever we're chatting and I digress from the topic at hand (which *never* happens) and tell Natalia stories from my past, she says: "You *have* to write another book. I'm *serious.*"

After 2021's betrayal, Natalia sent me a gag book in the mail. On the cover I'm

speaking at an animal rights conference (from which I would be banned) along with the title: "I'M SO FUCKING SICK OF ALL THESE FUCKING MOTHERFUCKERS." (That was a catchphrase I learned in Cincinnati, and exactly captured my 2021 mindset after being fucked over by these fucking motherfuckers yet again.)

Natalia and I share a medical affliction that has caused us great agony. (We'll get to that.) We also worked together at two different organizations, which has given us the opportunity to talk a lot over the past years. She Googled my name to find the picture for *I'm So Fucking Sick of All These Fucking Motherfuckers* and to find out more about why I was fired from our first common employer. This led to comments like, "I didn't know Gary (*et al.*) hated you so much! You need to write another book. I'm *serious.*"

Of course, Anne is the primary reason I'm speaking these words into my phone. I assume that is obvious by now.

Writing actually started when I hit on the working title *The End of Veganism.* But I have talked too much without even giving a hint of that thesis, so here goes:

When the weather turned briefly cooler a while back, Anne and I did a taste-test of the Beyond Meat chicken tenders versus Impossible Foods' chicken nuggets. I blogged about this and posted the blog on social media. (Excerpt from blog: On Beyond's package, they loudly say "NO GMO's." I remember listening to multiple interviews with Beyond's Ethan Brown, who said, "People tell us they don't want GMOs." I have to say, with all due respect, you are talking to the wrong people, Mr. Brown. What people want is cheap meat. Full stop.)

The picture that came along with those social posts was a bag of the Impossible Foods nuggets, winner of the taste test. (Anne still prefers Gardein's.) That picture prompted some vegans to think that the best use of their time was to angrily comment about how Impossible's products AREN'T VEGAN! This is because their plant-derived heme – the ingredient Impossible uses to give their beef products that slight "metallic," bloody taste – had been tested on animals so it could be approved by the FDA. So: Animal killing that is somehow connected to a company at any point = all their products are NOT VEGAN!

But of course, harvesting "vegan" food kills many animals. Rodent control programs on farms growing vegan food and in facilities producing vegan food kill many animals. Trucks transporting products kill many animals. And so on.

I briefly tried to reply constructively. ("I understand that you're upset about this. But I don't care if something is vegan. I only care about what can actually help a lot of animals.") As is always the case, engaging enrages them further.

Of course, NOT VEGAN Impossible Foods has helped many animals by producing products chosen by people who would otherwise eat animal meat. But it sure hasn't made them popular with (many) vegans. ("The Impossible Burger Debate Was A Test For Vegans, And We Failed.")

"Vegans or animals" is what ended my career. "Vegans or animals" was the driving force behind our current very non-vegan organization, One Step for Animals. I've seen this dynamic for the 35 years since I first stopped eating animals. It took me quite a while to recognize it, being in the vegan bubble myself. But if looked at objectively and without personal ego invested or identity involved (which is not easy) the reality is clear:

Veganism has been terminally poisoned
by people obsessed with protecting their vegan identity.

For this very vocal and visible minority – and yes, it is only a minority of vegans – veganism is only about *them* and defending *their* strict rules of being "vegan." (Or "Vegan," as some write it.)

At least this is true in the United States. From my time in Germany, for example, it doesn't seem to be the case there. While editing this chapter, I came across Kenny Torrella's "How Germany is kicking its meat habit" at Vox. But Deutschland shows the "unintended consequences" of focusing on meat instead of animals: Although per-capita *meat* consumption is down there, each German is consuming one more factory-farmed *animal* than ten years ago. That means that despite a large drop in meat consumption, many millions more animals are suffering on factory farms. Not cool.

Another perfect example of vegans caring about themselves *über alles*:

> One: Publicly refuse to eat animals – live vegan
> Two: Publicly refuse to sit where people are eating animals
> Three: Encourage others to take the pledge
>
> –The Liberation Pledge

Doesn't that say it all? "Publicly refuse to sit where people are eating animals." So it isn't just about the purity of what you *consume*, but also the purity of anything you *see*.

Of course, this removes opportunities to *actually help animals*, because the only way to actually help animals is by being with non-vegans and persuading them to take animals into consideration.

The Liberation Pledge is only one example. My pal Ken recently suggested I listen to an interview with a "vegan advocate" he thought I'd like. In the interview, it was all "advocating veganism," "promoting veganism," "making veganism mainstream," "repeating the case for veganism over and over." The advocate went on to say *his* new book was going to be *the* comprehensive and irrefutable case for veganism.

If only someone had thought of that before.

I wonder how many vegan advocates actually listen to what they are saying. It is all about promoting *their* diet, *their* lifestyle, *their* beliefs. Not actually about animals.

Back in 2016, I was excommunicated from the national animal rights conference and fired from my full-time job. My sin? Quoting, with source, what celebrity chef Anthony Bordain said about vegans. With all the suffering in the world, and all the many people allowing and even perpetuating this cruelty, it was a founder of One Step for Animals who became the *bête noire* for Gary and his fellow fanatics.

In case it isn't clear: I did not say anything bad about vegans. I was merely noting what *a famous celebrity* said about vegans. And for that, I was banned. That is truly some insecure theocratic bullshit.

Paul and I have a saying: The biggest impediment to the spread of veganism is vegans. While I was writing this today, he sent me yet another news story to prove it: A vegan saying drinking pee as the key to longevity. (There was once a table at Vegetarian Summerfest promoting this.)

Don't get me started.

Over a quarter century ago, our Best Man Mark said, "I grow weary of the term 'vegan.' It has just become a label for moral superiority." And he said this after being a founding board member of our national vegan group.

You might wonder why I'm so strident in my attack on the vegan fanatics, especially since I'm on good drugs and supposedly so mindful. It is because I helped create them.

Of course, even before Jayne went on her crusade, some vegans have hated me. Eventually, even my long-time best pal turned on me for annoying the Vegan Police. But despite all my efforts to make the focus actually helping animals, I did spend two decades working every day to build up a "vegan" group.

Oops.

It would be one thing if "vegan first, vegan only" was actually helping animals. But if promoting veganism worked – if the next leaflet, book, video, movie, website was really going to make a difference – we would have seen it by now.

How do I know? *Because I did the projections.* Decades ago, I calculated what would happen if every vegan converted *just one other person every five years.* Have we seen anything like that? No. When Animal Charity Evaluators did the most thorough metastudy of surveys about vegetarianism and veganism, they found: "Around 1% of adults both self-identify as vegetarians and report never consuming meat. [This is important because many people call themselves "vegetarian" but still eat meat.] It seems that this percentage has not changed substantially since the mid-1990s."

What I didn't realize when I built those projections was that the vast majority of people who "go vegan" subsequently quit veganism. Unbiased surveys show that over 80% revert. (And then, of course, spend the rest of their lives badmouthing veganism.)

Why? One survey of former vegans found that the top reason for quitting was that they couldn't take the pressure to maintain the level of purity demanded by other vegans. Again, vegans are "the greatest impediment" to the growth of veganism.

But really, vegans *don't matter.* It is *irrelevant* how many vegans there are.

The only thing that matters is how much *suffering* there is.

Think about it. If you were to promote a position that would lead to more suffering than an alternative, would you do so? There might be strange edge cases, but choosing to create more suffering than an available alternative strikes me as pretty much the very definition of immoral.

And on that measure, the world has gotten *way* worse for non-human animals since Anne and I stopped eating animals and co-founded a group promoting veganism. On average, every person in the United States eats more animals today than ever before in history. This is true globally as well. Those are the simple, bottom-line facts, the facts that all vegan advocates have to answer for.

Everything I've learned indicates the United States would be a better place for animals if we ended veganism. Not that you should eat animal products. (You can, as we'll get to.) But we should never utter or use the word "vegan" again.

Still think we need to promote "vegan"? A 2017 survey found that vegans are viewed more negatively than atheists, immigrants, homosexuals, and asexuals. (*Really* hard to be atheist, vegan, and asexual. Yikes. Sorry.) The only group viewed more negatively than vegans is drug addicts. Another 2017 survey found "Meat-eaters are being put off going veggie because of certain aggressive vegans." In 2018 – the year I stopped collecting these stories –

Protesting milk at trade joes lol

researchers found that "vegan" is the single worst word you can possibly use to describe a product – worse than "diet," "sugar-free," or "low-calorie."

As a long-time reader noted:

> I've become almost embarrassed to say I'm vegan ... not because of what it stands for, but because of the negative impression people have been left with due to other vegans and their negative behavior and words.

I talk about this more, with many documenting links and graphs, in my 2017 post, "How Vegans Hurt Animals." In that blog, I go into more of why vegans are so unpopular. (Tl;dr: It is because they are [justifiably] rage-filled and just can't get past that.) It is my second-most-popular post of all time, having been hate-linked by many vegans in their ongoing campaigns against me.

Think about it this way: If we want to help animals, *why* would we use – let alone promote – a word that has such negative baggage? A word that makes people think of pee drinkers, screamers in restaurants, and terrorists. (The latter is what Anthony Bordain called them.)

What reason could there be to use that word? What *possible* reason, other than an unwillingness to put helping animals first?

So what is the alternative?

We could and should put the focus entirely and always on the others who need our help.

I certainly don't think it would hurt if we were all "animal advocates" instead of "vegans" or "vegan advocates." Never talk about ourselves, never talk about our diet, never talk about our rules or dogma. *It should never be about us.*

And of course, I say this as a person who cofounded Animal Liberation Action but allowed the name to be changed to be about veganism instead.

Sorry.

PS: Since it is unlikely everyone will take my advice above, a variety of admirable people are working to both support current vegans, in part to lower the recidivism rate and also change the public's view of vegans. World of Vegan is a prime exemplar of this.

PPS: In case it isn't clear, I'm not "Vegan." I'll outsource this to Vincent, the head of One Step for Animals, Australia, who blogs at theanimalist.medium.com:

> **Even if all vegans were nice and friendly, the point of my article is that veganism in itself as a movement is not something I want to be a part of.** A broader, more inclusive approach focusing more on the animals and less on every detail of an individual's current lifestyle is more effective. Either way, [veganism] remains nothing but a tool amongst many that can be used against speciesism, for animal rights. It isn't a goal and it shouldn't be a dogma (a principle or set of principles laid down by an authority as incontrovertibly true).
>
> I have called myself a vegan and worked at changing veganism but I have come to the conclusion that veganism is what it is and that it is a

closed club, which is detrimental when it turns it into **a rigid dogmatic venture based on personal purity and exclusion**. Veganism as a movement to fight speciesism is not something I embrace or even condone any more.

I still don't consume sentient animals and their by-products and I still want to encourage others to do likewise, in a friendly and pragmatic manner. Promoting an animal friendly lifestyle is a tool, not an end.

Or, as Margaret Atwood put it on Ezra Klein's podcast:

Is it about how virtuous you are?
Or is it about actually trying to better conditions?

Day 16 Continued:
Test Your Marriage!

You know, Mrs. Buckman,
you need a license to buy a dog, or drive a car.
Hell, you need a license to catch a fish!

But they'll let any butt-reaming asshole be a father.

*–Tod Higgins as played
by Keanu Reeves in the movie* Parenthood

Anne's father's death (and our super-happy-funtime trip from Colorado to Michigan) was *not* the worst catastrophe in the summer of 1995. What would *eventually* turn out to be the worst calamity occurred later, when Judas, who was now my best male friend, was dumped by his fiancée. He then drove his beater car from Tucson (where he was living at the time) to our rental house in Boulder and moved into the living room. It was then we decided to try to make our nonprofit a real thing.

At the end of the summer, he came with us back to Pennsylvania.

For the next two years, we rented a small house across the street from Anne's colleague Chris and his family. Judas lived in the downstairs room which was also the living room, TV room, my office, and the baby's playroom. (As they started to be able to control their life by walking and talking, EK became less screamy and more an actual person.) We made a go at the nonprofit using Anne's money, e.g., Anne bought Judas a decent car and paid to print tens of thousands of booklets. He went on the road for weeks at a time, staying with animal advocates around the country and leafleting at various colleges.

Having survived the Summer of Catastrophes, having EK in daycare, and having our own room did wonders for our married life. We were still young enough that the mood could strike even in the middle of the night ("Are you up?" Um, *yeah* – don't need to ask me twice!) so we could finally take full advantage of the vasectomy I had gotten right after the baby was born. As Anne tells it: "After watching the birth, Matt ran straight to the closest vasectomist."

Getting "fixed" was yet another example of how society promotes procreating. As happened to all my friends who got vasectomies, I was questioned *very seriously* if I really wanted this. (YES.) (Although it was uncomfortable, and seeing *smoke* rising ... down there ... well, there were moments....)

But no one grills you about *bringing an entirely new person into the world*. No one questions you about that decision *at all*. That. Is. Fucked. Up. Reverse that – make everyone who wants to breed pass an inquisition and let anyone who wants a vasectomy get one free and without hassle – and the world would be a vastly better place.

But in addition to wingflaps, our story shows public policy's profound impacts on people's lives. If we both had been given parental leave (and if a different combination of our genes had led to a happy baby; I know they exist – our pal Michelle's son seems to be a delight) then maybe it wouldn't have been an all-out sprint to Vasectomies-Я-Us. (On the other hand, I'm not sure if any combination involving my genes would have led to a happy baby. Sorry.)

By late '95, I was also under treatment following my Crohn's diagnosis.

For the year following Worst the First, it felt like I spent more time in doctor's offices than in the classroom. Once I spent most of a day in the ER waiting for treatment for fistulas; I was gone so long that Anne called the hospital to find out what had happened. Another time, I was lying ass-up when the doc brought in a group of med students to see. She said, "This is Matt...". I cut her off, squealing, "Names changed to protect the naked!"

After what felt like an endless string of proddings and probings (one of which was *really bad!*) I was finally seated in front of Dr. P. After my much-repeated litany, he said, "You have Crohn's. We'll need a colonoscopy [a word that sent me into a panic] to confirm, but I'm shocked none of the other doctors saw this."

Given how awful it had been to have a scope shoved just *a little* way up, I was *completely* freaked-out about a colonoscopy. The prep, as you hopefully don't know, is terrible. (It was much worse back in 1995.) The highlight, though, was when Anne gave me multiple hanging-bag enemas the next morning. Want to test your marriage? Give each other hanging-bag enemas following a night of shitting more than you could have ever imagined shitting.

I was truly terrified, so much so that I was trying to get Anne to go into the operating room with me. But the procedure itself was fine! It was actually interesting. They gave me enough drugs to keep me calm and relaxed, and I could watch what was going on and hear what Dr. P was finding. During a later colonoscopy, I asked Dr. P why he chose gastroenterology. He said, "I didn't want to deal with death all the time, so oncology was out. I don't like kids, so no pediatrics. In the end, I went with the cool tech."

When I had my first colonoscopy here in Tucson, they thought I was crazy to want to stay awake. The doc finally said I could be awake for the removal. (I definitely needed to be out for my later endoscopy. Yikes.)

Having the Crohn's diagnosis led to treatment with many drugs. Famous vegan doctor Michael Klaper had a long call with Anne and me, yet none of his many suggestions, including an elimination diet, made a difference. But the drugs did.

I've not yet had to go on any of the newer immunosuppressants, but I'm glad they're around. Dr. C, my encyclopedic and gregarious primary care doc since 2007, said that when he started his residency, he would see loads of patients hospitalized with uncontrolled Crohn's. Now there are almost none. (Sadly, two of my friends developed Crohn's since I've known them. Oddly enough, they both live in Sacramento. I've met a number of other vegans with Crohn's.)

Back in '95, the high doses of the steroid prednisone helped the Crohn's, and had many side effects, too. The obvious was increased energy. (So it was good we had our own bedroom.) Also increased appetite – I thought about food a *lot* – and water retention. Pictures from that time show me with a more rounded face, but not quite the dreaded moonface. At my peak, I weighed over twenty pounds more than I do now. Before the diagnosis, I was down to 130, thirty pounds *less* than today.

The longer-term effect, though, was on my bones. These days, doctors know to give a bone-density drug along with the prednisone. But instead, my prednisone use back then exacerbated what is now degenerative osteoarthritis.

Oops.

Day 16 Concluded:
Money might not buy happiness, but lack of money can bring unhappiness

I don't care too much for money,
Money can't buy me love.

But also:

Just give me mo-ooo-ney.
That's what I want.

–The Beatles

Money was the only point of contention Anne and I experienced. She was tired of living like students. She had a professional career now, and she needed to look the part, especially to become better known.

I, of course, well ... you know. Money = freedom, therefore spending money = bad. <sigh>

But even though I didn't like it, I knew she was right, so at Shelley's suggestion, I took Anne shopping. At the mall, I kept the (still unhappy) baby, and Anne and I agreed to meet at a certain place. In a Three-Stooges-esque comedy of errors, we kept missing each other. Eventually, Anne had the mall page me. The baby was unamused.

When we got to the car, I kinda lost it. In what was probably the angriest I've ever been in our marriage, I *pounded* the steering wheel. We now refer to this episode as "The Mall of our Discontent."

(My steering wheels have gone from comforting me to suffering my abuse. After Gretchen came on to me, I extricated myself in a flustered panic. [A girl? Interested in me? *That way?*] I went out to my Buick station wagon's and put my head on the steering wheel, thanking it for being cool against my feverish forehead. When Diane and I were driving from West Palm back to Cincy after my time at Pratt & Whitney, something went wrong with my Chevy Citation's engine. I eventually lost it then, too, also pounding the steering wheel. The next day, I was surprised to note my hands were sore. I looked at them, saw bruises, and wondered, "What happened? Oh...yeah." Oops.)

Things weren't going any better with our nonprofit.

Once while our part-time roommate was on the road leafleting, we got a message from a major animal rights organization. They wanted to make our work one of their projects. This was very exciting, as we were going nowhere fast on our own. However, we just couldn't come to an agreement. So it goes.

Shortly after that, in the fall of 1996, Anne, Judas, and I were standing in the baby's room. (I don't remember why we were there and not downstairs.) We hadn't had any success raising funds, and Anne said she couldn't keep paying for everything. We had rent, daycare, car payments, student loans, and professional expenses. And we needed to get a place in a good school district. As you might guess, we didn't live extravagantly – we took no vacations, didn't go to movies or out to eat – not even our beloved Taco Bell Bean Burritos *sans* cheese plus potatoes. We made no decisions that afternoon, yet it was clear things were coming to an end.

The next day, the mail brought a check from Nalith, a foundation whose board members included George Eisman (from the "Freezing, Snuggling, and Wine Undrunk" chapter). And the course of my life changed again.

However, Judas had had enough of living like an activist. He decided that after leafleting that school year, he was going to go back to school to become a chiropractor so he could live a comfortable life. (Years later, while driving Anne and me past expensive houses in San Francisco, he half-moaned, "I always wonder: Why can't that be me?") We would count on having a network of leafleters in place by then. As Executive Director, I would continue to do all the paperwork, newsletters, legal filings, correspondence, and fundraising.

On occasion, we would all hang out with Glenn, the head of the Pittsburgh animal rights group. Glenn, an interesting and funny fellow, was also the nephew of a relatively famous actor. (He was the first person who told me about the multiplier effect: that giving money to poor people can grow the economy by more than the initial distribution. At the time, I didn't believe him.)

He had been a lawyer when his dad (also a lawyer) had an affair and left his mom. This was also the time Glenn was becoming politically active. These two events led him to quit being a lawyer and pursue activism. He also cut himself off from both parents – his dad for being an ass and his mom for not standing up for herself. (Mostly, I think, because he wanted to be his own person.) His uncle had fellow actor Martin Sheen – who Glenn greatly admired – futilely urge Glenn to reconcile.

Glenn moved in with two brothers, Scott and Bill, with whom I remained Facebook friends for decades. (Sadly, Scott died recently.) For money, Glenn cleaned hotel rooms.

He was also my first example of a very smart person being susceptible to conspiracy theories; his was that HIV doesn't cause AIDS. This will be a problem for me going forward. For example, Ross, the vegan grad student in engineering, would adopt "the moon landing was fake." ["Why wasn't any dust kicked up?"] See also "The Mind is Fragile" chapter.)

Glenn was a kick to be around. We would always know when our housemate was on the phone with Glenn, because we would hear bursts of laughter. Unlike many other animal advocates, Glenn was kind to the baby, bringing them gifts, including a very loud toy that *mysteriously* broke.

For our first three years there, Glenn was the Pittsburgher we hung out with the most.

And then he was dead.

It turned out that a childhood disease had damaged his heart. And one night, it just quit.

Marcia, Glenn's mom, looked to us to find out what his life had been like. We stayed friends with Marcia until she died, exchanging letters every year.

It never occurred to me to think that my childhood Scarlet Fever (the first time I almost died, but I remember nothing of it) might have damaged my heart. Luckily, I had warning, after which I wondered if Glenn had experienced any symptoms but ignored them because he had no health insurance. (The importance of public policy.) As you'll see, that nearly happened to me.

Money makes the world go 'round, but your time will run out.

Lessons from a lifetime of bad decisions.

> Markets can remain irrational
> longer than you can remain solvent.
>
> *–John Maynard Keynes*

Value your time more than your hourly wage.

If you follow the advice below, you will die with money in the bank. But you won't have any time left. In other words: your time is more valuable than the money you could earn with that time.

Try to have a balanced approach to money.

Don't skip memorable opportunities in order to pay more on your car or house. On the other hand, don't buy coffee or lunch if you can just as easily make them at home. Your own cooking will be way cheaper and healthier. (Restaurants are an expensive way to get fat.) On the third hand, going out to social events can often be important networking and/or social opportunities.

You will make money mistakes. I've made a book's worth of screw-ups. That's just the way life goes. Learn the lesson and move on; beating yourself up serves no purpose.

(Also, if you are vegetarian, *definitely* don't say you won't come to something if meat is being served. Please just get over your personal discomfort and/or moral outrage. Instead, think about helping animals. Boycotting gatherings won't lead to fewer animals being eaten, but it *will* lead to people to think *even less* of vegetarians.)

Value your future time, but not more than your current time.

You will be old for a long time (hopefully) and you don't want to be broke and broken down during all that time. So save, exercise, and eat well. On the other hand, you will never be younger than you are right at this moment, so take advantage of it. Better to visit Germany at 40 (or 54) than 80.

Build up a cash reserve for emergencies and opportunities.

Today (2022) inflation makes savings worth a lot less from year to year, but inflation won't last forever. Also, you can put up to $10,000 a year in I-bonds that earn interest equal to inflation.

More importantly, you never know if you'll have a calamity that insurance doesn't cover or doesn't cover fully. (Know what that is? rhymes with *boremadowing*.)

Or an opportunity might come up to take a bucket-list trip on a mistake fare – follow Scott's Cheap Flights for more on this. (That is how we are in Germany this month on tickets that cost barely more than what EK is paying to go to a conference in Austin next month.)

Have between two and four credit cards

In case one isn't working for some reason, or you have to cancel one because of fraud. In general, get a standard cash-back card. Our second card is Amazon's Visa, which gives you five percent back on Amazon and Whole Foods purchases. If you want to do more with credit cards – and have the time to get into the weeds – follow "The Points Guy."

You can actually have too *few* lines of credit. When we finally paid off Anne's student loans, our car, and our house, our credit score went down. How crazy is that? Keep your mortgage if you have a low interest rate and invest the extra money.

Don't buy things.

Natural selection has, of course, programmed us to want to accumulate. In the evolutionary past, those with the most reproduced the most. But the happiness you get from "things" fades – we acclimate to everything new. Then we want more. Then the cycle repeats – the hedonic treadmill. Get off the treadmill, get rid of stuff, and look to buy memories instead. Like going to Germany and Prague.

Stuff also ties you down. The fewer things you must manage, the less mental energy you need to spend on them. And then the few things you *do* have can provide ongoing happiness with their functionality and/or attached memories.

Stuff story one: Stereo.

When I was eleven, I *really* wanted a stereo. The child's record player and transistor radio weren't cutting it. I did *tons* of my own research – at the library, not on my uncle's Facebook feed – and worked and saved. When I finally got it in 1980, I was ecstatic. (Thank you, Panasonic! Your cameras served me well, too.) One time, I walked into my room and got a thrill seeing it. "I'll never get tired of it!" Of course I did tire, but only of its looks.

Napping with TS in my boots and gloves on the famous futon, stereo and CD player just above TS's head.

What I didn't tired of was its ever-changing music. I kept that stereo for decades, adding a CD player to it once those were affordable. I played it for friends, I played it for every woman I wooed, I played it out the window while washing the car. It moved all over the country. Its speakers on either side of the famous futon, Anne and I listened to Wynton Marsalis, Shostakovich, The Beatles, Michael Hedges, and many more. The first music our offspring heard emanated from that stereo. I still associate a certain U2 album with the baby's inconsolable screams; once, I turned *Achtung Baby* way up (on my Sony headphones plugged into the stereo) to drown out the howls. Sorry Bono.

Stuff story two: InstaPot.

In 2019, Anne's then-boss (and future back-stabber – *never question an insecure boss!*) sent her an Instant Pot. We are not ones for kitchen gadgets (except bread machines) so we didn't know what to think of the Instant Pot. But it's great! There are so many recipes online, and you can explore various ideas, especially with spices from Savory Spice Shop's online store.

Stuff story three: Art.

Art is the stuff we have that isn't functional like an Instant Pot or stereo. (Although we no longer have a stereo, just an old iPod dock Jhini gave us long ago.) Most pieces we display are by Team Green-Ball. Within my line of sight here at my desk are three framed sunflower photos by EK and a big painting they did from their photo of a Ferruginous hawk. There are also a bunch of pictures of Anne stuck to my monitor, and a head-on photo of the first 747 I was ever on. (Denver to Frankfurt, Lufthansa flight 447, May 2016.)

In addition to being aesthetically pleasing, each of those photos elicit fantastic memories. But we also have a few framed posters by Georgia O'Keefe and Vincent Van Gogh. These we got because of the depth of their aesthetic interest. They don't seem to get old. They were also the only good thing about my otherwise unpleasant and far-too-long mushroom trip.

My childhood walls were covered with awards. But in college, on an outing with Guido to look for non-teenager clothes, I got two framed Ansel Adams photo reproductions. The first thing I would do in every new apartment was hang them up. Then the place felt more like home.

PS: I still had most of those non-teenager clothes when I met Anne, including the shirt, tie, and belt I wore for our legal marriage ceremony. I kept those for many years until they fell apart.

Whenever you can, put money aside for retirement.

Putting money aside is more important than pre-paying installment loans like cars and houses, as your net return will be higher in the long run. (But *always* pay off credit card debt; better yet, never have credit card debt.) If work offers you a 401(k) with matching, do that. The matching is *free money*. If you are taking the full match, put extra money in a personal IRA. (Work retirement plans tend to have hidden but often offensively-high fees. A full 1% a year? For what?)

If you aren't earning much that is taxed highly on the margin – below about $60,000 if you are single or $110,000 if married – put your money in a Roth IRA. Otherwise, use a standard IRA. (You can only contribute so much to an IRA each year.)

Regularly and methodically, put your money in a simple index fund, not a target fund date unless you are over fifty. Vanguard is an excellent place to invest your money, as they are known for offering low-cost funds.

Don't pay attention to the market.

There will be several scary financial times in your life. As an earning adult, I've lived through 1987's Black Monday, the bursting of the tech bubble in 2000, the collapse following 9/11, the Great Recession of 2007-08, the market cataclysm early on in covid, and the current (2022) bear market. *The worst thing you can do is react to market conditions.* The best thing you can do is keep to your investment schedule no matter what. Some of the best market gains follow the worst declines.

Note: I am not a licensed financial advisor. But I already have your money (thanks!) unless:

1. You got a review copy of this book. In which case, please tell your audience, "I laughed, I cried, it was better than the butthole cut of *Cats.*"

2. You got the book from the library or downloaded it for free. In which case: Huzzah! You are acting frugally! But you *can* make an exception, *just this once.* (Or make a tax-deductible donation at OneStepForAnimals.org.)

Please keep in mind: **no one is on your side when it comes to your money**. That is the most important line in the entire book. Real estate agents – both buyer and seller – want to make as much money for as little work as possible. The same goes for financial advisors. Anyone who is talking to you about your money is doing so because they want your money, no matter what they say.

If you want to learn more about money and investments, please check out the 2022 edition of Andrew Tobias' *The Only Investment Guide You'll Ever Need*.

Another original painting by EK

Day 17: To the Exurbs – and Beyond!

Suburbia
where the suburbs met utopia.

–Pet Shop Boys

By the time I stood for my Engineering and Public Policy (EPP) PhD qualifying exams in late 1995, my first advisor had turned on me. Tip: don't make a preening liberal who has power over you ashamed of eating meat. At the time, I didn't care too much, as I thought I knew my topic – the role of particulates in global warming – inside and out. After my presentation, however, the first question was one for which I couldn't quite remember the answer. It was the *only* question I couldn't recall – I did have a slide about it, deep in the "grab this one if you get the question" pile – but I had forgotten about that slide. It threw me, leaving me flustered. Even so, the one professor I thought liked me told me after, "I was going to vote to pass you, but then I heard you had done a bad job in the forestry class." (I hadn't gotten the professor the media attention he wanted because I literally had my hands full with a baby.)

So it goes.

They gave me a master's in EPP and I moved over to Environmental Engineering with Statistics Mitch as my advisor. I crushed the exams there. (But remember: quadratics have two solutions; solving them in Excel will only give you one of them.) My Department of Energy fellowship ran out and I landed a research position in the Biology Department at the University of Pittsburgh. Then I passed my dissertation proposal – modeling a lake north of Pittsburgh to test various remediation options – and got maybe thirty pages written.

But I just … couldn't.

For one, I was dealing with Crohn's. Second, although EK was happier now that they could talk and walk, I was the primary parent. Third, I just didn't give a shit about modeling a lake – it just didn't matter. Very little really matters.

Feeding the neighborhood chickens.

Finally, I felt compelled to do something to help animals. With Anne working and Judas at chiropractic school, if our nonprofit was to accomplish anything, it was on me.

It was also the time when we started looking for a house in the Fox Chapel school district. Boy did we luck out! We got a place that was just about perfect, including great neighbors. I lived in that house for longer than anyplace else before – a bit over ten years. (I've lived in our Tucson house for 15 years and counting.) Confident and happy, EK made friends at their new preschool, running right into the fray without even a glance back. Once in elementary school, they were in the gifted program for English, and their IQ tested one point higher than mine had back in the day.

Being out in the exurbs meant Anne had to commute about a half hour each way, on windy roads and highway. (People who know her might find that unlikely, given that she doesn't like to drive and generally only gets behind the wheel for medical emergencies.) But Anne had no issues driving. (While I had several, including a time when the Altima was slipping backwards on an icy hill toward a line of stopped cars: "Fuck!" EK, then two and in the back seat, happily warbled, "Fuck! Fuck!" Yup.) Pittsburgh's Carnegie Library system was fantastic, with loads of books on tape for her beater Chevy Nova, and then on CD in her Honda CR-V. Anne consumed more books in those years than any other time.)

Sometime around 1995-96 was when, after trying other antidepressants, I ended up on Zoloft, which made my mood more "even" and winters less horrible. And then, when EK was in first grade, Anne got her only semester sabbatical of her entire fourteen years at CMU.

Isn't this easier than driving your Nova?

Day 17 Continued: Time the Second

It's a sunny day in California
But that old sun is shining on me
Here at home

It makes for a good day

For some serious reflection
And massive rationalization.

–Lyle Lovett, "Good Intentions"

It might be cheating, but vacations with Anne are very often times when life is obviously and recognizably Perfect. Traveling with her is almost always an absolute joy. Her planning and organizational skills shine; we can go two weeks just living out of our carry-ons. I don't know if *all* the prep time we put in is worth it – there must be diminishing returns at some point – but the effort generally makes trips amazing.

We are more flexible than it sounds – we can adjust on the fly if things don't go as planned or if there is a better option. There isn't a lot of spontaneity, though, but spontaneity is significantly overrated.

Example: In 1990, when I was working at Pratt & Whitney (with lasers and holograms!) dad came down to visit. He didn't want to make any plans, so we didn't. We ended up at a St. Augustine motel with blood on the stairs and – I'm not making this up – blood on our room's ceiling. But he got his oysters, so he was happy.

Were you wondering when I was going to get back to my "you can eat animal products" point from The End of Veganism chapter? Here it is: Eat all the bivalves you want. Oysters, clams, scallops – go to town. Also, don't sweat any minor ingredients or trace amounts. *It just doesn't matter.* Very little actually matters. But try to avoid situations like the one I had when mom came to visit in Florida:

At the time, I was vegetarian but not yet vegan. (I still ate dairy – *tons* of cheese, OMG – and eggs.) At a local restaurant, we were given a sampling of spreads and fresh breads. One of the dips was amazing, so I asked the waiter what it was. "That's 'gater." *Ewww.*

Back to the second time "normal" life – i.e., not a vacation – was recognizably Perfect: Anne's sabbatical.

That fall, the weather was magnificent, so lovely as to make up for a fraction of the winter to come. (A *small* fraction.) The internet, which we accessed through a screechy dial-up modem (and later a satellite dish that didn't work in the rain) allowed distance collaboration. Anne was working on an innovative new teaching project with three colleagues around the country.

EK was ever more independent. They agitated: "We go for kids' rights! We want freedom from adults!" And when Anne went to wash their bedding, they staged a beanie-baby protest complete with signs: "You don't know what you're doing to us!" "The sheets smell fine!" I guess this was payback to taking them to protests while still a baby in the sling.

One day, they arrived home and announced that they had joined the "Peace for the World" club. We thought it was great that the school had such a club, but it turned out that EK had formed it.

Like the other two times life was perfect (as well as vacations) Anne and I spent concentrated time together, much of it outside. We were still young and did not waste it. (It was around this time that the picture referenced in the "Stone Cold" chapter was taken. Yowza!)

On a sunny fall day, Pittsburgh is pretty freakin' amazing. The city has many parks, and the Audubon Society's Beechwood Farms was right by us, almost directly across from EK's Fairview Elementary. June 1994's *exceedingly* memorable Hartwood Acres park was up by the middle school.

But of course, a sunny fall day was the exception. At least in Pittsburgh.

People ask how we can deal with the Tucson heat. As I mentioned, the mornings are often cool, especially before the summer monsoon season. And it really is a dry heat – I once ran three miles when it was 102°, no sweat. (Well, almost no sweat.) Back east is far worse. While they were in high school, EK came with me on a work trip to the D.C. area. We went for a run the first morning when it was only 80° but very humid. I thought I was going to die. (Figuratively, not literally.)

Pittsburgh's universally sticky summers and oppressively cold, dark, and dreary winters – ugh. During one cold snap early on in our time there, it was too cold for Anne to walk to campus. The school didn't close, though. Another time, the wind-chill didn't get above 0° F for *three straight days*. I think that was what prompted us to get new, double-paned windows for the entire house.

Early in EK's school days, the three of us came to Tucson for the first time. (Anne had been pregnant when we were here in '94, so that time was two-and-a-half of us.) We did the walk-through for the house my folks were buying, and we hung out with my cousins. EK organized a concert, dragging in their reluctant cousin Peter, who is two years younger. (And now a *jet pilot!*) Their guitars-and-maracas concert of Beatles covers ended with "We rock! We rock! We totally rock!"

But that wasn't when we first had the idea of moving to Tucson, though. Those plans would start after we visited in the depths of winter and realized we didn't have to be depressed from Seasonal Affective Disorder for months on end.

(Actually, I'm only now remembering that when I was in fourth grade in Toledo Ohio, we were assigned to write a "future autobiography." In it, I had Future Matt living in Tucson. At that point in my life, I had never been west of Michigan.)

It was also on one of these "flee Pittsburgh" trips that I met Kari, who became one of our best pals. She was a member of our nonprofit, and knowing we were coming to Arizona, organized a talk for me in the Phoenix area. (Which went great! The Q&A went on for hours!) When Kari and I met beforehand for lunch, she asked if the restaurant was OK, as the food was potentially sloppy.

As she tells it: "And you answered, 'It's fine. I have another shirt in the car in case I goober.' That's when I knew we'd be pals."

The next year, she organized a talk at the library, and the room was so full I'm sure it broke fire codes. There were literally people sitting next to where I was standing, giving me almost no room to stalk around. Kari stood in the doorway (as seen above).

Driving down I-10 to my parent's Tucson house following the library talk, we hit some of the scariest rain I've ever encountered. The same thing happened in the winter of 2019 after I testified before a committee at the state house in Phoenix (below; screenshot by Kari).

FYI: Arizona gets both summer and winter rains, making the Sonoran Desert far more diverse and interesting than any other. The sky islands – tall, isolated mountain ranges over 9,000 feet – allow you to drive from the desert to a Pine-and-Aspen biome and climate like Colorado. In the winter, you can ski or sled, then come back down to warm weather.

Jumping back in Pittsburgh: Around the turn of the century was when I started poisoning Bonnie and Tom's oldest, Catharine.

Given that I love meat, I was happy to find recipes for seitan – aka "wheat meat." Seitan was the key ingredient in a casserole I often made when our two families would get together.

Catharine referred to it as "Matt casserole," and it was her favorite. It took a while for them to connect her stomach issues with Matt casserole. Eventually, though, she was diagnosed with Celiac disease, which is an actual physical reaction to wheat gluten. And I had been giving her *pure gluten* in the Matt casserole. Yikes.

Sorry.

This led to the cards on the Christmas counter in 2002. Bonnie and Tom had moved into their big house and invited us and my parents, as well as neighbor friends, for dinner. Bonnie's parents were there as well. We all brought dishes that were labeled "Vegan, not gluten-free," "Vegetarian, gluten-free," etc. Tom's excellent wine flowed freely (except to me – I was driving) as the adults crammed around their dining room table, extended to maximum length. Non-adults ate in the finished basement/game room.

There was *much* laughter. My memory is that Bonnie's dad was quite loquacious, and one of their friends was cutting and acerbic. A young guy came over to pick up one of the older kids for a late Xmas date, and we all drunkenly razzed him. Sorry kid.

Back at our house, my parents were in our room, and Anne and I added another memory to the pleasure-filled famous futon in the basement. It was not better than Christmas '93, but it was the most indelible.

Flashback to our first winter. *Brrr!*

Brains! Redux: The Mind Is Fragile

One of the saddest lessons of history is this:

If we've been bamboozled long enough,
we tend to reject any evidence of the bamboozle.
We're no longer interested in finding out the truth.
It's simply too painful to acknowledge,
even to ourselves,
that we've been taken.

Once you give a charlatan power over you,
you almost never get it back.

–*Carl Sagan,* The Demon-Haunted World

There was a clip that went viral sometime in 2021; it even made the late-night shows. (*Please* watch Colbert. He will make your life better. I swear. You can watch at least the monologue on YouTube, and if you use AdBlock, you don't have to see any commercials.)

In the clip, Joanna Overholt is testifying before an Ohio state house committee, screaming that she had been magnetized by some insidious plot. She keeps pressing bobby pins against her skin to prove it, but they don't stick.

While funny, it is striking and at least a little terrifying to realize that she truly – and furiously – believes this. She is educated, functions in society, is a nurse (!), and might be a wife and/or mother. And she believes some nefarious plot has made her magnetic.

Although maybe not as crazily laughable, we all have our psychological quirks and blind spots, even people who make a living railing against unreason. For example, in early 2022, author (██████████) and podcaster ██████████ took a break from maligning misinformation to defend his friend Joe Rogan.

At first glance, this seems at the very least unnecessary if not absurd. But to me, it makes perfect sense. Even though he is one of the worst sources of misinformation, Joe Rogan is much more famous than ██████████, and Rogan has repeatedly been deferential to and promotional of ██████.

Even though Rogan is a significant net negative for the world, our minds are simply not built to do utilitarian calculations when it comes to interpersonal dynamics. The human brain evolved dealing with small groups of people who we see every day. So if someone with more social power praises us, our brains simply can't help but view them as "friend."

This is true for me as well. For decades, one of my best friends was someone who yearned for fame and fortune. I should have realized this when I heard him talk with envy about famous vegans or lust after big houses. But I remained blind to his true nature until 2014, when my blindness cost me nearly everything I had built professionally.

Yet sadly, I didn't learn my lesson, once more mistaking personal kindness for character until it yet again cost me dearly in 2021. Fool me once....

One thing these situations have in common is having a mutual "enemy." Because some people are mean to him on Twitter, ██████ shares that enemy with Rogan. With me, the "enemy" was animal exploitation, as well as the general assumption that vegans are inherently good people. (Ha-*ha.*)

I think this also explains a lot about Mar-a-Lardo's appeal. He is supposedly rich and powerful, and he says nice things about certain people ("I love the poorly-educated!") and speaks harshly about "the enemy" – immigrants, Muslims, the press. Many people thus see him as on "my side," even considering him a "friend." This is straight from great despots' playbook: Create an "us vs them" dynamic and demonize "them" – Jews, Tutsi, Blacks, Mexicans, Commies, Hippies. Given Traffic Cone of Treason's success, it is reasonable to fear for the future of democracy in the U.S.

Although con men and despots have existed forever, it seems easier to get suckered in today. For example, a very smart, dear, and long-time friend of ours has now made "anti-vax" their identity. Their Facebook feed became just one long string of anti-vax posts. They no longer work for animals, as they had for decades, because they won't get vaccinated.

This process started in 2016 with their capture by the Bernie Bros contingent. It wasn't Senator Sanders' ideas; if politically possible, we would gladly support those ideas – the United States would be a better country if we had Scandinavian policies. Rather, the pull was the anti-Clinton and then anti-establishment left-wing fringe. Then it morphed into acceptance of "everyone is out to get me and my small group who know the truth" conspiracies: "So-and-so SILENCED!"

The problem is that this evolution is entirely understandable. You read more and more, deeper and deeper, until it is all of a piece and no one else can be believed. This would have happened to just about anyone with the same background and the same media consumption.

The same is true for people who grew up listening to Rush Limbaugh and then started watching Fox News. Racists. Sexists. Anti-LGBTQ fanatics. They didn't start "bad" – they were programmed by cynical and/or fanatical groups and "news" networks that use our mental shortcomings to warp our reality and take our money. Bigots and haters and conspiracy theorists all believe what they believe because that is what got into their brain.

It's the same for growing up in a religion. What we believe is what we see, and vice versa. Our brains are not rational machines, but *rationalizing* machines. We want an identity. We need a tribe. We'll believe anyone for that. We'll give up anything for that.

It is crushingly sad, often without any consolation.

The more you invest in a set of beliefs –
the greater the sacrifice you make in the service of that conviction
– the more resistant you will be
to evidence that suggests that you are mistaken.
You don't give up.
You double down.

—*Malcolm Gladwell,* The Bomber Mafia

Day 17 Concluded:
Dazed and Delirious in Deutschland

This is what love is for
To be out of place
Gorgeous and alone
Face to face

−Wilco, "Impossible Germany"

The July before 9/11, with David Duval about to win his first and only major at Royal Lytham & Saint Anne's, Anne and I left for the Pittsburgh airport.

I had taken Saint Anne to the airport many times before. Once, a day before she was supposed to fly to Amsterdam to start a tour with other German teachers from around the world (including Russians who really could pound back vodka) I drove EK to the library. Leaving them there − EK loved the place and was well-known by the staff − I drove down to the Blawnox post office to mail booklets.

That's when the Crohn's attack started.

I was in bad shape by the time I picked E up – so bad that I stopped at friends who lived closer to the library. But E went to the door and found that no one was home. I took some deep breaths and drove home. Walking carefully and painfully from the detached garage to our house, I ███████████████.

Anne had to delay her trip a day.

Speaking of the library, there was a woman there who had a crush on me. On one of the rare occasions Anne was there too, the librarian tilted her head in Anne's direction and spat with disdain, "So that's *the wife?*"

External attention like this was *much* more common for Anne, e.g., old male colleagues would call or email her out of the blue. One time, while meeting with an art dealer who was a potential donor to our nonprofit, I was utterly invisible – he stared at and flirted with Anne the whole time. "Um, dude, her husband and father of her child is *right here!*"

As the punchline to a longer conversation, JL concluded, "Anyone in their right mind is at least a little in love with Anne." Sorry fellas – for some reason, she chose me.

Back to David Duval:

This summer trip to the airport was different, because <drumroll please> *I was going with her.* That's right! Insular Midwestern boy was leaving this hemisphere! (Unless you're reading this in Europe. Then it would be "leaving that stupid hemisphere." Apologies to Canada.) We were flying to Frankfurt.

Shockingly (and shamefully) I don't remember if the flight was direct from Pittsburgh. (The next time, 2005, we connected in Philadelphia – a nightmare that involved moving to an entirely new plane and losing one full day of the trip. The next year we connected in Cincinnati.) But this flight, like every other until 2016, we were on a Boeing 767 with a two-four-two configuration.

Anne and I had two seats together, gorgeous and alone on the starboard side. (As we did this year, in the way back of our 777s.)

On this 2001 767, we watched *Traffic* together (this was the first plane I'd ever been on with screens for every seat) and then other movies I don't recall.

As you would expect, I didn't sleep at all. I have *never* slept on a plane, regardless of what I drink, what drugs I take, or how tired I am. (Not even earlier this month, with my overall sleep the best it has ever been. Lately, I've hardly taken any sleep meds at all!) Anne, the World's Greatest Sleeper, eventually dozed off, after which I experienced that period of exquisite sleep-deprivation torture. Then we flew into daylight and landed.

Sleep deprivation plus the incredible excitement of being *on a new continent* left me in a dream-like state. I have vivid yet gauzy memories of walking through the airport – especially the huge baggage claim area. (We never check bags; Anne always packs so we get by just with carry-ons.) It was almost an out-of-body experience. Like I was floating.

Here's the thing about being in Germany with Anne: I'm *completely free.* I can even be happy when *cold.* (As seen above at Cologne's Chocolate Museum.)

Generally, I like planning and being in control, but for the first three times we went, I did exactly squat. *Nada.* We only walked and took trains – no driving – and Anne handled all that. And the hotels and restaurants. But moreso, *I talk with no one but Anne.* In Germany, Anne handles *every single interaction. I don't even know what is being said.* I don't know what the signs say, what the menus say, or what the announcer on the train is saying. ("Meine Damen und Herren....") In 2016, as a grown-ass adult who had been to Germany three times before, I was ~~terrified~~ nervous when she sent me alone to the store for supplies. In *Berlin,* one of the most cosmopolitan and English-speaking cities in the world.

Overlooking Passau, Bavaria, 2018

On this 2022 trip, I went to get Indian take-away in Erfurt by myself, but only after she had written it all down.

I took two years of German from a nun who insisted that "Fräulein" is how you address any unmarried woman. So ... not awesome. Frequently at home, I will speak Germlish ("Willst du ein haircuten mir gibt?" "Herr part oder nichten Herr part?") or terrible German ("Wir gehen zu haus" "Essen wir uns?"). Still, thirty years on, I get a laugh. (*Score!*) In Germany, I will sometimes be unable to resist being a ten-year-old boy. But seriously: "Wir suchen dich"? *Come on!* How can I be expected to resist? "Dich" is everywhere in Deutschland! It must be a gay guy's paradise!

After passing through customs in 2001, Anne took me *zu* Freiburg (street performers above – look closely). That is where we may well end up living if Velveta Voldemort gets back in power. There, she bought a bunch of books. (On our first three trips, Anne was always on the prowl for things to use in the classroom. This involved buying lots of *Kinder- und Jugendliteratur* which we would then haul back to the States, along with German chocolate.)

Then she took me to an Ethiopian restaurant where they seemed shocked to see us. The place was a Fußball club – a long bar, TVs, and two small tables out front. Anne ordered a Weinschorle for herself and a half-liter Hefeweizen for me. (Wheat beer is something I only discovered in Germany.) Anne started looking at her receipts while we sat and drank. She found a mistake on one right before the second round of drinks arrived. "Oh, we'll have to go back and get this fixed." Then we saw someone rush in with grocery bags just before the third round came, bringing me to 1.5 liters of beer on an empty, jetlagged stomach. Only *then* did we start to smell cooking. At this point, mellow Anne said, "Oh well, we don't have to go back."

The food was good, but by then, we had switched to water. (Which you pay for there! Even just tap! Germany isn't a desert, WTF?) Probably because they saw us eating, another couple came in just before we left. I wonder if they got to spend a pleasant hour-plus drunkening while waiting for their food.

Day 18: Time of Your Life

Another turning point, a fork stuck in the road
Time grabs you by the wrist, directs you where to go

–Green Day, "Good Riddance (Time of Your Life)"

The long Flagstaff travel note from this Day – "So happy it's scary" – has been moved to later.

From what I remember, even being raised atheist and vegan by two freakishly brilliant and beautiful parents, EK had a pretty normalish grade school experience. They didn't come home crying all the time like a certain memoirist, so I take that as a win. And there were other kids in the gifted program.

EK went to birthday parties, so *suck it*, haters! E went trick-or-treating with Emma and Greta, after which they would trade the treats. One day in first grade, the students were describing their family. E said, "My mom's a German teacher. My dad's an engineer." Then Emma said the same thing, and the teacher thought she was just copying EK. But she wasn't! In a picture from this time, EK and Emma look like siblings.

In seventh grade, Emma and EK joined the cross-country team. In what wouldn't bode well for the next nine years of competitive running in Arizona and Southern California, the colder it was, the better E ran. In their first (hot) race, I hollered, "You can rest when you're dead!" EK then puked in the finishing chute. (Sorry slower kids!)

But in their last cross-country race in Pittsburgh (which was too cold for us to attend; we love our kid and all, but c'mon – it was below forty!) EK kicked ass. Emma's mom Cathy – a *truly*

dedicated parent – called us right after, shocked and excited. During the coolest meet of the spring track season, E set a huge personal best in the 1600 meters (basically a mile). Above is a great picture from that race: E is running alone, eyes straight ahead with a look of complete focus. One of the coaches is in the infield calmly encouraging E to keep an even stride.

By this time, our nonprofit had grown past the point where we needed another full-time person. Anne had had enough of the petty office politics, which hadn't stopped even after she was promoted to Full Teaching Professor. At dinner one evening, EK said it would be fine if we wanted to move. Toward the end of the term, in the face of the "You'll never work in academia again!" threat from the department head, Anne quit and applied for COBRA health insurance. (Thanks President Clinton!) We flew to Tucson over spring break (mid-April) to find a house. It snowed upon our final return to the 'burgh – again: *in mid-April* – as if fate wanted to reinforce our decision to move.

We sold off a bunch of stuff, including both sets of the big fancy stereo speakers I had lusted after for so long. A moving company packed up the rest and Team Green-Ball headed west.

Two good and eight tough months later, at eighth grade talent night, EK played guitar and sang Green Day's "Good Riddance (time of your life)." Indeed.

At the Freiburg market

Day 19: Wolf Park, Dog Camp, and Time the Third

Maybe the sun will shine today
The clouds will blow away

–Wilco, "Either Way"

The first stop of 2007's Westward trek was at one of Anne's friends in Indiana who lived near Wolf Park. Unlike their parents, EK is an animal lover. They had a home-lettered t-shirt and a custom-stitched sweatshirt that read, "May I please pet your dog?" Dogs and wolves are their favorite (pack loyalty) but Anne's allergies prevented E from forming their own pack. The closest they got was Sunny the Guinea Pig, whom we had rescued years before and who was now in the back seat of Anne's 1999 Honda CR-V. On our multi-day journey to Tucson, we would let her out to munch on grass whenever we stopped. (Sunny, that is. Not Anne.)

After Wolf Park, our next stop was Shelley's place in rural Illinois, where she had moved to have more room for more dogs. EK stayed there for Dog Camp as Anne and I continued to Tulsa (where preparations were underway for the PGA Championship, which Tiger Woods would win in triple-digit heat), Albuquerque (where we had a lovely meal sitting outside at El Patio de

Albuquerque), and down to Tucson. We watched Netflix DVDs on our Dell laptop every evening, including the wonderful dystopian nightmare – or utopian fantasy, depending on your view of humanity – *Children of Men*. Driving across northern New Mexico, we went through the most stunning thunderstorm either of us had ever seen, with *crazy* lightning across the high desert plain. We should have stopped to take it all in.

As we pulled into The Old Pueblo (as Tucson is known) we stopped at PetSmart to get Sunny's supplies. It was late June, and the signs said it was 105°. I said to Anne, "If this is all it is, this is nothing." It certainly was nothing compared to the bitterly cold and miserably dreary winter days up north. (To paraphrase something I vaguely remember maybe Bill Bryson saying about the New England's cold: "It wasn't just uncomfortably cold. It was 'crawl over your own mother to get back inside' cold.")

After we moved in, we went over to my cousins' several days in a row to take care of their animals, including Maggie (above) the golden Lab who would stay with us on-and-off for the next nine years. (And who didn't respect the boundaries of Anne's garden.) EK was still in Illinois. Carl and Lori had gotten out of town, off to somewhere cool. And as their thermometer reached 115°, Anne and I *very much* took advantage of their shady, secluded, private pool.

Life was again Perfect. I was high on actually *living* somewhere completely sunny and entirely foreign to my previous experience. Not as high as meeting my soulmate and enjoying the *heck* out of each other for thirteen months, but noticeably high.

As they often do, boys would ruin a good thing.

My sister said this book is too painful to read, so I can use this:
A Blacktail Rattler and I get up-close and personal.

Bonus Tips

My tasks involved the making of mistakes,

Then discovering how to resolve those errors
without being an asshole

A search that I now understand will never end.

–*Nick Offerman,* Where the Deer and the Antelope Play

1. Kindness (usually) costs nothing.

I used to say, "Kindness costs nothing" but then realized this isn't always true. For example, when dealing with someone who gets their kicks abusing people. (Google "rolling coal.")

This isn't to say you *shouldn't* be kind to those who abuse others, if only to influence others. As mentioned, reacting to the screaming dairy farmer with calm politeness led Joe to stop eating animal products, and then become a leading activist and co-found One Step for Animals. And I remained friends with Benedict for 21 more years after he voted Green in 2000. However, I did end a friendship with a vegan who spent every day ranting against Hillary in 2016 – I just couldn't take it anymore.

But in *most* cases, kindness costs nothing, even with people who voted Republican or Green. <shudder>

Every day, we can improve our corner of the world by being nice. Reading a nametag and asking people, by name, how they're doing. Saying "Thank you!" more frequently and sincerely. Going slightly out of our way to wave to people in the restaurant's kitchen, or in the back office, or elsewhere behind the scenes. If you can lift a person's spirits by saying something kind or listening to them briefly, you've made things better with basically no cost to yourself.

2. If you are ever on high doses of opioids...

...for the love of all that is decent, err on the side of too much poop med. Trust me on this.

3. Recognize the three types of people.

A. Some people suffer and then don't want anyone else to suffer.
B. Other people suffer and then want *everyone* else to suffer.
C. Still others have never really suffered and have very little empathy. They assume life has been great for everyone and the rest of us are just whiners.

The distinctions between these types of people aren't always obvious at first, but these different life experiences lead to big differences in any long-term relationship – partnership or friendship.

Also remember that 50% of people are below average: below average in intelligence, below average in compassion, below average in driving ability, below average in rationality....

Bonus bonus tip: Visit Yosemite! Try to go in the off-season.

4. Don't read the comments.

Comment sections – especially on local news sites and YouTube – are the ugliest places on earth. Unless you have nothing you'd rather do than become angry and/or depressed, don't ever read comments.

5. The (initial) key to happiness is:

Low expectations.

But expectations ≠ assumptions:

Well-being isn't about *expecting* the best.
It is about making sure you don't *assume* the worst.

–Adam Grant

You might think this is snark or a joke, but I'm entirely serious. The less you expect – especially of other people – the less you'll be disappointed. The less you expect, the more you'll be grateful when things actually work out or people do what they say.

But always *assuming* the worst leaves you with no room for growth. It is a subtle but important distinction.

Arizona's high country, where a lot of this book was edited. Driving here, a bag of tortilla chips in our back seat exploded due to the pressure difference.

Day 20: "*That's* a high math score!"

Hey bulldog!
Hey man, what's that boy?
Woof!
You've got it, that's it!

–The Beatles

A cool morning – only 66° at five-thirty, although it will get to a hundred degrees later. I'm listening to George Winston's sublime *Autumn*. The pain is about average, so with the phone's voice recognition, I should get through today's chapters.

EK had the fourth-grade teacher every kid needs and deserves. She taught her students how to organize and insisted everything be organized *the right way*.

Folders were color-coded by subject and had to be kept neat. Assignments were to be turned in on time and completed as instructed or they were done again. More so than any particular knowledge imparted, the overarching lesson was that students needed to get their shit together.

Fourth grade is the time to do it. As Malcolm Gladwell makes clear in his "Carlos Doesn't Remember" Season 1 episode of his

Revisionist History podcast, college is too late to lift people up. High school is too late. You have to get kids when they're young, before puberty, before they are given over entirely to their peer group.

I saw this strikingly when I went to a parent conference EK's first year at Dorseyville Middle School. Walking the halls while classes were in session, I saw sixth grade kids sitting at attention, while next door the eighth graders would be slouched over as though trying to melt onto the floor. They were looking everywhere but at the teacher.

The difference was night and day. Just *two years* separated them. It was startling. If it had been presented in a TV show or movie, it would have come across as heavy-handed.

The vice principal was late for the Individualized Educational Program (IEP) meeting. But the person in charge was there and prepared, so he started reviewing EK's status. I was an old hand at this by sixth grade, so I listened politely but trusted their expertise. They'd dealt with hundreds of gifted students before, having gone to school to learn the field's accumulated wisdom. Who was I to question them?

Then the vice principal walked in, sat down, and started ruffling through EK's file. Clearly, he hadn't reviewed them beforehand, because while the other person was still talking, the vice principal blurted out, "*That's* a high math score!"

Once we got to Tucson, this would cause some challenges, but an ultimate victory, both later that school year and down the road. Anne and I convinced Esperero Middle School to put EK in eighth grade advanced math. This, in turn, threw E in with the pack of boys who "had a good thing going until you came along."

For the first time since babydom, EK was miserable.

By working harder than ever (shades of my ninth-grade biology class) EK made it almost to the top – just short of another interloper, a seventh-grade whiz kid who put them *all* to shame.

Succeeding in that class allowed E to take both AP Calculus I and II in high school, which allowed them to get in even *more* math at Pomona. This fulfilled the main lesson EK took away from adopted brother JL: "Take all the math you can."

More than that, though, this single math class toughened EK up. They still mention it from time to time, how they were different after that. Less of a kid anymore. It was painful to see at the time, but I wouldn't spare them that experience if I had it to do over. (And believe you me, if I could, I would do many, if not *most* things differently as a father.)

In addition to a smaller pool of smart kids, the pool of other dedicated runners also dwindled in the desert. At cross-country that fall, EK found no one else on the girls' team to run with; only one sixth grader even wanted to be there. (When a freak rainstorm canceled a meet, most of the kids celebrated. This confused and angered E: "Why are they even on the team?") So E practiced with two of the boys – a seventh grader named Harry and a quiet math classmate named Jack, the first of many Jacks in EK's life. Jack the First and E would shadow each other for the next five years, running every season and taking the same advanced classes. Jack would be on a state championship XC team, and both E and Jack would win state championships in individual Science Olympiad events as part of the high school's dominant team.

Harry's mom was very nice. We took care of the family's incredibly, um, *striking* bulldogs when they were out of town. After talking with Anne several times, Mrs. H switched over to Lightlife's plant-based ground beef for Taco Tuesdays. No one noticed – not Mr. H, Harry, or his younger brother. (Today's ground beef products from Impossible Foods and Beyond Meat are even better.) Sadly, Harry and family left after that year.

"Math Math Math" brother JL came to visit, too. We went to the Pima Air and Space Museum, where he told us that as a kid, he had written to the Secretary of the Defense to tell him to stop making the F-104 Starfighter – the plane Chuck Yeager crashed trying to set an altitude record. (An event made famous by the stunning Sam Shepard in the movie version of *The Right Stuff*.)

We also went to the Titan Missile Museum, a previously-functional nuclear missile silo that is now open to the public. (You can see it in *Star Trek: First Contact*.) This led to discussions of nuclear strategies, including why the Titan, with its one incredibly powerful bomb, was retired in favor of missiles with multiple smaller warheads. ("Smaller" being relative – only twenty times more powerful than the city-destroying Hiroshima bomb, compared to *three hundred* times larger.) That discussion led to this exchange three years later, while driving from our visit to Stanford down to L.A. to visit Caltech and the Claremont Colleges:

> JL: So while I was working on existential risks at Oxford, we examined whether a terrorist could set off the Yellowstone Caldera with a big nuclear bomb. Fortunately, it isn't possible.
>
> EK: What about smaller bombs used in series?
>
> JL: Um, we didn't think of that.

Boom.

Day 20 Concluded: Running to Stand Still (*SportsBall!* redux)

> You can go your own way.
>
> *–Fleetwood Mac*

Next month, we'll stay at my cousin's cabin in the mountains. There, we'll hike and edit this book. (FYI – *far* more time will be spent editing than writing.) Free time at the cabin is "payment" for fifteen years of taking care of their beasts. Not just feeding, scooping poop, and mopping up barf, but cleaning up after Peter's chickens were slaughtered, probably by a bobcat. (His high-school class had seen *Fast Food Nation*, which prompted him to pursue backyard egg production.) Feathers and blood *everywhere*. Given that we work every day to help chickens, "ironic" might not be a strong enough description.

I should come clean and admit that I was a bad *bad* helicopter dad. When I said there were many things I would do differently, this is one of them.

After playing "Time of your life" and graduating eighth grade, EK started high school cross country (XC) in June 2008. Practice at six a.m., Monday through Saturday, from June to the dark November mornings prior to State. E was the only new person joining the team, which added to my protective instincts.

The following year, EK was joined by fellow sophomore Sage, a nice young person and great runner. (E only finished ahead of her in one race; E finished ahead of everyone at least once. Aren't you glad you know that?) Sage and family would move after junior year, though, leaving EK as the single senior on the team, and thus the sole captain for the XC team. This was the *only* year they had just one captain. And it was, by far, the biggest XC team of E's four years, as E recruited graduating eighth graders and potential runners at the high school. Years later, EK said being cross country captain was their single greatest challenge of high school.

Honestly, I don't quite understand why I was so … crazed … when it came to their high school running. At one big meet at Randolph Golf Course, when the coaches had moved E down to the JV race, I thought I might have a heart attack (*foreshadowing*) while walking out to take up first cheering position. They finished in the top-ten there, as they had in their very first high school race, the JV race at famed Buffalo Park in Flagstaff.

As with seventh grade, we missed their best high school XC race. It was one of those rare, cool, drizzly days, and the team was down south in Sierra Vista. EK kicked ass, finishing the 5K in twenty-one minutes. But sectionals and the state championship were sunny, hot, miserable affairs.

EK was also the only ninth grader on the track team, and oddly the only one *at the entire meet* to run in every single distance event at sectionals that year: 800, 4x800, 1600, and 3200.

The 4x8 was the first race of the first day, a hot May afternoon. EK was the third leg, Neda handing them the baton with the lead, a handoff immortalized in the local paper (and now in this book). On their first lap, another girl pulled up right behind

E. Neda screamed, "Don't let her catch you! *I worked too hard!*" E pulled away in the second lap, handing the lead to Izzy, who cruised to victory.

The two-mile was the last race that evening, under the lights. Neda and another nice young woman from Sahuaro were favored. An 800 specialist from Pueblo went out with the two favorites for the first mile. Starting the very first of eight laps, EK was running

Tonja Greenfield/Foothills News
.... baton to **Ellen**

alone, in the no-man's-land between the lead pack and the trailing. After a mile, E was a hundred meters back, but Pueblo started to fade. Over the concluding mile, as though they had been running for decades and had perfected chases, E slowly reeled Pueblo in, passing strong right at the *very end* of the very last turn, blazing down the final straightaway to qualify for the state championships.

Screaming, I leapt up, catching maybe *four full inches of air*. In that moment, I was ecstatic. Sister-Rita-level rapturous. Maybe the single happiest minute I've ever experienced.

Yeah, that is *messed up*. Sorry.

As with cross country, State was a hot, miserable affair. EK's legs locked up in the last hundred meters of their relay leg, and the 4x800 team finished outside the medals. After the race, E puked and puked and puked, and they looked like it while running the two mile shortly thereafter. During those torturous thirteen minutes, I kept thinking, "Should have pulled [them]. Shouldn't have let [them] race after all that puking." But E didn't seem too troubled about it: "If I hadn't raced, I would have always wondered."

Day 21: Sowing the Seeds...

I'm
taking a ride
with my best friend.
I hope
he never lets me down
again.

–Depeche Mode

Although we were very different, Judas and I eventually became best pals after Phil moved in with Robbie. Unlike Phil and Guido – and just about everyone else I've ever been close with – Judas was an extrovert. (After Judas ███████████ to ███████████ ███████████, Benedict, also an extrovert, eventually became my next best male friend. Oops. *Somewhere* in there is a lesson. Hmmm....)

In all the time I knew Judas, ███████████████████. He would go from obsession to obsession. He obsessed about ███████ ███████ and then ███████████████████████. He was sure raw foodism was The Way. He was also involved in many "get rich" schemes, including renovating and flipping a house (ended up a nightmare), opening a vegan store, and selling The Ultimate Meal (blech) and other supplements.

He also ██ ██████. He argued *vociferously* to include a rice recipe in our nonprofit's booklet. Why did he want to use our limited space to distribute hundreds of thousands of rice recipes to college students? Because *he*, a long-time vegan, liked the recipe.

Despite ██ ███████████████████. A vegan cookbook author convinced him that our group *had* to promote veganism instead of vegetarianism. She did this ██ ██.

Anyway, he went to chiropractic school. Then he transferred to the dietician program. Then he came to work for our nonprofit.

Around this time – the mid-2000s – I started having real doubts about the efficacy of our work. A decade before, I had published the results of my models showing what we should expect if promoting veganism was successful. A decade later, there was no indication that we were having any impact. There was a slight dip in per-capita meat consumption during the 2007-08 Great Recession. (At the time, we made a big deal of that dip!) But then the trend reversed and continued to its current record levels.

It was even worse than that, given that people were eating more chickens while chicken "production" was "intensifying" i.e.: becoming more brutal. (Google "John Oliver chickens" for details of how chicken farmers are treated by big ag.)

As noted, I had written pieces and given talks that had pissed off vegans; recall Jayne's jihad against me for noting that many more animals are killed for food than in labs. Promoting the long, slow work of "winning friends and influencing people" drew the ire of those who wanted to act on their anger now now *now*.

Our group had also once published a guest piece that dared to question the claims and methods of one of veganism's cult leaders.

The *immediate* threats of lawsuits led us to quickly scrub the article. Even though the facts were clear, we didn't have the money to hire lawyers. Unlike the cult leader, we couldn't charge $20,000 per speaking gig, an amount that still amazes and galls me. (Con man Bernie Madoff fleeced that particular leader, after which his closest apostles pleaded for everyone to send Dear Leader money.)

In 2004, when I accepted Benedict's Animal Rights Hall of Fame award, I had fun with the speech. Since I figured I'd never be back there, I referenced all our differences of opinion. Before I delivered the plaque to him, I even put a post-it over his name and wrote in mine, since I simply assumed that taking a selfie with the doctored award was as close as I would get.

(The "Hall of Fame" was set up by one man – let's say Zeke – who ran it as his own personal fiefdom. He took himself off the committee so he could be inducted, then took it over again.)

The next summer, Anne and I were in Germany. One day I went to an internet cafe and saw an email claiming that I and Judas had been elected to the Hall. I thought it was a joke, and, once I thought about it, a pretty funny prank at that.

But it wasn't a joke, at least not in *that* way. We were told to write our own introduction and give it to Zeke before the ceremony, which I did. He removed any mention of "influential essays," talking only about leafleting and his personal history with Judas.

(This was Zeke's pattern. When Paul was inducted, I leaned over to Anne and whispered, "Watch. I'll bet you that he makes it about himself." And sure enough, Zeke's introduction began: "When I opened the door in 1998 and saw tonight's inductee standing there, I knew I had someone I could mold into a great activist....")

The senseless ceremony in 2005 was probably the high point of the work Anne, Judas, and I would do together.

Yeah, you're smiling now, silly boy. But the seeds have already been sown.

Day 21 Concluded:
"You're Matt Ball?"

I think I've kind of been mistaken for somebody
who's trying to be a spokesperson for animal rights,
and the fact is I'm not qualified to be a spokesperson.

I am passionate about it,
but I'm not trying to make other people do what I do.

–Neko Case

In the summer of 2001, Anne, JL, and I drove to the national animal rights convention in DC. While in the lobby Friday evening, someone looked at my nametag and excitedly exclaimed, *"You're Matt Ball?"*

Up in our room, I told Anne this story, laughing. "He was so excited. It was like I'm a celebrity."

The next morning, I gave my regular "How Vegan?" talk, where I tried to get people to stop thinking in terms of rules and instead think in terms of impact. (A short excerpt is at the end of this chapter.) The room was packed, with people standing along the walls and out the door, which is why I didn't notice Professor

Peter Singer until he came up to me to introduce himself after the question-and-answer session ended.

My immediate reaction – which I luckily didn't say out loud – was, of course, *"You're Peter Singer!"*

In case you don't know, Peter has been called "the most influential philosopher of our time" in an article about him entitled "Unspeakable Conversations." He is famous not only for kick-starting the global animal advocacy movement with his article and then book, *Animal Liberation*, but also for controversial views that follow logically from his utilitarian premises.

I immediately asked him if he had plans for lunch, which he didn't. I rounded up Anne and JL, and we piled into our Altima to drive to a nearby Asian restaurant. Anne and Peter happily spoke German in the back seat.

During lunch, Peter told us that he was struggling with what to do with the money his foundation had. Should he hire someone to figure out how to spend it, or give it to groups doing good work? Anne leaned over and said, "We prefer the latter."

We kept in touch after that. In late November 2006, Peter invited me to Princeton to speak on a panel with Jonathan Haidt, the author of *The Happiness Hypothesis*. Jonathan's thesis that evening was, "Why Good Intentions Don't Lead to Good Actions." My talk was titled, "Causing Good Actions Anyway."

Anne was at a big teaching conference, so EK, who was in seventh grade at the time, came along to New Jersey, handing out copies of "A Meaningful Life" to the crowd.

In his presentation, Jonathan said that whenever he spent time with Peter, he would decide to go vegetarian. Then when he would get home, he would slowly fall back into his old ways. (He showed a slide where his face slowly migrated from a picture of Peter over to a burger.) Of course, this is a typical story, given that the vast majority of people who give up meat revert back.

To give a sense of the stakes, my talk began with a short film about the conditions on factory farms. Then I pivoted to how food tech could help us overcome people's inertia. If we could give people the burgers and the nuggets they wanted without killing animals, then good intentions *would* be enough.

(Producing meat without animals was an idea JL had told us about when he lived in our basement. [We let him out for meals.] In 2004, he started actively promoting the idea of cultivated meat – aka "clean meat" or, inaccurately, "lab meat" – actual animal cells grown in a clean manufacturing facility. That year, he founded New Harvest to promote research into cultivated meat. JL flew to Europe and convinced the Dutch Agriculture Minister to provide funding for research.)

The author Jonathan Safran Foer (*Extremely Loud & Incredibly Close, Eating Animals*) was in the Princeton audience for my talk, and he came to the dinner afterwards. That is also where I met the great Bob Wright in person.

The dinner, however, was a mess. It was as though the cook had heard my talk about giving people tasty animal-free food and said, "Hold my beer and watch this." The main course was a slab of barely warm tofu with a slight drizzle of sauce. It could *not* have made vegetarian food look worse. I'm *serious*.

Sitting across from me was a grad student. She started holding forth on how her mom was a dietitian and had proven that while adults *could* be vegan, it was *impossible* to raise a child vegan. She went *on and on*, digging herself in deeper and deeper.

When she stopped, Peter, at the head of the table, nodded to his right and calmly said, "I think we should let EK handle this one."

Beautiful.

Professor Haidt emailed me about a month later, saying that after they saw my talk, he and his wife had *committed* to being vegetarian. They really meant it this time!

After we moved to Tucson, Peter was our first guest. He stayed in the spare room, which we have since called "The Peter Singer Room." Our friend Zak asked if it is a utility closet. That's a philosophy joke. Any funnier than the engineering joke?

Excerpt from "How Vegan?"

When I first got actively involved in animal rights around 1990, the question "How vegan?" had a simple answer: either something is vegan or it isn't. The way to tell was to compare all the ingredients against lists of all possible animal products. This list eventually became an entire book, *Animal Ingredients A to Z*, which was the best-selling book at Vegan.com for many years.

This simple means of defining "good" and "bad" attracted many of us because it was so straightforward. But even before the list began to grow into a bible, it was inconsistent. The production of honey kills some insects, but so does driving and harvesting foods, and sometimes even walking. Many soaps contain stearates, but the tires on cars and bicycles contain similar animal products. Some sugar is processed with bone char, but so is much municipal water. Adding "not tested on animals" to the definition of vegan added a whole new level of complexity....

It is not enough to be a righteous vegan, or even a dedicated, knowledgeable vegan advocate. The animals don't need us to be *right*, they need us to be *effective*. In other words, we don't want to simply "win an argument with a meat eater." It *isn't about winning*. Instead, we want to open people's hearts and minds to a more compassionate lifestyle.

To do this, we must be the *opposite* of the vegan stereotype. Regardless of the sorrow and outrage we rightly feel at the cruelties animals suffer, we must strive to be what others want to be: joyful individuals with fulfilling lives. Only then can we do our best to really make a difference for animals.

Biting the Philosophical Bullet

Philosophy is the talk on a cereal box.
–Edie Brickell & New Bohemians, "What I Am"

This chapter and the next get *way* into the philosophical weeds and can be skipped with no consequences. But then you won't know Phil and I saw Edie in concert! Her album was like tater tots – i.e., highly addictive – when it came out in 1986.

Several years ago, as I was beginning to wrestle with the implications of the logic below, I emailed JL, asking, "Has anyone ever thought (*brief version of below*). He sent a link to an article in which the authors say, in passing, "Of course, no one thinks (*brief version of below*)."

Um, yes, at least *one* person does!

I still don't know where I'm wrong. The only counters I get are appeals to moral intuitions ("But if you're right, that would mean ...") not flaws in the logic.

Certainly, I *could* be wrong. I *hope* I'm wrong. But for now, here is my uncertain, unfinished [?] reasoning:

Generally, the people I ally with follow some form of utilitarianism. The one-sentence definition seems straightforward: a person ought to act so as to maximize happiness (or pleasure or "utility") and to minimize unhappiness (pain). Who could *possibly* disagree with that?

Maybe me?

We make decisions every day that involve trade-offs. We cause ourselves pain through exercise in exchange for feeling healthier and hopefully living longer. We restrain ourselves from eating the entire pint of Ben & Jerry's Colin Kaepernick's Change the Whirled in order to not look pudgy for our foxy Frau. (And to hopefully live longer with said Frau.) (And because pretty much everything is easier when you are thinner and more attractive.) We don't smoke because ... well, smoking is fucking disgusting.

Some of us – especially parents – have responsibilities that require denying others their immediate desires. For example, we set limits for our children so they learn good habits that will hopefully serve them well in the future. A large part of parenting is constraining a child's current desires for more future happiness.

Beyond that, our choices and policies often impact multiple others. We tax some to provide services to others. We mandate (when rational) masks to protect the vulnerable. (And, of course, to protect the masked as well.)

In general, a utilitarian will add up the good and bad, pleasure and pain, and pick the policy that maximizes the excess happiness (utility).

But unlike some vegans and effective altruists, I don't think this works in all cases. Thus, maximizing utility can't be our (only) ethical guide.

Parfit is wrong and Chalmers is *way* wrong.

Imagine the worst possible suffering. The person suffering, when they can form a conscious thought, actively wants to die. The worst torture ever conceived. On a suffering scale, make that a 1,000 out of 1,000.

Now imagine the briefest, mildest unpleasant experience. Not even a stubbed toe – maybe just a brief muscle spasm that you barely notice. Make that a 0.0001 on the suffering scale.

Is there any circumstance under which you would choose to save 10,000,001 individuals from the brief muscle spasm instead of saving the one person from torture?

And yet, that is what a strict utilitarian calculus would require – prevent the most total suffering.

Even stranger, strict utilitarian calculus would have us torture someone at level 1,000 to give 10,000,001 others the briefest, faintest pleasure.

People have spent entire careers arguing the above, but the short takeaway is that I don't see how morality can possibly be based on a simple summing across individuals.

This is relevant in many situations, not the least of which is how animal advocates think about insects:

Back in 2005, Dr. Michael Greger noted that talking about insects with the general public is so strategically misguided that it causes actual harm – it makes vegans look crazy and dogmatic and thus easy to dismiss. But I also think it is philosophically mistaken as well.

I would be very comfortable betting my life that insects do not have subjective conscious experiences. Not to get into the weeds, but I believe people too easily conflate *behavior* with *consciousness*. The ability to sense things – what some people refer to as "sentience" in its *broadest* meaning – exists all the way down to single-cell organisms. (As mentioned in Day 1, Carl Sagan once told me this is why he thought "sentience" *per se* couldn't be the basis of morality.) "Sentience" also exists, with ever-increasing sophistication, in our robots. (I don't see any reason to think consciousness is substrate-specific – there isn't anything magical about our neurons. This is one place where Chalmers is right.)

To me, all the evidence indicates that the ability to have conscious, subjective experiences – to be able to not just *sense* but to *suffer* – derives from and requires significant (neural) complexity. And once the appropriate level of complexity is reached for consciousness to (somehow) flicker into existence, further complexity can lead to a capacity for "greater" consciousness, e.g., a fertilized egg doesn't go from a total lack of subjective experience to full adult-level consciousness with the addition of just one more neural synapse.

In other words, the ability to feel feelings is not binary, but analog. (For much *much* more, see the Open Philanthropy Project's Luke Muehlhauser's "2017 Report on Consciousness and Moral Patienthood." I don't fully agree, but it is the most honest and thorough good-faith exploration of consciousness I've ever come across.)

So even *if* insects can have any subjective experience – and again, I would bet my life they don't – their most intense sensation would be the palest hint of a feeling, a tiny fraction of the worst suffering we can experience.

Just as no number of people having a brief muscle spasm could rise to the level of concern of one person being tortured, no number of insects experiencing their "worst" suffering rises to the level of concern of a single suffering human. Or cow. So please stop talking about bees.

Please note: I'm not saying I have a coherent replacement for classical utilitarianism. Believe me, I realize the seeming contradictions that arise from my view.

One obvious problem: just as I would save one person from being tortured instead of sparing a trillion people from experiencing a muscle spasm, my initial *intuition* would be to save multiple people from suffering at level 999 instead of sparing one person level 1,000 agony.

But our intuitions are terrible – racist, xenophobic, innumerate – so we can't trust them.

Of course, I'm still a consequentialist. That is, I still think the rightness or wrongness of an action is determined by the action's consequences, not by whether it follows some rule.

One person suggested I'm a negative utilitarian. While I appreciate that view – it is the closest to me that I've found – I think it is more complicated than that. Unlike Parfit, I see a fundamental discontinuity between summing *within* an individual vs summing *across* individuals.

As noted, I will cause myself to suffer some – not eating a donut ... or ten – to avoid worse suffering in the future – more heart surgery. But I wouldn't choose to have someone *else* to suffer so I could avoid suffering. And I wouldn't have someone else suffer so I could experience pleasure.

(Well, unless that someone else was Mitch McConnell. Or pretty much any elected Republican. Except Liz Cheney. How crazy is *that?*)

In short: summing across individuals ... really bothers me. Even though it *seems* reasonable at first glance, the more I think about it, the less it makes sense.

There is no entity experiencing "all the suffering in the universe." *Only individuals suffer* – the universe doesn't suffer. (That is the most important sentence in the entire chapter.)

For those deep in these discussions: this rejection of "total" utilitarianism also answers Parfit's repugnant conclusion to my satisfaction. Or, as Scott Alexander puts it in discussing the repugnant conclusion in the context of longtermism (emphasis added):

> [T]he conclusion's repugnance doesn't hinge on the lives of the people involved being especially bad. It hinges on people having to be sadder and poorer than the alternative, their standard of living forever capped, just in order to tile the world with as many warm bodies as possible. **I genuinely don't care how big the population is.** I don't think you can do harm to potential people by not causing them to come into existence. Hurting actual people in order to please potential people seems plenty repugnant to me regardless of the exact level of the injury.

Exactly.

I try again to catch Open Phil's attention.

Back in March 2022, I came across a discussion by Open Philanthropy's Holden Karnofsky: "Debating myself on whether 'extra lives lived' are as good as 'deaths prevented.'" His piece is useful in explaining where I differ from many utilitarians.

(In short, Holden concludes that starting with *any* particular position will lead to consequences that offend our intuitions. True!)

To me, this is the key section of Holden's argument:

> I'll give my own set of hypothetical worlds:
> - World D has 10^18 flourishing, happy people.
> - World E has 10^18 horribly suffering people, plus some even larger number (N) of people whose lives are mediocre/fine/"worth living" but not *good*.

There has to be some "larger number N" such that you prefer World E to World D. That's a pretty wacky seeming position too!

It isn't just wacky, it's wrong. I simply don't think there is *any* number N that works here. That is, I don't think you can offset horrible suffering with any number of other people, no matter their level of happiness. (Also: Utility Monster.)

Again, there is no entity experiencing the net summed happiness of the world – there are only individuals experiencing their own pleasure and suffering.

Neighborhood chickens in our Pittsburgh backyard.

<insertion>

Chicken Worlds

This is a very hard concept to convey to people. I have tried several times, and only Anne seems to really *get* it. (She is even more brilliant than beautiful. Really – it's true!)

So let me try again:

Imagine a universe that has only two worlds, World RR and World FL. In World RR, Ricky Rooster is the only sentient being and is suffering an absolutely miserable life.

This is bad. But *where* is it bad? In Ricky's consciousness. *And nowhere else.*

On World FL, Rooster Foghorn is living in one forest and Rooster Leghorn is living in a separate forest. They are the World FL's only sentient beings, and don't know each other. Their lives are as bad as Ricky's.

Our natural response is to think that World FL is twice as bad as World RR. But *where could it possibly be twice as bad?* Foghorn's life is bad in his consciousness *and nowhere else.* Leghorn's life is bad in *his* consciousness *and nowhere else.*

Where is their world twice as bad as Ricky's?

Nowhere.

Okay, yes, I admit it is twice as bad in *your* mind and my mind. But we are not part of that universe. Imagine that these worlds are unknown to any other sentient being. Then there is simply nowhere that World FL is worse than World RR.

In this example, there are *three* worlds and only three worlds: one in each of their minds.

Please tell me where I am factually wrong. Seriously, I'm asking. My life would be much, *much* easier – and happier – if you did.

Don't say the implications of this insight leads to absurd conclusions that offend our intuitions. I already know that! Just tell me where I am factually wrong.

I know (oh, yes, I *know*) that this seems like it can't possibly be right. This is because *we can't help* but be utilitarian in this regard, just like we can't help but feel like we are in control of our consciousness and our decisions and our choices.

But I can see no way around this simple fact: Morally-relevant "badness" (and goodness) exists only in the singular consciousness of an individual.

Then why, you may ask, am I working for a world where there are fewer suffering individuals, when there will always be at least *some* suffering individuals?

An obvious but insightful question! The answer is simple:

I can't help myself.

(More below.)

</insertion>

Back to OPP's Holden, who notes that taking my non-utilitarian position leads to some counter-intuitive outcomes, like not valuing more happy people over fewer happy people. But again: There is no entity experiencing all the suffering – or happiness – in the universe. Only individuals suffer or experience happiness. The universe doesn't experience aggregate utility.

It is only our *intuition* that more is better. I held the "more is better" view for most of my life, but it now seems clear that this intuition is flawed. It just *feels* right to want more total happiness, but *it doesn't actually matter* in our universe, a universe where only individuals experience (finite) happiness. There is absolutely no ethical relevance to "the total net happiness in the universe." Aggregate utility is a fantasy that only exists in the minds of utilitarians. A seemingly useful fantasy, but a misleading fantasy.

Once you see the folly in maximizing a fictitious variable, you can avoid other morally offensive conclusions. For example, you aren't ethically obligated to torture someone in order to provide a slight pleasure to N others (or allow N individuals to avoid a slight discomfort). You also aren't personally ethically obligated to have as many "lives worth living" children as possible, a consequence of utilitarianism that Holden tries but fails to hand-wave away.

Of course, I certainly could be wrong *yet again*. That seems more likely than not. But I've read loads of very smart, thoughtful people, and no one has shown me where I'm factually wrong or offered a philosophy that takes Chicken World into account.

The Chicken Conclusion: Marginal Impact

I realize the above seems to contradict my concern for chickens. The reason isn't a love for chickens, but rather, marginal impact.

Someone could *easily* convince me that I should do something to help individuals suffering worse than chickens. But these would have to be individuals who would not be helped if not for my specific efforts – i.e., no one else would do the work I'd do, or I would do it significantly better. I've not yet figured out what that job could be.

I've seriously thought about being a counselor. Given my many terrible experiences with therapy, I have thought I could do it better. However, Anne rightfully warns that unless I get *way* better at mindfulness (possible—see later chapters) I would be endlessly frustrated when my patients inevitably refuse to act in their own self-interest; for example, cutting off contact with toxic family members and/or colleagues.

Hmmm.

Loads of people care about mammals and loads more care about humans. Few people care about chickens even though the average chicken is basically tortured. Even assuming chickens have a lower *capacity* to suffer than a cow, I'd rather be reincarnated as your average steer than your average chicken, because the chicken is treated *much worse*. (I'd easily choose being reincarnated as a bug over either of those options.) Yet most of our dietary / vegan advocacy leads to many chickens suffering far worse than cattle.

Not cool.

Cabrillo National Monument, San Diego.

My Expected Value Is Bigger Than Yours.

I welcome our robot overlords and you should, too!

And all the answers that I started with
Turned out questions in the end

–Alison Krauss, "Gravity"
(OMG is that a beautiful song)

If you don't know what longtermism is, please skip this chapter. Yay you!

Longtermism ≈ the interests of oodles of sentient beings / robots in the future is more important than any other concern.

I disagree.

The smartest person I know disagrees with my disagreement.

███

███████████████████████████████████

[Longtermists believe] summing up all the possible future joy from (hopefully sentient, but probably not; how could we ever know *for sure?*) robots vastly and absolutely swamps any concerns of the moment. So keeping humanity on track for this future is what truly matters.

But as far as I can tell, humanity's continued existence is *not* a self-evident good. I know Effective Altruists (EAs) tend to be well-off humans who like their own existence and thus personally value humanity's existence. But this value is not *inherent*. It's simply a *bias*. It's simply an *intuition* that makes EAs and others *assume* that humanity's continued existence is unquestionably a good thing.

That aside, basing decisions on "add up everyone" is where I get off the EA / utilitarian train, as per the previous "Biting the Philosophical Bullet" chapter.

Yes, I understand expected values, but let's think about what these longtermist calculations say: A *tiny* chance of lowering existential risk – a vanishingly small chance of improving the likelihood that quadzillions of happy robots will take over the universe – is more important than, say, stopping something like the Holocaust.

I'm serious. If a longtermist had been alive in 1938 and knew what was going on in Nazi Germany, they would have *turned down* the opportunity to influence public opinion and policy: "An asteroid might hit Earth someday. The numbers prove we must focus on that."

Over at Vox, Dylan Matthews' "I spent a weekend at Google talking with nerds about charity. I came away … worried" captures these problems. Excerpts:

> The common response I got to this was, "Yes, sure, but even if there's a very, very, very small likelihood of us decreasing AI [artificial intelligence] risk, that still

trumps global poverty, because infinitesimally increasing the odds that 10^52 people in the future exist saves way more lives than poverty reduction ever could."

The problem is that you could use this logic to defend just about anything. Imagine that a wizard showed up and said, "Humans are about to go extinct unless you give me $10 to cast a magical spell." Even if you only think there's a, say, 0.0000000000000001 percent chance that he's right, you should still, under this reasoning, give him the $10, because the expected value is that you're saving 10^32 lives. Bostrom calls this scenario "Pascal's Mugging," and it's a huge problem for anyone trying to defend efforts to reduce human risk of extinction to the exclusion of anything else.

Ultimately you have to stop being meta ... if you take meta-charity too far, you get a movement that's really good at expanding itself but not necessarily good at actually helping people.

(By the way, if you don't buy five more copies of this book for your friends, humanity will go extinct. You've been warned.)

Or, as Matt Yglesias put it in "What's long-term about 'longtermism'"?

> Suppose right now there's a 0.001 percent chance that climate change could generate a catastrophic feedback mechanism that leads to human extinction, and doing a Thanos snap and killing half of everyone reduces that to 0.0001 percent. A certain kind of longtermist logic says you should do the snap, which I think most people would find odd.

Furthermore, no one can *know* what the impact might be of their longtermist efforts. This is called sign-uncertainty, aka cluelessness. We simply don't *and can't* know if our actions aimed at the long-term future might have a positive or negative impact.

There are plenty of examples, but one involves work on AI. Think about efforts to reign in / slow down the development of AI in western democracies – e.g., to force researchers to first address the alignment problem. This could lead to an unfettered totalitarian AI from China pre-empting every other attempt. Oops.

Another example: EAs talking about the threat of an engineered virus (ala Margaret Atwood's fantastic *Oryx and Crake*) might be what gives real-world Crake his idea to engineer said virus! This is not a fantasy; as Scott Alexander explains, "al-Qaeda started a bioweapons program after reading scaremongering articles in the Western press about how dangerous bioweapons could be."

Or longtermists could inspire the creation of a malevolent computer system, as noted in this great thread on longtermism.

Alexander Berger, the very wise co-head of the Open Philanthropy Project (and someone who I hope will someday fire me) made yet another important point in his 80,000 Hours podcast:

> I think it makes you want to just say wow, this is all really complicated and I should bring a lot of uncertainty and modesty to it. ... I think the more you keep considering these deeper levels of philosophy, these deeper levels of uncertainty about the nature of the world, the more you just feel like you're on extremely unstable ground about everything. ... my life could totally turn out to cause great harm to others due to the complicated, chaotic nature of the universe in spite of my best intentions. ... I think it is true that we cannot in any way predict the impacts of our actions. And if you're a utilitarian, that's a very odd, scary, complicated thought. ...

I think the EA community probably comes across as wildly overconfident about this stuff a lot of the time, because it's like we've discovered these deep moral truths, then it's like, "Wow, we have no idea." I think we are all really very much – including me – naïve and ignorant about what impact we will have in the future.

I'm going to rely on my everyday moral intuition that saving lives is good ... I think it's maximizable, I think if everybody followed it, it would be good.

And from his interview with The Browser:

I'm not prepared to wait. The ethos of the Global Health and Wellbeing team is a bias to improving the world in concrete actionable ways as opposed to overthinking it or trying so hard to optimize that it becomes an obstacle to action. We feel deep, profound uncertainty about a lot of things, but we have a commitment to not let that prevent us from acting.

I think there are a lot of ways in which the world is more chaotic than [we think]. [S]ometimes trying to be clever by one extra step can be worse than just using common sense.

Awesome.

Edit: Hardcore Effective Altruist Kat Woods' "The most important lesson I learned after ten years in EA":

To be an EA is to find out, again and again and again, that what you thought was the best thing to do was wrong. You think you know what's highest impact and you're almost certainly seriously mistaken.

Every single time I have been so damn certain that this was the time we'd finally found the thing that totally definitely helped in a large way.

And when people think they have the answer, and it just happens to be their math, sometimes sarcasm works best:

Backstory: EA's determine an issue's worthiness based on three variables: 1. Scale, 2. Neglectedness, 3. Tractability. (A calculation like this is what led to One Step for Animals.) Taking this literally leads to D0TheMath's post on the EA's Forum, "Every moment of an electron's existence is suffering." Excerpts:

> Scale: If we think there is only a 1% chance of panpsychism being true (the lowest possible estimate on prediction websites such as Metaculus, so highly conservative), then this still amounts to at least 10^{78} electrons impacted in expectation.
>
> Neglectedness: Basically nobody thinks about electrons, except chemists, physicists, and computer engineers. And they only think about what electrons can do for them, not what they can do for the electrons. This amounts to a moral travesty far larger than factory farms.
>
> Tractability: It is tremendously easy to affect electrons, as shown by recent advances in computer technology, based solely on the manipulation of electrons inside wires.
>
> This means every moment of an electron's existence is pain, and multiplying out this pain by an expected

10^78 produces astronomical levels of expected suffering.

This is funny, but it is very close to how some EA's think! (And some people *really do* believe in panpsychism. *Not funny.*) (More funny.) I knew one EA who stopped donating to animal issues to support Christian missionaries. There may be a small chance they are right about god, but if they are, the payoff for every saved soul is *literally infinite!* He actually put money on Pascal's Wager!

I don't know that I'm right; as I mentioned, I've changed my mind before. I understand that many smart people think I'm entirely mistaken. But I would at least like them to regularly and overtly admit the opportunity costs, e.g. that writing an endless series of million-word essays about a million years in the future means you are *actively choosing* to not help those who are suffering *right now.*

You might wonder why I continue to flog this issue. (I blog about it regularly.) It is because I am continually saddened that, in a world filled with so *much* acute and unnecessary misery, so many brilliant people dedicate their 80,000 hour career trying to one-up each other's expected value.

PS: The day after I finished this chapter, an essay by Open Philanthropy's Holden Karnofsky landed in my inbox: "AI Could Defeat All Of Us Combined."

My first reaction was: "Good."

He is worried about the previously-mentioned "alignment problem" – i.e., that the artificial intelligence(s) we create might not share our values.

Holden writes:

> By "defeat," I don't mean "subtly manipulate us" or "make us less informed" or something like that – I mean a literal "defeat" in the sense that we could all be killed, enslaved or forcibly contained.

Note that we humans enslave, forcibly contain, and kill billions of fellow sentient beings. So if we solved the alignment problem and a "superior" AI actually *were* to share human values, it seems like they *would* kill, enslave, and forcibly contain us.

Holden, like almost every other EA and longtermist, simply *assumes* that humanity shouldn't be "defeated." Rarely does anyone note that it is possible, even likely, that on net, things would be much better if AIs *did* replace us.

The closest Holden comes is when he addresses objections:

Isn't it fine or maybe good if AIs defeat us?
They have rights too.

- Maybe AIs should have rights; if so, it would be nice if we could reach some "compromise" way of coexisting that respects those rights.

- But if they're able to defeat us entirely, that isn't what I'd plan on getting – instead I'd expect (by default) a world run entirely according to whatever goals AIs happen to have.

- These goals might have essentially nothing to do with anything humans value, and could be actively counter to it – e.g., placing zero value on beauty and having zero attempts to prevent or avoid suffering).

Zero attempts to prevent suffering? Hey Holden, aren't you mistaking AIs for humans? Humans are the *cause* of most of the world's unnecessary suffering, both to humans and other animals.

Setting aside our inherent tribal loyalties to humanity and our bias for continued existence, it is likely that AIs defeating humanity would be a *huge* improvement.

Please convince me otherwise. I would much rather be optimistic.

PPS: I posted this chapter to the Effective Altruism Forum to make the case that we should focus on suffering now instead of happy robots in the future. Also, I even *explicitly argue against* even *talking* about engineering viruses.

This comment came in within three minutes:

> I find it hard to believe this is a position in good faith. Do you think we should kill all humans e.g. by engineering deadly viruses and releasing them into every population center in the world?

<sigh>

Day 22: The Shocking Inevitability

Best friend on the payroll
Oh no no no
It's not gonna work out

–Morrissey

Relatively early in our time in Pittsburgh, Anne and I went to a gathering of vegans. Many of them were so arrogant and mean that on the drive home, Anne said, "I want to go eat a burger so I won't have anything in common with those people." Turns out the feeling was very mutual.

I've been putting off writing this chapter, as it is still raw, even eight years later. So I'll try to rush through it

After EK went off to Pomona College in Southern California, tension continued to build between Anne & me and our former housemate. Judas and a ███████████ leafletter pressed their efforts to make our organization more vegan-friendly. Anne and I argued that the organization needed effective messages – e.g., more focus on chickens, no mention of cattle, no rice recipes. We also wanted to update our methods. It wasn't 1990 anymore – we didn't have to go to concerts to have tens of thousands of 16-page booklets simply thrown on the ground. There were more efficient means of reaching people. For example: the Interwebs. One Step for Animals mostly does easily-testable online outreach, although we've also advertised on podcasts and in computer games.

Anne and I also thought we should continue to take nonprofit salaries and put more of our donors' money into our actual outreach. In retrospect, if we had wanted to keep our jobs, that's where we should have given ground. But also in retrospect, it was clear our position in the group was untenable. People want to be popular with the people they know, and for Judas and his sidekick, that was the loudest vegans.

One spring day in 2014, Anne and I received notices from Judas' college roommate (and board member who had taken Best Man Mark's position) that our services were no longer required. Behind my back (in addition to being Executive Director, I was Vice President of the board) Judas and his college roommate had convinced their other pal on the board to fire us.

And just like that, we had a kid in college, a mortgage, a car payment, and no income. They were free to have the group ███████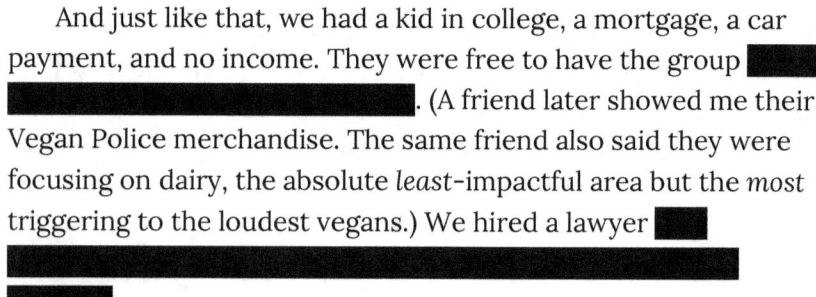
████████████████████████████. (A friend later showed me their Vegan Police merchandise. The same friend also said they were focusing on dairy, the absolute *least*-impactful area but the *most* triggering to the loudest vegans.) We hired a lawyer ████
██
███████.

One of the first calls I made after being shitcanned was to Benedict. Oops.

A majority of people I considered friends took the vegan side. (Veganism *über alles!*) One later contacted me with the news that the coup-supporting leafletter had left the group for an actual animal advocacy group. "I thought he would never leave," she wrote. "I guess you were right."

Ya think?

For the first time since Diane, I broke down and sobbed. Twice. No money, no career, no friends (relatively speaking), no prospects. It was bad. Really bad. But it wasn't yet one of the Worst.

The only saguaro we've ever seen with
an arm on an arm on an arm.

Day 23: Flashback to Worst the Second

Grown-up love means actually understanding what you love, taking the good with the bad and helping your loved one grow.

–Al Franken

Lies & the Lying Liars Who Tell Them:
A Fair & Balanced Look at the Right

In August 2003, in a motel room in Florence Oregon, I had the second and shortest of my Worst experiences. It was the most violent Crohn's attack I've ever had. During those hours, when I had any coherent thought at all, I wanted to die. Literally, not figuratively. But I was mostly just a ball of writhing, wordless agony.

Before this and after, Anne has gotten me to the emergency room for Really Bad Crohn's attacks, including while on vacation. Once, when we were visiting my parents in Tucson from Pittsburgh, she and my dad took me to Northwest Medical Center. While waiting, I was bent over, convulsing in waves of anguish. My dad, who had never seen me like this, was angry with the staff, berating them, "Can't you see how much pain he's in?" Anne, on the other hand, was used to sitting and waiting while I moaned for hours. At least I wasn't puking *that* time.

They finally put me on a gurney in the hall and pumped me full of prednisone and opioids. Drifting in and out of consciousness, I heard Anne talking to a nurse originally from Oregon. The nurse said the first time she got out of the shower in Tucson and grabbed her towel, she was shocked: the towel was dry.

Back to the Oregon coast where I was trying to turn myself inside-out from both ends.

This time, there was no hospital. I couldn't be moved from the toilet. All Anne could do was flush and haul out bags of barf. Several lifetimes later, it was over. Anne and EK dragged me to bed, where I watched the PGA Championship (to tie this back to Day 19 and the final of my three Perfect times). They opened the window and went to find a laundromat.

Here's the thing: That Oregon trip was one of our best family vacations ever. *Psych!*

I'm not saying all other vacations sucked. Far from it! We've been to awesome places and had wonderful times all over the world. For example, we went to Germany right after EK graduated from Pomona; I had some Crohn's on that trip, and EK was quite sick for a bad travel day, but overall, that trip was amazing!

The 2003 Oregon trip started with a lovely sunny day at several parks in Portland. As we strolled (and Anne and EK danced to a guy playing a hammered dulcimer) I was cogitating on the talk I was to give that evening.

The next day, we started a stunning drive down the Oregon coast. The weather was perfect and the sights spectacular. (Still some of the best pics I've taken – see above – even though it was one of the early, low-rez digital cameras.) We went across the mountains and up the other side, stopping in Bend, which was then a lovely little town I'd like to visit again, although I'm told it has really built up since.

Multnomah Falls, Columbia River Gorge

After driving through an eerie haze of wildfire smoke, we headed back to Portland via the Columbia River Gorge, which has some wonderful waterfalls.

For me, the highlight had been back in Portland. That was the time I actually became a public speaker, rather than a scared guy trying not to choke. This must be what people call "finding your groove." Finally, I knew what I wanted to say and how to tell the story. I *owned* it. (Later, I turned that talk into the essay "A Meaningful Life," which received a fair amount of play within the

quiet, sane wing of the animal advocacy movement.) And for the first time, the crowd was really with me. I could see it. I could *feel* it.

The Q&A session was even better. I handled everything well. I was engaging and funny – the crowd actually laughed. (Wish I also could have told my high school self that real laughter *and* women were coming. No *way*!) I'm generally not humorous in prepared remarks, but oddly, something about "doing it live" prompts my brain into witty banter and joke mode. (A change from my generally boring engineer self. Have I told you how they redesigned the F-102 fighter jet?)

Not that every talk from then on out was great. *The very next one* is the perfect example. It was just a few months later, in Albuquerque, as I helped my mom drive their minivan to Tucson. (On that trip, I made her listen to Al Franken's latest book. I very much miss Al Franken as a public figure.) Unlike Portland, where I had some general notes, I prepared the *shit* outta this talk. I pressed my shirt, had my tie on just right (*How to Win Friends and Influence People*) and strolled into the room, brimming with confidence.

There were five people there. They only wanted to talk about the local rodeo.

An even worse train wreck came in the winter of 2017 when I spoke at the Scottsdale Vegan Fest. (Trouble was *right there* in the name. I had a *much* better time speaking to the national convention of Future Farmers of America. No joke.) This time, I took a different tact with "Learning from History to Maximize Our Impact." Instead of making a specific argument, I told my life story (get it?) and the lessons I've learned. ("Lesson number six: Avoid chronic diseases." "Lessons nine *and* ten: People don't act the way they say they will. This is a hard lesson to learn.") The crowd seemed mostly indifferent except for two punked-out hard-corers who were just chomping at the bit to lay into me. They couldn't wait to scream at me about how terrible "fake meat" is, how immoral "lab meat" is, how I was a shill for the meat industry. The master of ceremonies did nothing to help, and no matter how kindly I tried to get them to back off, they wouldn't. Finally the MC came up and said, "Well *that* was interesting."

Our Phoenix pal Kari was there; she took the picture of me flailing. Afterwards, we went to a local place and I called Benedict while Kari went to get her order. He didn't believe me when I told him how bad it was. I put Kari on and he asked her what really happened. In a classic understatement, she replied, "It wasn't pretty."

The punks weren't the first or last vegans to hunt me. I was once doing an evening webinar for a California-based group and someone kept cutting in and talking over me. Eventually the host had to mute him, after which he took to the chat to continue his attacks. It turns out he was in Europe and had stayed up until the middle of the night to heap abuse on me.

One last story:

Probably the highest-energy talk I gave was before hundreds of people in Wisconsin at the 2016 Mad City VeganFest. The camera doesn't closely pan with me, so in the video, my stalking back and forth looks like I had just done a speedball. (In my experience, people find it easier to pay attention if there is movement. Engage as many senses as you can!) If you watch, you'll notice my shirt is untucked and I have no tie, so I couldn't use my standard opening: "Good afternoon. I'm

Matt Ball. I haven't had an interesting life, so I wear a tie."

Why do I look like I just fell out of bed? When the previous session had ended, I *had* been all put together, with the shirt and tie as seen on the cover of I'm *So Fucking Sick of These Fucking Motherfuckers*. But that session had gone over time. This left the

A/V people in a rush to get me mic'd-up. (With two separate wireless mics! Never had that before.) So the tie came off and the shirt came out.

Whatever. The punchline comes later.

As I mentioned, it was a high-energy affair. Laughter, applause. During the Q&A, I jumped off the stage, dislodging one of the mics. Sorry.

(Note: I've only watched a few minutes of this talk, which is more than I've ever watched or listened to of just about anything else I've done. I know that supposedly everyone hates their own voice [except Alison Krauss. She had damn well better love her voice, as it is ah-*may*-zing] but my voice is *truly terrible*. Be thankful you aren't listening to this book read by me. <*shudder*>)

So after the Q&A ended, I'm all jazzed up. Here comes my very famous friend of many years, Dr. Michael Greger, all pressed in his suit. (And, since I finished on time, fully mic'd up in advance.)

MATT BALL: CHANGING THE WORLD BY EXAMPLE, ADVOCACY

Still flying high from my talk, I ask, "Did you see that?" He is busy getting organized and doesn't even look at me.

"See what?"

(Story on previous page at bit.ly/MattBallAZ)

Anyway, back to Oregon, August 2003, two days before the second Worst moment of my life. After the talk and all the discussions that followed, Team Green-Ball heads back to our hotel. We got one of those super-cheap last-minute deals in downtown Portland's tallest hotel. I take nine-year-old EK to the bar on the top floor, where I have a Rusty Nail and we look out over the city at night.

It was a *fantastic* vacation.

Day 24: Prelude to Worst the Third

Laughing like children, living like lovers
Rolling like thunder under the covers…

And I guess that's why they call it the blues

–Elton John / Bernie Taupin

On Sunday, Cinco de Mayo 2013, while still Executive Director of the organization I had co-founded with Anne over 20 years before, I woke up with a weird sensation in the left side of my chest. I didn't know what it was, but certainly didn't want to go to the ER – I (wrongly) figured I would wait at least six hours with "weird sensation in my chest." Maybe I could "walk it off."

The feeling didn't change, but I did notice it got … weirder if I bounced up and down. Eventually, I emailed my cousin Lori, a nurse and administrator at the largest hospital in Tucson: "Hypothetically, when is the best time to go to the ER?" She said a bit before six a.m., as everyone who came in during the night has been dealt with and the shift is about to change.

The next morning, I called my doctor's office. When I told Alice I had a weird sensation in my chest, she told me to go to the ER. (*Foreshadowing!*) But given my past experience, I didn't want to go to the hospital unless I was dying. (*More foreshadowing!*)

Finally she agreed to let me come in to see Dr. C. He gave me an exam and nothing seemed amiss. But the weird, disturbing feeling persisted.

The following morning, I woke Anne up a little after five and said I thought we should, yet again, go to the ER.

At least it wasn't the middle of the night.

Lori was right – Tucson Medical Center (TMC) was a ghost town. But here is the key advice if you ever go to the ER: *always* say your chest hurts. You'll be seen quickly. Once when Anne took me to UPMC back in Pittsburgh, I mentioned my chest in addition to my Crohn's symptoms. (I wasn't lying – my chest did hurt.) Then, as in 2013, I got right back.

At TMC's Emergency Department, I explained what had been going on. First they tested my heart, which seemed fine. Then they gave me an x-ray. Then sent me for a CT scan. On one of the trips, I asked the attendant about himself. (It is *especially* important to be nice to people with medical power over you!) He told me about his love for Elton John, how seeing Elton live was the highlight of his life, and other Elton stories. I nodded and smiled and made appropriate noises. When we got back to my cubby, Anne listened in and then said, "Matt doesn't even like Elton John."

NOOOOOO!

And that's not even true! I just don't like him at *the same level* as Anne or the attendant. *Rocketman* is an inventive, fun movie that we saw at the $1 Tuesdays theater – it is a good big-screen pic! – and then again with EK. The songs are *fantastic*.

Finally, a diminutive doctor (her size will be relevant in a minute) came in and said they had finally figured it out: My left lung had partially collapsed. It was the CT scan that revealed the problem. Dr. C hadn't thought of a pneumothorax, nor had the ER team at first, because my blood oxygenation was nearly 100%.

(When I saw Dr. C next, he apologized profusely. He then told me about a young man who came in with his dad. The kid had a classic tension pneumothorax, which means that the bubble of non-lung air in the chest presses on the heart and trachea. Dr. C was going to call an ambulance, but the dad said he could get him to the hospital faster. After extracting a promise that they go *straight there*, Dr. C sent them off and called the hospital to get the kid straight into surgery. And this– *ta-da!* – is *even more foreshadowing!*)

Back to the ER in May 2013 where the doctor is telling us she'll have to pump my chest to get the air bubble out and let the lung re-expand. And no, they have no idea what caused this spontaneous pneumothorax, except that I'm a tall, skinny guy, although outside the normal age range. (BTW, this is the malady I share with Natalia.)

Now remember, other than my "muscular but still can't dunk" legs, I'm really skinny. Like "*You need to eat a pie*" skinny. (Ever since my high doses of steroids for Crohn's, however, I've had a problem with a blubbery belly, given that when I'm happy, I like to eat and drink. And when I'm unhappy, I drink.)

The doctor started to drill into my upper left chest. *Owww!* Then she climbed up on a stool and leaned all her weight into it: "This is really tough!" Squeezing Anne's hand like there's no tomorrow, I squealed, "How can that be? I have no muscle there!"

When the doc was finally into my chest cavity – and this is 100% true, I shit you not, you can ask Anne – she pulled out what looked like a child's toy air pump. Bright yellow and cheap plastic. She hooked it up to the tube she'd stuck into my chest and started pumping the little toy handle. And it squeaked this grating squeal that belied its tiny size: SQUEAK! SQUEAK!

What. The. Living. Hell?

As she pumped, I started to feel *real* pain. Not that the earlier pain of her drilling wasn't real! Oh, *it was!* But this new pain was all through my chest, back, and neck. Once she finished and my full respiratory capacity was restored, he gave me a shot of morphine. This provided a wonderful wave of relief that I felt flow into my body from the IV point.

Ahhhh.

Morphine didn't quite cover all the pain, though, and what was left came creeping back. The pulmonologist who came in said that pain management in these situations is hard. (Which, luckily, isn't true for Crohn's: a bunch of steroids and a shot of the doc's favorite opioid and I'm out of the doom loop and on my way to sleep and recovery.) It ended up that Dilaudid worked best for me at this point, but it wasn't perfect. They gave me a fancy hot-water system and continually tried to keep me comfortable.

Also, *everyone* I met told me how lucky I was to have the upper chest drilling: "They used to have to open a huge hole in your side." (Guess what that is? It rhymes with "*Morebadowing*.")

By the time Anne visited that evening, I was able to get out of bed with a wireless transmitter in my robe pocket and walk outside. We watched the bats come out from under a bridge.

The next morning, slightly over 24 hours after we arrived, I was on my way home.

Let me say here: I do not think this hospital stay could have been better.

The last nurse's assistant I had was only interested in sneaking off to text her boyfriend. But other than that, *every single person I met* – and there were *dozens* – was incredibly competent and friendly. It was an absolute model of professionalism and compassion.

I recognized and appreciated it then. But not nearly to the extent I would in 14 months.

The Oregon Coast. Note the lighthouse.

The Interesting Life of
an Uninteresting Person
(but really: Drug-Aided Meditation)

I am thoughtful –
full of thoughts, all the time, inescapably, exhaustingly.
But I am also mindless –
acting in accordance with default settings
I neither understand nor examine.

–John Green, "The Anthropocene Reviewed"

This chapter title was one of the many working titles of this book. Really, I'm just a boring Midwestern guy, but many interesting and improbable things – good and bad, fortunate and un – have happened to me.

But this chapter isn't really about that. It is about mindfulness. Run away, run away!

The "interesting" event today was that Google cut off access to my email from within Outlook. The first fix I found didn't work, and then it was time to go for our jog.

Previously, computer issues used to be the one sure way to set me off. When Anne's pals Shelley and Katherine met me during 1992's Time the First, I was, as mentioned, totally blissed out. (That is: not my normal self.) They asked Anne, "Does Matt ever get upset about *anything*?" Anne replied: "Well, he does yell at his computer."

Guilty!

Even in November 2019, when setting up this new Dell, I would be triggered by problems. (I do a lot of customizations that weren't working as they should, and I couldn't install Office 2019 to save my life. Next time, I'm going to move to a Mac full-time; my current laptop is a Mac.) Anne and I went on what should have been a lovely hike at Saguaro National Park East but I fretted the entire time about the problems I was having with this Dell.

When faced with today's (2022) computer problem, however, I knew eventually everything would work out. And in the end, we're dead anyway, so do the quirks of Outlook 2016 really matter?

Of course, I am fully aware this is the Wellbutrin talking. But it has been my long study of mindfulness, my regular meditations, and continual re-readings of *Why Buddhism Is True* that allow my brain to take advantage of the drug's help.

Mind you, I am absolutely no expert on mindfulness or meditation. I've never been on a retreat. I might have spent about as much time reading and listening to podcasts about these topics than actually meditating.

From the beginning I was biased toward the analytical. But I honestly think that

A. An intellectual understanding of what mindfulness is going for

is more important than

B. Actually meditating.

Obviously only up to a point. Knowing can't actually help if we never stop to observe our thoughts.

For me, being mindful all day long is the ultimate goal, not sitting on the bench my pal Jon hand-made for me. (Thanks!)

Not that I'm anywhere near enlightenment. Ha-*ha*! Yet I think that to get the "point" of mindfulness meditation, you have to embrace a paradox. The first step is realizing that "thoughts think themselves." No matter how it *feels*, it simply can't be otherwise. We don't have free will, no homunculus in there making choices of what to think or do. It is just neuronal interactions –chemical reactions following the causal laws of physics.

Observing my thoughts led me to realize many don't even take root, they simply come and go. (Except songs. Those suckers get stuck in there.) Even when I'm on a train of thought, the original impetus was random. That is, when I "choose" to think about something, the initial thought for that chain ("I'm going to think about mindfulness") just arose on its own, triggered seemingly at random or by an external force – an alarm, a previous thought, recognizing a bad mood, listening to a podcast.

As discussed in the BRAINS! Chapter, there is the *experiential* self – the entity feeling lust, the person taking pain medicine, the inner ear hearing The Mountain Goats' / John Darnielle's "This Year." ("I am gonna make it | through this year | if it kills me.") But I am not *controlling* my thoughts, so they can't be me.

I am not my thoughts.

And yet, paradoxically, we can "choose" to program ourselves such that, at some level, we observe our thoughts. Being mindful is like having someone ask, over and over again, "What are you thinking about?" Except we regularly interrogate ourselves to observe our thoughts.

By observing our thoughts and realizing the thoughts are not us, we can "choose" to let negative thoughts go. We don't *have* to hold on to any thought. (Except when a *Hamilton* song gets stuck in our heads – can't get those out! Just avoid "It's Quiet Uptown" – that one is *really* freakin' sad.) By reading books or listening to podcasts or following guided meditations, we can alter our programming so we can better learn to drop negative thoughts. Instead, we can feel gratitude that we had the good fortune not to have been born in Syria.

An example: At the library today, a woman was standing there, no mask, talking loudly into her cellphone. My initial, visceral response was a mix of anger and revulsion, followed by a thought that included bad language. (I'll spare you.) But then, realizing I wasn't going to act on those feelings – e.g., I wasn't going to say anything to her – I let the feelings go.

Of course, this is easier said than done. I have noted that depression is an issue that can, at least *sometimes*, be treated with drugs. (And sometimes therapy, according to others.) The last time I was seriously depressed, I was able to *recognize* negative thought patterns and diagnose my depression. But I wasn't able to "mindfulness" my way out of it. (Kinda like trying to stay awake for days with "willpower.") It is only after getting to a better place with the help of medication that I'm able to use mindfulness to any good effect.

Don't take my word for it. From pages 20-21 of *Why Buddhism Is True* (don't tell Bob I'm outsourcing so much of my book to him):

> In mindfulness meditation as it's typically taught, the point of focusing on the breath isn't just to focus on your breath. It's to stabilize your mind, to free it of its normal preoccupation so you can observe things that are happening in a clear, unhurried, less reactive way. And "things that are happening" emphatically includes things that are happening inside your mind. Feelings arise within you – sadness, anxiety, annoyance, relief,

joy – and you try to experience them from a different vantage point than as usual, neither clinging to the good feelings nor running away from the bad ones, but rather just experiencing them straightforwardly and observing them. This altered perspective can be the beginning of a fundamental and enduring change in your relationship with your feelings; you can, if all goes well, cease to be their slave.

After devoting some attention to the overcaffeinated feeling in my jaw [while on a meditation retreat], I suddenly had an angle on my interior life that I'd never had before. I remember thinking something like, "Yes this grinding sensation is still there – the sensation I typically define as unpleasant. But that sensation is down there in my jaw, and that's not where I am. I'm up here in my head." I was no longer identifying with the feeling; I was viewing it objectively, I guess you could say. In the space of a moment it had lost its grip on me. It was a very strange thing to have an unpleasant feeling cease to be unpleasant without really going away.

There is a paradox here. (Don't say I didn't warn you!) When I first expanded my attention to encompass the obnoxiously intrusive jaw-grinding sensation, this involved relaxing my resistance to the sensation. I was, in a sense, accepting, even embracing a feeling that I had been trying to keep it a distance. But the result of this closer proximity to the feeling was to acquire a kind of distance from it – a certain degree of detachment (or, as some meditation teachers prefer, for somewhat technical reasons, to put it, "nonattachment"). This is something that can happen again and again via meditation: accepting, even embracing, an unpleasant feeling can give you a critical distance from it that winds up diminishing the unpleasantness.

The desert in bloom

A Personal Request from Me to You

If you're giving a speech, be vulnerable.
Fall on the audience and let them catch you.

*–David Brooks, "The Greatest Life Hacks in the World
(for Now)"*

Before we get into this last stretch:

If you have found this book worth reading (well, maybe not all of it, but some of it?) please share it with friends, enemies, and anyone else you think might find it worthwhile.

If you'd like to do more, please consider a contribution to One Step for Animals' efforts to reduce suffering. It would mean *a lot.* More than I can tell you.

Thanks!

PS: If you'd like to leave on an upbeat note, you can stop reading now. I'm not joking. Sorry. Life is what it is.

Along Rattlesnake Trail, Sabino Canyon Recreation Area

Day 25: The One Who Got (Inside) My Heart

And all that could befall a heart
Or break this perfect life apart
The swords we carried could not do a thing about them

–Mary Chapin Carpenter

You might think that a collapsed lung, scoliosis, Crohn's, and degenerative osteoarthritis would be enough. But the trials of my torso were just getting started. As I wrote at the time (October 2017):

Tl;dr – Kindness should be our baseline.

Friend and One Step advisor Ginny recently co-authored a book entitled *Even Vegans Die*. If you haven't read the book, it is important for at least two reasons. The first: because of our understandable yet generally impotent anger over how humans treat other animals, many vegans are simply cruel. These angry vegans often aim their cruelty at other vegans. This is especially true when it comes to "health."

The second reason is that not feeling healthy is a leading cause of people going back to eating meat. Many vegetarians and vegans oversell their diet as the cure-all, so when others stop eating meat and then feel worse rather than the "awesome" they were promised, they go back to eating animals. Furthermore, these now former-vegetarians tell all their friends and family about how terrible vegetarianism is. This is one of the main reasons the percentage of the population who don't eat animals in the United States has basically remained unchanged for decades.

Many if not most of my friends have learned to avoid vegan fanatics, especially online. In *Even Vegans Die*, Ginny and her co-authors give examples, so I won't tell my stories.

Except just one....

Relative Number of Farm Animals Harmed by Average American Consumption of Different Foods

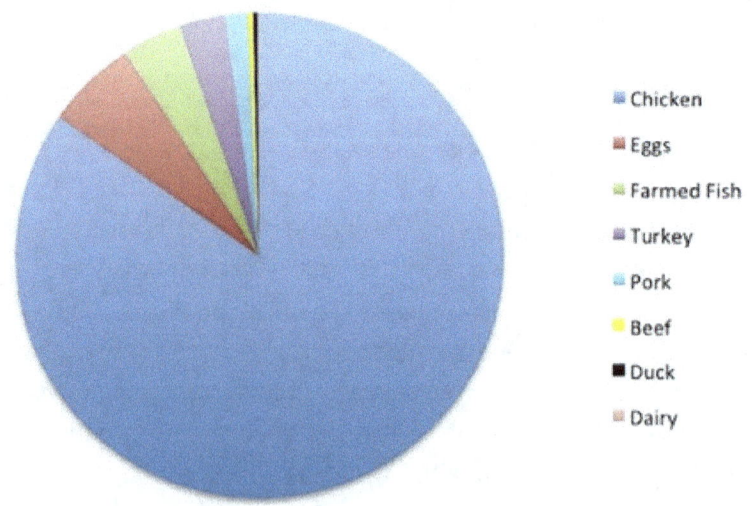

- Chicken
- Eggs
- Farmed Fish
- Turkey
- Pork
- Beef
- Duck
- Dairy

A vegan once attacked me for referencing a simple, factual graph showing that orders of magnitude more chickens are killed every year than dairy cows. (You can see the graph on the "About" page at OneStepForAnimals.org.) She claimed I would cause more people to get Crohn's disease by "promoting" dairy. Little did she know that I have had Crohn's for decades, having come down with it well after going vegan.

It is frightening how many of my fellow Crohn's victims developed the disease after going vegan. Sometimes, if I mention having Crohn's in an online forum, I will be told I just need to go vegan. Some even imply I *deserve* Crohn's for not being vegan.

How to win friends and influence people.

Now to my personal update.

Note: I had not planned to have any of the below known publicly. But for a variety of reasons, the story is creeping around and I'd rather people hear it from me instead of via a game of telephone. Also, a wise person reminded me it is arrogant to attempt utilitarian calculations for one's friends. Sorry, I can't help it!

...I started having some discomfort in my chest while running.... When the pulmonologists didn't find anything, he sent me to a cardiologist.

The cardiologist scheduled a stress test for September 28 (2017). I failed that *badly*; they immediately scheduled me for heart catheterization the next Friday, October 6 at Tucson Medical Center. The surgeon was fully booked, so they created a slot for me *before* the normal schedule started – that's how concerned they were. At that time, angioplasty with contrast would allow them to look inside the arteries and heart. This would determine if I could get by with stent(s) or if I needed open-heart bypass surgery.

They also put me on a beta blocker, which lowers the heart rate and blood pressure. (*Foreshadowing.*) The next day, Sept 29, I went back to the cardiologist for an echocardiogram. That was perfect – could not have been better: muscle strong, valves all in good shape, aorta looked clear.

Side note back to my opening point about vegans: I asked a vegan doctor what preparation advice they would have if someone might be having bypass surgery in a week. This person basically said not to have the surgery but go vegan instead. I asked what to do if that wasn't an option. I never heard back.

After a *very* stressful week (even popping the anti-anxiety medicine clonazepam like candy) Anne and I got to the hospital at 4:45 a.m. that Friday. (Not the first time driving to that hospital in the dark, nor the last.) In surgery, I asked to stay awake. Although surprised, they acquiesced on the condition I be on the "calming" meds. (Yes, please!) This allowed me to watch the screen as the doctor went in through my upper thigh, threaded his way up to the heart, and checked (with contrast) every aspect of the arteries and the heart. (It was when he was *literally inside my heart* that I asked for extra medicine.)

Modern medicine sometimes seems like magic!

Punchline: One 8 mm section of a major vessel was 95+% blocked (occluded). The nearly-closed artery was the left anterior descending artery, also known as "The Widow Maker." That is why they had rushed me into surgery – but they only explained *that* part to us afterwards.

The occlusion was entirely obvious even to my untrained eye – it was so bad I thought I must be misinterpreting what I was seeing.

Given that only one small segment of only one artery had any blockage at all, the doctor speculates that sometime in the past, somewhere in this small segment, there might have been some kind of injury or other trauma – maybe my childhood Scarlet Fever, maybe Crohn's related – that caused it to accumulate deposits over time. (Flashbacks to Glenn.)

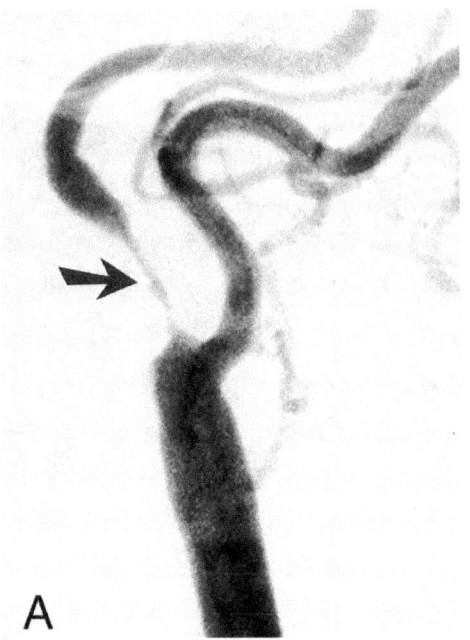

A

Everything else was absolutely fine – no sign of a problem anywhere in the heart or any of the other arteries. The entire occlusion was between arterial branches, so the doctor was able to stent it open. (No open-heart surgery!) I watched as he retested that artery after the stent, and blood flow was 100%. It was *amazing*. Magic! The doctor then closely checked all my other coronary arteries again in case the procedure had caused a change; they were all perfectly clear. While I was still on the table, the nurse gave me a big dose of aspirin and Plavix, another blood thinner. I had also taken my beta blocker that morning.

So at this point – about 9 a.m. Friday, October 6 – I was absolutely ecstatic. Heart fine, muscle strong, valves good, arteries clear. I was discharged at 3 p.m. and Anne drove me home.

You know it doesn't end there.

At some point shortly after we went to sleep early Friday night (it had been a long day) I got up and walked into our bathroom. The next thing I knew, I was on the floor. I must have passed out. In retrospect, I should not have gotten up on my own, being on blood thinners *and* beta blockers, on top of low blood pressure to begin with. It just hadn't

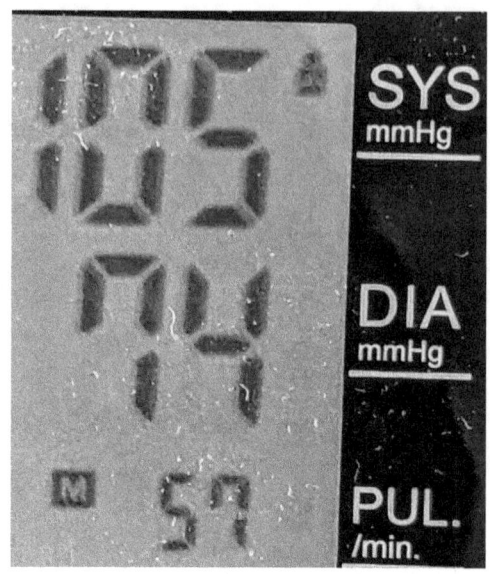

occurred to me to worry about it – I had walked around just fine during the day.

I hit the back of my head (I have a contusion there) and utterly mangled my torso. It hurt to breathe and was agony to move at all. After I crawled back to bed and spent several torturous hours trying to sleep, I realized this wasn't just a temporary injury. Once again, I woke Anne and had her take me to the Emergency Department. Every movement hurt. (See, I told you there were more nighttime trips to TMC – not even 24 hours later!)

Over the eight hours we were there, they gave me morphine (did nothing), Fentanyl (helped a little), and, at the end, Dilaudid (also helped a little). I had a CT scan of my head and chest. That is where they found one cracked rib. (I still can't believe only one.) The stent was still in place.

But here's the kicker: the CT scan also revealed a small pneumothorax in my lower left lung.

That's right: a small section of my left lung was collapsed. *Again*. Number three. The doctor couldn't say if this pneumothorax was from the fall or if it had been there before. I certainly couldn't feel it at any point; I still can't. The doctor decided to leave it untreated.

Note: In 2014, a surgeon had glued this lung in place so it *could never collapse again.* [Story still to come.]

I am still in a great deal of pain, but somewhat better day-by-day. Ultimately, though, the bottom-line take-away is the same as my Crohn's and never-ending lung collapses: the damage to this one tiny segment of my artery was just a fluke. Yet *another* fluke. Because of the miracles of modern medicine, it was found and fixed. Once I heal up from my fall, I can go back to running, hiking, and biking – there will be no lingering issues.

Again, I didn't want to publicize this, because I think it creates more suffering for my friends than glee for the many who loathe me. Saying all this is self-indulgent [ha-ha!] and doesn't help us help animals.

But if you take one thing away from this story, though, please let it be that our baseline should be kindness. If you take away something else, realize that decades of veganism, healthy living, and relative youth won't necessarily protect you from heart disease, lung collapses, Crohn's, chronic back pain, or even tinnitus.

Life can be cruel. All the more reason to be kind to one another.

My deepest thanks to everyone who has supported Anne and me through this and everything else we've gone through since March 2014. As another long-time friend sent:

I expect to pass through life but once.
If therefore, there be any kindness I can show,
or any good thing I can do to any fellow being,
let me do it now, and not defer or neglect it,
as I shall not pass this way again.

–William Penn

I love this picture by the great Ned Harris for two reasons.
One reason is Anne's obvious delight.
Is there anything better than the smile and laughter of a loved one?.

Day 26: The Green Party Fucks Us Again

Bernie or Bust!

–Rich white people insulated
from the true meaning of "Bust"

Its 4:30 a.m. and my sidebar says 59 degrees. The house is wide open, filled with the plaintive cries of mourning doves, the only noise other than my cicada-like tinnitus. Headed up to the high nineties, so this is the last time we'll see temperatures in the fifties until we're in the White Mountains in a few weeks.

Note: these next few chapters are neither fun nor funny nor helpful or important to the plot. Sorry. Please feel free to skip to Travelog for Introverts, with a brief stop at the pictures. Thanks.

When news broke on October 28 2016 about Comey reopening the investigation of Hillary's emails, Anne came into my office asking what I thought might change. I was pretty shaken. I had a bad feeling right through to Election Day, and I convinced Anne, as well as EK out in DC, to go to bed without looking at the news at all.

Doctor, cure thyself.

Of course, I watched the trainwreck unfold on my laptop. The cheap whiskey I was guzzling didn't take the edge off or make me sleepy. It just made me more depressed.

When it was clear there was no hope, I texted EK and asked them to call as soon as they got up. Although young and progressive like typical Bernie-ites, EK and others in their Trans community knew how much elections matter, how many lives would be devastated if the hateful bigots took power.

The phone rang early, before the sun had risen here, not waking me from hours of agony on the couch. Sobbing, EK's rage wasn't at the system or the Electoral College. Rather, they cried, "I hope they are happy. *I hope they are fucking happy!*"

We both knew who "they" were. The Bernie Bros. The women who "just didn't like Hillary." Everyone who insisted on making the perfect the enemy of the not-horrible. Everyone who made the election about their personal feelings instead of concrete policy.

Everyone who insisted on being promised *everything* they wanted, thus unleashing the monsters.

As in 2000, the 2016 votes for the Green Party in key states were greater than Traffic Cone of Treason's margin of victory.

This coalition of the Green Party and the GOP (Guns Over People) has, since their first collaboration in 2000, given the White / Christian Nationalists a stable majority on the Supreme Court that will reign for decades. That in turn has released America's Taliban on everyone who isn't a straight white Christian male. They now have the ability to build their theocracy, imposing their fanatical views on every aspect of our lives, society, and "democracy."

Yes, it is true, as Ben Rhodes tweeted: "George W. Bush and Donald Trump both lost the popular vote and appointed five of these judges who will shape American life (and, on climate, life on Earth) for decades. Some democracy." But the choice of Gorsuch or Garland was *right there* for people who *claim* to care about human rights, the climate, and life on Earth. Instead, they chose their ego, giving us Brewskie Kavanaugh and Amy Handmaid's-Tale and their witch-hunting heroes, condemning a generation of those already marginalized and oppressed to an even worse fate.

The Oregon shore; look for the people for a sense of scale.

Climate activists are to blame for some of the suffering caused by climate change

Come on, children, you're acting like children
Every generation thinks it's the end of the world

–Jeff Tweedy / Wilco, "You Never Know"

Simple summary: By being anti-nuclear power and attacking any work on adaptation or mitigation, (some) climate activists have made, are making, and will continue to make climate change much worse than it needs to be.

(A reminder: I was a Department of Energy Global Change Fellows. I'm not talking out my ass.)

To summarize the chapter another way:

It is factually incorrect and counterproductive to say climate change will make the earth "uninhabitable."

If you take climate change seriously, it is ethically wrong not to promote adaptation and carbon removal.

It is *especially* wrong to ignore all of today's suffering by claiming the future is more important.

I have been told (on Facebook FWIW) that these points are "trivial." OK then.

The argument against pursuing adaptation and mitigation is that people might feel free to continue burning fossil fuels. This claim is either willfully ignorant or malignantly narcissistic.

There is simply *no possible past* in which anyone anywhere would have burned *more* fossil fuels if we had been pursuing research into adaptation and carbon removal. People have been sounding the alarm about how greenhouse gas emissions will disrupt our current equilibria for decades. Even I, as a Department of Energy Global Change Fellow from 1991-96, was sounding the alarm!

And yet emissions today are higher than they've ever been.

(And they would have been *even higher* if not for nuclear energy, along with many more dead. Climatologists James Hansen and Pushker Kharecha calculated that the use of nuclear power between 1971 and 2009 avoided the premature deaths of 1.84 million people by preventing air pollution from burning coal. And if, following Fukushima, Japan and Germany had reduced coal power instead of nuclear, they could have prevented twenty-eight thousand premature air-pollution-induced deaths and twenty-four hundred million metric tons of cumulative carbon-dioxide emissions. The stats are clear: Anti-nuke = pro-death & pro-$CO2$.)

Would anyone have bought a bigger SUV if we had pursued systematic research into ocean seeding? Does anyone *truly* believe CO_2 levels would be higher if we had given more money to the Department of Agriculture to develop and distribute drought-resistant strains and more productive crops? (Google "Fixing a flaw in photosynthesis could massively boost food production" for what is possible. And "Scientists use gene-editing in cereal crops to boost yields without nitrogen fertilizer."

More GMOs will reduce hunger and disease and make the world better; therefore, it is clear that blanket opposition to GMOs is immoral.)

There is actually a near-perfect parallel with promoting veganism here. For decades, the most vocal vegans have opposed and attacked both adaptation – promoting plant-based meat and supporting the development of better slaughter-free meats – as well as mitigation – a harm-reduction message like One Step for Animals' "Please don't eat chickens." It had to be their way – their exact version of Veganism – or nothing.

What do we have to show for all those decades of promoting veganism? The average person in the United States and the average person in the world eats more animals today than ever before – *far* more than when Anne and I co-founded a group to promote veganism.

Yes, it is hard to give up purity for pragmatism. It took me decades to get to this point. But really, you can only say that consequences matter.

Anyone who cares at all about the consequences of climate change needs to *pay attention*. The United States will *never* take all the necessary actions on climate change. It is very simple: despite what people *say*, they are not willing to make any meaningful sacrifice. (Another perfect parallel with veganism.) As soon as gas prices go up a bit, Democrats' approval goes down, and Republicans take power. We've seen up-and-down again with Biden's approval rating.

And please don't tell me that people care about the climate. As Matt Yglesias noted in "Is quiet climate policy enough?" (emphasis added):

Reuters did a survey recently that showed 69% of Americans say the United States should take "aggressive" action to combat climate change, but only 34% would be willing to pay $100 more per year in taxes to achieve that goal. A hundred bucks is not a lot of money. People spend that on Halloween decorations. A nice dinner date could cost you more than that.

[W]hat we've seen time and again is that there just really isn't a public appetite for this. Washington State tried the neoliberal idea of a revenue-neutral carbon tax and it got crushed in a referendum. So then they tried the left idea of a carbon tax to fund progressive stuff and it also got crushed. When the price of gasoline goes up, people freak out. Fundamentally, the lobbyists are not the problem. People really like cheap energy, and the communities that have significant natural resource extraction industries really like them and want to keep them. You absolutely can chip away at this stuff at the margin, but it's always going to be pretty marginal.

He expanded on that in "How the Green New Deal became the Inflation Reduction Act."

[I]n the most recent Gallup poll asking people about the most important problem facing the country, about 2 percent of voters named climate or environmental concerns … behind race relations, poverty, family values, crime, gun control, immigration, oil prices, "economy in general," and inflation.

And this is pretty consistent. In a pre-election Pew poll, voters ranked climate as their 11th priority out of 12. In a pre-election Gallup poll, 55 percent of voters said climate was either very important or extremely important, which sounds good but puts it behind healthcare, terrorism, gun policy, education, the economy, immigration, abortion, inequality, the budget deficit, taxes, race relations, and foreign affairs.

So let's deal with reality. Let's stop making the perfect the enemy of the better. Please.

PS: Of course, the "Green" party explicitly chose to run in swing states in 2000 and 2016, putting G.W. Bush and Hair Furor in power. These should be recognized as two of the worst, most harmful choices in all of human history.

Three blog posts on climate change + bonus

Yes, I know it is lazy to just reproduce blog posts. But writing a book is *hard!*

See if you can find the common theme in these posts.

1. Some notes on global warming and progress

I heard David Wallace-Wells talking about his book, *The Uninhabitable Earth* (based on the article of the same name) on Ezra Klein's podcast. I am not a fan of disaster porn, but wanted to give the book a chance.

That isn't easy, because to start with, the title is a lie. He admits this on page 6, saying "According to some estimates" (a sign that cherry-picking is about to start) *some* regions of the world would be uninhabitable by 2100.

Or maybe not *uninhabitable*: "Certainly it would make them inhospitable."

Greenland is pretty darn inhospitable much of the year. Heck, 115 degrees Fahrenheit here in Tucson Arizona is quite uncomfortable, although not as bad as Pittsburgh from November through March.

People live *everywhere*. Lots and lots of people! But I guess *The Somewhat More Inhospitable Earth* didn't test well as a book title.

Also of note: during the Cretaceous Thermal Maximum, when the dinosaurs found the world quite habitable, the global temperature might have been about 15°C hotter than it is now! That means where it is 70° F now, it would have been 96° F then!

It also doesn't help that David gets basic, easily-Googleable facts wrong. For example, he says on p. 8 that 15% of all humans who ever existed are alive now. That is twice the actual percentage.

What makes it worse is that he *goes out of his way* to be an arrogant prick: "I'm not about to personally slaughter a cow to eat a hamburger, but I'm also not about to go vegan. I tend to think when you're at the top of the food chain it's okay to flaunt it, because I don't see anything complicated about drawing a moral boundary between us and other animals, and in fact find it offensive to women and people of color that all of a sudden there's talk of extending human-rights-like legal protections to chimps, apes, and octopuses, just a generation or two after we finally broke the white-male monopoly on legal personhood."

Yeah? Well FU.

And "top of the food chain" is simply saying "might makes right." It isn't any different than saying "God gave us the Earth to use."

Note: *David didn't need to say anything about veganism.* Shitting on farmed animals and vegans had nothing to do with his (dishonest) case that the world was going to become "uninhabitable." He knows Ezra Klein and knows that Ezra is a cool vegan. But David went *out of his way* to claim that the people who care about other animals are the ones who are being "offensive."

So I don't like hyperbole, I don't like factual misstatements, and I don't like rationalizing "I got mine" assholes.

But the worst is implying everything is just fine right now and will be bad only in the future because we are short-sighted and selfish.

Of course, things are not great today for the majority of sentient creatures – in large part because of speciesist sods like Wallace-Wells.

More than that, however, things could get much, *much* worse for humans and, in terms of percentages, still not be as bad as things were *mere decades ago.*

The percentage of people living in absolute poverty, the percentage dying from preventable diseases, the percentage held as chattel – all of these and more were unimaginably worse just a few generations ago. As Yuval Harari summarized in *21 Lessons for the 21st Century:* "For the first time in history, infectious diseases kill fewer people than old age, famine kills fewer people than obesity, and violence kills fewer people than accidents." (If you doubt this, please Google "Seven charts that show the world is actually becoming a better place.") Within my grandparents' lifetime, things were, on average, *much* worse than under the *worst* projections of climate change.

Just consider basic life expectancy. From The Roots of Progress' summary of Steven Pinker's *Enlightenment Now: The Case for Reason, Science, Humanism, and Progress:*

> Life expectancy is up, from a world average of less than 30 years in the mid-18th century to over 70 years today; and the increases are seen by all age groups and all continents. Child mortality and maternal mortality in particular have been drastically reduced: "for an American woman, being pregnant a century

ago was almost as dangerous as having breast cancer today."

That last bit amazes me every time I read it.

Addendum: Well after I wrote this blog post, and two weeks after I put this chapter together, Ezra Klein published "Your Kids Are Not Doomed." In it, he cites just how bad it was for the average human for nearly all of human history, concluding, "No mainstream climate models suggest a return to a world as bad as the one we had in 1950, to say nothing of 1150."

More from Ezra's column:

> As my colleague David Wallace-Wells … wrote to me, "What looks like apocalypse in prospect often feels more like grim normality when it arrives in the present." Oof.
>
> This is no mere abstraction or prediction. The evidence that we ignore mass suffering is all around us. We are ignoring it right now, just as we did yesterday, and just as we will tomorrow. "An estimated 20 million people died of Covid, and now we're over it. What do we make of that?" Wallace-Wells wrote to me. "Ten million people a year are dying of air pollution. What do we make of that? And what does it tell us about climate change, which is quite unlikely (as I wrote in my big piece on pollution) to ever kill as many as now die from particulates?"

Remember, Wallace-Wells is "famous" for his book *The **Uninhabitable** Earth*, in which he says civilization and agriculture

– you know, the things that ultimately increased life expectancy by decades – were mistakes (see below). But don't expect old David to change his diet or not have kids. *It is almost as if he doesn't really believe what he says in his book.*

Or, as Ezra said in his June 2022 Ask Me Anything:

> So if you're saying that the kinds of outcomes that we think we're going to have for the next, let's call it 100 years, are so grievous, decimating, right, to use that language, that it would be immoral to bring a child into them, I think what you're saying on some level, whether you know it or not, is that it would have been immoral for most people, most human beings, to bring children into the world any time before 1975 or something.

He's not wrong. BTW, I was born in 1968; Anne in 1963.

History didn't start in 2019. We have made *unbelievable* progress. We can *and should* learn from that. (For more on this, please check out Matt Ridley's *The Rational Optimist*.)

We can do *a lot more* to reduce suffering in *many* ways – from harm-reduction advocacy to disease eradication to climate change adaptation and mitigation. But writing self-important hyperbolic disaster porn does not help. By exaggerating, lying, and being so self-centered, David Wallace-Wells is actively making things worse.

PS: Oh yeah – and vote Democratic at every opportunity. If that isn't your message, STFU.

PPS: You want uninhabitable? Google "Snowball Earth."

2. Hysteria is not constructive

Earlier, I found that David Wallace-Wells' book *The Uninhabitable Earth* was off the rails by page 8. But I wanted to see if he redeems himself in the rest of the book.

Not so much.

On pages 198-199, he says that agriculture and civilization were mistakes. *That* – not a concern for making the current world better – is where he's coming from. He doesn't *really* want us to deal with climate change. He wants humanity to be a handful of hunter-gatherers.

But in the meantime, he wants to live in comfort, eat meat, and breed to his heart's content.

To kick off his penultimate chapter (pages 204-205) he features what appears to be a paranoid schizophrenic who, years ago, predicted that humanity will be extinct within ten years. (And who also claims to have been surveilled by the "Deep State" since 1996.)

Then, on page 221, David goes on to claim that not only is climate change going to kill us all on Earth but is also why there is no intelligent life in the universe.

That is simply an *amazing* level of hyperbole and arrogance. As a duck would say: Quack Quack Quack!

In case anyone reading this is looking for some actual, sane, and reality-based writing on the topic, please check out Project Drawdown.

But if your first, second, and third priorities aren't winning elections, then you are *wasting your time*.

3. The World of Tomorrow

Imagine that tomorrow, we discovered a world orbiting the Sun opposite of the Earth, i.e. the Sun is directly between our Earth and Earth II. It has the same inclination and the same size moon. It has an average temperature of 65° Fahrenheit, with oceans covering 73% of the world, and ice covering 7% of the world. It is teaming with life, although there are no humans or humanoid species.

It would be a miracle, no? We would definitely stop planning to go to Mars, with its average temperature of -81° Fahrenheit and no readily-available water.

Get this: The mirror Earth described above is what our world will be under climate change – except for the no-humans part. Under every climate change scenario, there will still be lots and lots of humans.

Again, I don't mean to imply that climate change is not serious. It is, but not because the world will be "uninhabitable." Climate change will cause a lot of suffering because we have set up our civilizations under the previous climate – living along current coasts and river deltas, growing certain crops in certain (often unsuitable) places, suppressing fires that have normally been a part of the ecosystem, etc. If we *actually took suffering seriously*, we would be hard at work adjusting civilization to the coming new norms. But instead, many of us just keep demanding zero emissions while emissions continue to rise.

Meanwhile, despite the Sunrise Movement's strident opposition to him, Biden and the Democrats (including Senator Manchin) quietly passed the nation's largest-ever climate investment as part of Biden's 2021 infrastructure bill. (Update: Democrats, including Coal Millionaire Manchin, passed an even bigger climate package via *compromise*; e.g., the Inflation Reduction Act includes provisions that will make it easier to build pipelines and easier to secure new oil and gas leases.)

This work could have started in the U.S. in 2001 but for the "Green" Party running Ralph Nader in Florida.

Winning elections is what matters. Full stop.

"Green"land – *even snowier than Pittsburgh!* From a 747 window.

Greta Thunberg's misery is the result of child abuse.

There might not be a world to live in when she grows up.
What use is school without a future?

–Our House Is on Fire:
Greta Thunberg's Call to Save the Planet,
a dishonest picture book aimed at traumatizing kids ages 3-8

Even on the spectrum, Greta could and should have experienced a better, more materially-secure childhood than 99% of all humans (and 99.9999% of all sentient beings). Instead, she's been pushed into believing the world is going to end and then exploited by the climate community and the media. She has been reduced to futility crying "You have stolen my dreams and my childhood."

Sorry, but it wasn't the world's politicians who have stolen your dreams and childhood.

Meanwhile, the United States elected Boiled Ham in a Wig and will probably elect the Human-Toupee Hybrid again or someone as bad. China and India continue to go full-bore into coal.

Humanity blows past every "this is our last chance" moment with carbon emissions going up and up and up. So what exactly has Thunberg accomplished in exchange for being utterly miserable, other than making other impotent, self-absorbed liberals swoon?

Climate change matters in as much as it causes suffering. We should not use the topic to cause additional unnecessary suffering, like by terrifying and traumatizing little kids with utter lies like "There might not be a world to live in when she grows up."

PS: We should all be very careful as to whom we lionize. Google "How Rachel Carson Cost Millions of People Their Lives" and "Cancer, Carson, Chemicals and Smoking."

With all that said, here are the Grand Tetons, a great place to visit. This is nowhere near as good a photo as Ansel Adams did there.

Extinction Is No Big Deal

Humans are not the protagonists of this planet's story.
If there is a main character, it is life itself,
which makes of earth and starlight
something more than earth and starlight.

–*John Green,* The Anthropocene Reviewed

Extinction is certainly not the huge deal many people make it out to be. 99.9% of every species that has ever existed on earth is extinct. That is, for every 1,000 species that have ever existed, 999 *are extinct.* We wouldn't be here today if not for extinction on an unimaginable scale.

All the arguments about why (more) extinction theoretically matters – potential medicines, ecosystem balance, loss of life – are *trivial* compared to the reality on the ground. We can design medicines at the molecular level now, which is almost infinitely more efficient than testing various things found in a rainforest. We humans are destroying ecosystems for reasons – growing food, grazing cattle – that can be addressed head-on, rather than by saying "extinction!" or "biodiversity!"

In 2017, I snapped and wrote this rambling, ranting open letter to Ezra Klein after he interviewed Elizabeth Kolbert, the author of *The Sixth Extinction: An Unnatural History*. You can skip ahead without consequence.

Hi Ezra,

I've written to you before about how many people dismiss the unimaginable suffering in the world *right now*. I appreciate that you regularly make this point.

My main question regarding your recent podcast: What global warming impact did Ms. Kolbert document that is actually so terrible? Some people use boats instead of dogs. Elephants and giraffes aren't reproducing as fast as they are dying. And then there is her claim that people could potentially face starvation as optimal growing areas shift north. (Although she said people would have to move, this is obviously not true – farming and maybe a handful of farmers might move, but the vast majority of people won't.) People can live in "115 degrees" Tucson, "no potable water nearby" Los Angeles, and "sub-optimal for agriculture" Iceland. Food gets imported, water gets desalinated, life goes on.

But doesn't the claim of *potential* starvation and migration beg the questions: How many people are suffering from starvation and forced migration *right now*? How many people are suffering from horrible but curable diseases? How many people are living indescribably miserable lives from crushing poverty while billionaires build personal yachts the size of apartment complexes?

Consider the past. Stalin's purges, the Great Leap Forward / Cultural Revolution ("From 1958 to 1962, [Mao's] Great Leap Forward policy led to the deaths of up to 45 million people – easily making it the biggest episode of mass murder ever recorded"), and even the partitioning of India that followed independence (aftermath) – all these caused human suffering on a scale beyond anything we in developed countries can imagine today. Yet most people *don't even know those events happened.*

The Spanish Flu ... well, that goes without saying. If that happened today, developed countries would treat it like the end of the world. [*Prescient in 2017.*]

Less speculative: you, Annie, your kids, and your grandkids are way, way more likely to die from an antibiotic resistant infection than global warming.

Haven't there *always* been environmentalists yelling "the sky is falling"? Hasn't *every single one* of their doomsday predictions from the 60s, 70s, and 80s been proven wrong?

Shouldn't this give us pause when evaluating new doomsday claims?

And not to be cynical, but if global warming truly is The Worst Thing Ever, why is geoengineering a topic we can't even discuss? Ocean seeding and enhanced weathering – these aren't even part of the discussion. Increasing albedo is *verboten* because the sky would look different? A slightly-less-blue sky overrides The Worst Thing Ever?

<insertion>

Vox's Bryan Walsh wrote in July 12 2022's Future Perfect: "To argue, as the climate activist Greta Thunberg did in a tweet earlier this month, that nuclear power can never be considered 'green' is to implicitly reveal that your fear of nuclear trumps your fear of climate change. And if that becomes the norm, the climate will pay the price." Or, as James Lovelock put it decades ago: "Some time in the next century, when the adverse effects of climate change begin to bite, people will look back in anger at those who now so foolishly continue to pollute by burning fossil fuel instead of accepting the beneficence of nuclear power."

</insertion>

One closing question: Why are so many liberals so *overwhelmingly* concerned about global warming – something potentially bad in the future – while they *actively take part* in what you recognize as today's horror: factory farming?

I understand it might seem abstract to consider what is needed for the people of India and Africa to get out of crushing poverty. But eating factory farmed animals is not an abstraction. It is directly – and knowingly – contributing to absolute horrific and undeniable brutality.

But it is much easier to talk about potential Big Bad Things in the future than actually care about suffering we are directly connected to, and could help end, *right now*.

And, of course, factory farming contributes significantly to climate change. It is telling that before you brought it up, Ms. Kolbert didn't even know that meat production causes as much global warming as transportation. But like your standard liberal, she brushes it off: "I don't think it does rise to that level ... people have to eat."

Nothing to see here – look over there!

By being inefficient in resource use, eating animals also plays a role in global hunger and starvation. It will almost certainly be the source of our next pandemic [*prescient once again*] and it is driving the antibiotic resistance that really does threaten you and your future descendants. But almost no one talks about it, because it implicates them personally. Better to fret about the future.

I'm neither a right-wing head-in-the-sander nor a techno-utopian – although everyone who talks about what the climate will be in 100 years is hugely underestimating how much everything will have changed by then. I'm simply a painist who just wants to reduce suffering.

Thanks again for all your amazing work, especially your insistence on always bringing up chickens.

I Take the Colbert Questionert

All my life
I never knew
What I could be, what I could do

Then … one lucky day
You came along.

–Paul McCartney, "New"

You can easily skip this chapter – it is fluff. Anne insisted it be cut, and for several months of editing, it was. But the end of the book is so heavy, I put it back in today (September 12 2022) during editing. For background, see TheColbertQuestionert.com.

• **What is the best sandwich?**

I grew up loving Reubens, fully prepared (grilled then baked). In 1997, when Tiger Woods was winning his first Masters, we were in upstate New York trying to raise money for outreach. There was a place in Ithaca that made the best vegan Reubens, OMG. I got five to go when we left.

And to anyone who puts tempeh on a sandwich they call a "Reuben," I'll see you in Hell!

• **What is the one thing that you own that you should really throw out?**

If it was up to Anne, these pants.

Anne is the least sentimental person I know. She is *constantly* looking to get rid of stuff. If we haven't used something in a year, it is out the door! But for years, I've worn these pants every day it has been under 80 and they're just now getting good.

• **What is the scariest animal?**

'iders. <shudder>

• **Apples or oranges?**

Of course apples. You can spread peanut butter on them!

• **What is your favorite action movie?**

Crouching Tiger, Hidden Dragon. Simply amazing (non-CGI) and beautiful action sequences.

It also has what I hope to say to Anne with my last breaths. Chow Yun-fat to Michelle Yeoh: "I would rather be a ghost drifting by your side as a condemned soul than enter heaven without you. Because of your love, I will never be a lonely spirit."

• **Have you ever asked someone for their autograph?**

Wynton Marsalis in 1985. He signed the insert that came with the roll of film I was using. I kept it in my wallet for years.

When I met Tom Scholz, I didn't think to ask for his. Tom is, for all intents and purposes, the rock band Boston. Similarities: He was born in Toledo, is very tall and skinny, trained as an engineer but went into a different field, stopped eating animals later in life, doesn't like the limelight, and is dedicated to animal causes (his DTS Foundation has supported my projects. Like a lot of people, I listened to Boston's 1976 and '78 albums *over and over and over.*

This money was raised by fans of the band BOSTON, and donated to my DTS Charitable Foundation. We are donating the entire amount to you, along with an announcement on our websites. Keep up the good work!

Tom Scholz

Speaking of Boston's Tom Scholz: I *did* get his autograph!

• **What do you think happens when we die?**

Hopefully someone remembers us for a bit and doesn't judge us too harshly for our mistakes.

• **Window or aisle?**

Aisle for my knees. However, I love the view, so if I'm with Anne on a 767 or at the back of a 777 or 747, we will switch back and forth.

• **What is your favorite smell?**

Fresh pine at the holidays. Garlic frying in sesame oil. Tater tots. Cherry or blueberry pie.

• **What is your least-favorite smell?**

The aftermath of a double-barreled Crohn's attack.

- **Exercise: Is it worth it?**

  Yes, when I can. Being fit makes everything else in life better.

  As someone who has experienced significant health setbacks and problems, I have a deep appreciation for having the ability to exercise, to try to get stronger and more fit every chance I get.

- **Flat or sparkling?**

  Sparkling (if it weren't more expensive).

- **What is the most-used app on your phone?**

  The camera. Then email, then Photos, then text, then News. Then one of our meditation apps.

- **You get one song to listen to for the rest of your life: What is it?**

  "Everybody Wants to Rule the World."

  I thought about a longer song (e.g., The Beatles' "A Day in the Life") or even a classical piece (e.g., Shostakovich's 4th, 5th, or 7th), but nothing brings me happiness like "Everybody…".

- **Describe the rest of your life in five words.**

  Hopefully not painful or short.

Day 27: Burn the Heretic

The right looks for converts, the left hunts heretics.
They both find what they're looking for.

Good morning. Another 4:20 a.m. start. The pain is about average, so I'm again on my phone, walking the house while the eastern sky is still dark, and the early birds are singing. The tinnitus is *screaming*. I've been awake for more than an hour; the tinnitus kept me from getting back to sleep.

My neck scar is oddly prominent today. When I broke my neck last year, the surgeon actually went in from the *front* to fuse the vertebrae together. Isn't that amazing?

How 'bout if we start this chapter with an ego stroke? (Mine, sorry.) I mean, why else am I writing a memoir?

Over the past two decades, Matt Ball has had
a singularly profound influence on the animal protection
movement in the United States.

> Matt's reasoned, eloquent focus
> on having the biggest possible impact
> with the greatest possible efficiency
> has resonated with tens of thousands of individuals,
> and created fundamental, pragmatic change
> on every level of the movement.
>
> *–Michael Greger, M.D.*

When I was working at VegFund in 2015 (Day 30) Benedict was working at a different organization – let's call it Animal Asylum (AA). We were in regular contact, exchanging at least an email a day and a few calls a week. He was going to law school – AA said he could keep his full-time job but take time for school as needed.

One day he told me that he had an opening in his department and the job was mine if I wanted it. For most of the time he had been there, he had been his own media relations department, but now they were expanding their outward-facing work.

It seemed like a great opportunity, and I got the job. (I did more television during that time than any other.) Outside of my team, the organization's Chief Counsel became my best pal there. When he "left" AA, he joined the 80% and quit being vegan. The last I heard, he was much happier. So it goes.

Benedict left relatively soon after that to head a startup organization that will provide the stage for one of 2021's twin horrors. Despite the fact that I didn't want a leadership position ever again (see Harvard Business Review's "Why Capable People Are Reluctant to Lead") this left me as head of my department. (But not for long, don't worry.) There were two wonderful young people working with me, one of whom I had hired. I'm still sincerely sorry about that, DM.

When I started at AA, I talked with the Chief Counsel about the fact that Anne and I ran One Step for Animals. He told me that I just needed to keep my activities for One Step separate from my work for Animal Asylum.

A while later, Benedict was on the Ezra Klein podcast, back when Ezra was at Vox. (Having co-founded Vox, Ezra had wisely and successfully stepped back from a leadership position, being self-aware enough to realize it wasn't the optimal fit for him. Kudos, Ezra.) During the podcast, Benedict mentioned my work at One Step. This led Matteen Mokalla at Vox to contact me about doing a feature on One Step as part of their Vox Voices series.

Vox contracted with a local video production house where I gave my spiel about One Step. Afterwards, both of the video guys asked me detailed questions about changing their diet. Even though I had talked about not eating chickens, one of them planned to go vegan.

Everyone has met a vegan who has been rude to them

When the video came out in May 2017, Vox titled the article and video "Want to save animal lives without going veg? Eat beef, not chicken." Of course, I had never said that anyone *should* eat beef, but I understand exaggerating things as marketing.

The article (and description at YouTube) starts:

> "Go vegan!" and "It's not food, it's violence!" are two rallying cries that animal welfare activists have been chanting for years. But for activist and vegan Matt Ball, the purist ideologies espoused in those mantras might actually work against the goal of reducing and ultimately ending animal slaughter.
>
> Despite the animal advocacy from vegan and animal welfare groups, consumption of meat has grown in the United States from 183 pounds of red meat and poultry per capita in 1975 — the year Peter Singer's seminal *Animal Liberation* was published — to an estimated 217.8 pounds this year.
>
> Making matters worse, more than 80 percent of people who adopt a vegetarian (let alone vegan) diet ultimately go back to eating meat. According to Ball, vegetarians go back to their meat-eating ways in part because "they can't stand the pressure to maintain a pure diet."
>
> Although he is sympathetic to vegan and traditional animal welfare activism, Ball believes the time has come for activists to reconsider their tactics. That's why in early 2014, he co-founded a new organization called One Step for Animals. Their goal is not to get individuals to take on any given lifestyle or diet, but rather to convince as many people as possible to simply stop eating chicken.

The video, as you might expect, was controversial. I watched as it hit 100,000 views on YouTube, then 200,000. When it got to three hundred thousand and I saw the string of furious comments, I took our home address off the One Step website.

Yeah, I was kinda freaked out.

As of now, the video has 1.2 million views on YouTube. (I was told the inline version on Facebook had over 500,000 views.) It has almost 8,000 comments, with more dislikes than likes, so that might give you a sense of what people thought of it. When I look right now, the lead comment, with 1.8k likes, is by onie619: "It amuses me that one video would be so hated by both vegans and non-vegans."

What can I say except: You're welcome?

The video has also spawned a string of enraged "take-down" response videos and articles, where incensed vegans go into great detail to *prove* just how wrong I was to say *something I never said.*

That'll show me!

Being hated by vegans was nothing new. But being hated by *this many* was new. I hope everyone who disliked that video buys this book, because it will give them more of the furious self-righteousness for which they so feverishly yearn.

The video was the straw that broke the camel's back for Gary, one of veganism's main cult leaders. He turned his ongoing jihad against me to Animal Asylum. Rallying his rabid ranks, they posted everywhere, claiming Animal Asylum was promoting eating beef. Which of course is not true on two levels. I did not mention Animal Asylum at any point in the video, and Animal Asylum was not mentioned in any of the promotions for the video.

And of course, I *didn't say anything about people eating beef.* But ███████████████████████████████ . His mantra was: No drama. █████████████████████████████ . So I had to go. (████████████████████████████)

The true believers also turned their fury towards the national animal rights conference. I was excommunicated from that, twelve years after being elected to their Hall of Fame.

Purity *über alles.* The One True Faith must be defended against all heretics.

So it goes.

What do you see in these clouds?

Travelog for Introverts

I figured I had paid my debt to society
By paying my overdue fines
at the Multnomah County Library

–The Decemberists,
"California One / Youth and Beauty Brigade"

I didn't think I'd be getting in much writing this morning. We had a delightful time with my cousin Lori and her husband Carl last night, which kept us up well after our normal bedtime. Their house is absolutely lovely – since they bought it, they've spent a lot of time and treasure making a modern home out of a place that hadn't changed since the 1950s.

Even though the temperature was still in the 90s (a dry heat!) we sat outside and ate Lori's really excellent black bean and sweet potato soup. Then we made s'mores. Trader Joe's marshmallows have no animal products in them, and their graham crackers are Anne's favorite. We had dark chocolate from Germany, so we were all set.

While chatting (and laughing *a lot*) we remembered a story that I forgot to tell you:

The last time Anne and I had traveled before this month (May 2022) was March 2019. We flew to Las Vegas and had three excellent meals at VegeNation. We also saw a Cirque du Soleil show. (Their Beatles show *Love* at the Mirage is *really outstanding*.)

Other than *Love* and the food (VegeNation and Ronald's Donuts) I dislike Vegas very much. It is the embodiment of all the worst of humanity. But the Beatles show is absolutely stunning. Breathtaking. It is worth going to Vegas just for that.

We went to Vegas as the jumping-off point for Death Valley. It was hot, even in March. We are used to hot, but not being out in it all day. The park – the largest National Park in the United States – is definitely worth visiting. (The state parks near Vegas are great, too, although Red Rock Canyon is crowded.)

So it had been over three years of not traveling together when we drove through the end of night to Tucson's airport. When I had made the reservation for our first flight on the Airbus A321, I chose the aisle and window seats way in the back, hoping no one would pick the middle seat and we could have the entire row to ourselves. (This hasn't worked for us *yet* – the plane has been full every time.)

A nice young man came up and indicated he was in our row. We asked if he would like to have the window or aisle seat, and he took the aisle seat. I moved over and sat next to Anne.

Then a pajama-pants-wearing guy came up who didn't seem to speak English. He was gesticulating at the guy in our aisle seat, waving his boarding pass. It turned out that the nice guy was in the wrong seat. Pajama pants then sat down, put his bag under the seat, ran back to the galley and started barfing.

You can imagine how thrilling this was for us.

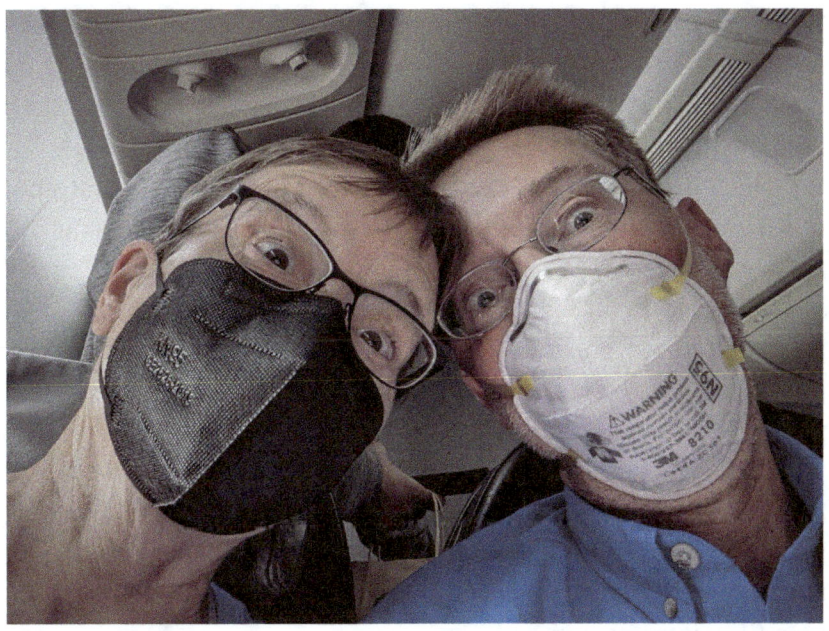

Here we were, at the start of a 13-day trip I had started planning in October 2019, *two-and-a-half years earlier*. We and our N95s had avoided covid until this point, and now a violently-ill guy is about to sit next to us on our flight from Tucson to Dallas.

Long story short (ha-*ha!*) the Captain eventually came back to the galley, got no response from pajama pants, and removed him from the plane. Score one for the Captain.

Anne pulled out her Clorox wipes and scrubbed everything down. The nice young man moved back into that seat, and we flew to Dallas.

And then on to Germany.

With all that said, I know you're wondering: "Is Matt still so happy it's scary?"

No.

When I was writing the first part of this book, I was quite excited. As mentioned, it was not painful to relive childhood events, as I don't identify with that person. He is long gone and doesn't solicit empathy from me.

The writing itself has also been joyful. Figuring out what to put down and what to leave out. (Yes, I actually *have* left things out.) Constructing sentences so they're easy to read. (I'm re-reading some "literature" at night, and while I appreciate long, well-constructed sentences and five-dollar words, that's not what I'm going for.) Arranging the book so it remains interesting even as you wisely skip chapters.

Then, of course, it was bliss to tell you about the best year of my life, even more so because by that point in the writing, we were in Europe. Combine writing with traveling and you have the best month of my life since 2007. Even with the SCOTUS leak about the inevitable end of Roe.

Our subsequent trip throughout the southwest (timed for the Ansel Adams exhibit in Santa Fe NM, which was, by far, the least interesting Adams show I've ever attended) was also fantastic. This made writing some of the less-wonderful chapters easier, because after writing I would spend the rest of the day by Anne's side, chatting about various things, looking at beautiful scenery, listening to podcasts, or just in companionable silence.

Don't get me wrong. It isn't that life is hard or bad now that we're home. Just less time doing fun things with my delicious and well-matched soulmate. And since we've been back, I've written some of the chapters I've been dreading, especially Day 30, which put me in a funk. And after writing downer Day 30, I wrote a depressing concluding Day 31, which I will probably change by the time you read this. (Update: Yup, changed. So note that Day 31 was originally *even more* dismal!)

But enough navel-gazing! You're not here to read about my mood swings. You're here for stories, digressions, sexual innuendo, cranky old man rants, and life tips. So back to it!

Our southwest circuit included three great places for introverts. The first is a little gem in southeast Arizona, Chiricahua National Monument (above). Since it is still a National Monument, Chiricahua doesn't get the people looking to bag every National Park. But it is incredibly beautiful, with the most amazing hoodoos and balancing rocks. A series of ~~tubes~~ trails allow you to hike as long as you'd like. There are no towns around. Wilcox is the closest place for gas and interstate access. Bisbee is the closest interesting place – a former mining community whose downtown is all funkified, including a great little vegan store and a brewhouse that serves good pretzels and plant-based chili. Downtown Bisbee is generally overrun with tourists when the weather is good. In what is becoming increasingly common, this prosperous liberal enclave is surrounded by resentment-inducing red-state poverty.

Continuing east is White Sands in south-central New Mexico, between Las Cruces and Alamogordo. (Pictured here.) It was a National Monument the first times we went there; it is now a National Park. Most of the park's only road is just compressed sand, and the route changes as the dunes shift.

The sand is very white, so it feels like you're in the aftermath of the most incredible blizzard ever. The five-mile hike through the dunes used to be deserted, but not so these days. We got there very early on a weekday, yet a dozen or so cars were already in the lot. Even with all of the others, we were able to spend most of the hike with no one else in sight, except when we passed a group of teenagers sliding, without a sled, 40 feet down the face of a steep dune, getting sand in every possible orifice.

It is a magical place unlike anywhere else on earth. The next largest gypsum sand field, in Mexico, is a tiny fraction the size. On our first visit to White Sands, the three of us did a sunset nature walk with a ranger, which was super-informative. Doing the five-mile hike the next day (above) we heard sudden, shocking sonic booms from fighter jets flying out of the nearby base.

The closest town is Alamogordo, where the Manhattan scientists stayed before the Trinity test. That first nuclear explosion, July 16 1945, exactly 49 years before Worst the First, was one of those moments that marks a sharp kink in the course of human events.

Up to the Santa Fe / Albuquerque area (plenty of fun stuff there) and then west towards Flagstaff will bring you to El Malpais

National Monument. This was our first time visiting, and it is another good place for introverts. Except for a pickup leaving as we got to the parking lot, we saw no one on our hike. It wasn't quiet, though – the wind was howling. At one point, up on the rim of a small volcano, we had to stop and bend down to avoid getting blown over.

El Malpais is very large, with two distinct sections that have no quick connection. As we were on our way to Flagstaff, we didn't have nearly enough time.

We didn't stop at all at Petrified Forest / Painted Desert National Park, which I-40 bounds to the north. It isn't the perfect place for introverts – in all the times we've been there, we've never been completely away from people. But it isn't mobbed like the Grand Canyon or Zion's main valley.

North of Flagstaff, just into New Mexico, is a place where you can *easily* be on your own. Cottonwood Canyon Road through Grand Staircase Escalante National Monument cuts through some of the weirdest landscape you'll ever see (below). It is the single most amazing drive we've ever done – and we've done Route 89A from Prescott to Flagstaff and Route 1 along the California coast.

We did the latter in 1995, right after the three of us got off the plane at SFO. That was my first time in California and it was beautiful! Two days later, I cut out of my conference to save Anne from baby boredom, and we drove California 1 again, this time all the way down to Point Lobos State Natural Reserve, a place Ansel Adams had photographed extensively. The naturalist who led our tour had known Ansel and told us stories about him. Then there was a strange cooing noise. We all stopped and listened, but no one could place it. Someone said, "It sounds like an exotic bird."

Turns out it was our baby, warbling happily in the baby backpack.

Cottonwood Canyon Road,
Grand Staircase Escalante National Monument

Death Valley – also good for introverts

Day 28
2021: A Suffering Odyssey

Well some say life will beat you down
Break your heart, steal your crown

–Tom Petty, "Learning to Fly"

Following my expulsion from AA (bad for financial security and health insurance, good for being freed from politics and machinations, bad for leaving my team unprotected) I focused on One Step for Animals while looking for another job.

Ever since it was formed, working for Benedict's new nonprofit was my dream. Founded on the ideas I outlined in my 2006 Princeton talk, the group focused on the supply side of animal advocacy: give people what they want but produced without cruelty to animals. No more fighting with vegans who insist the message must be "all or nothing!" (Although many vegans attack supply-side work, too. "My way or the highway!")

Although I was initially unsuccessful at landing a job there, this may have been fortunate, at least in the short term. Brad, the libertarian who got that job, would be fired and his entire department dissolved. (I can never see "libertarian" without thinking of this joke: "Mom, when I grow up, I'm gonna be a libertarian." "Well son, which is it? You can't do both." It's funny 'cuz it's true.)

But in 2017, I landed a position in the communications department. Until a few months before I was hired, my friend Emily had been the entire Comms team. However, Benedict hired Annie to head the Comms department shortly before I came on board. (Note: Ann*ie* = work boss. Ann*e* = life boss.)

At in-person retreats, it would be fascinating to meet folks I had only known as faces on Zoom. David, for example, a reserved, retiring scientist and ultra-runner, turned out to be about as tall as me! Annie turned out to be *physically* shorter than she projected, but *even more* excited and enthusiastic!

At last, for the first time since ███████████████ in 2014, I had what I thought and assumed would be my final job ever. Having seen the utter failure of demand-side work – convincing individuals to stop eating animals – I was committed heart-and-soul to supply-side efforts.

My initial job – media specialist – was very hard. That had been Benedict's job for many years at PETA and much of his time at Animal Asylum; his high energy and natural extroversion made him great at it. But Annie knew I was doing my best, so I kept my head down and plowed ahead.

She built an amazing team that did outstanding work. (I'm still in varying levels of contact with several of them.) Sadly, Emily left soon after I started, having burned out so badly she still hadn't recovered years later.

In 2018, Annie argued against putting on a conference, saying we were too small, too understaffed, and too unprepared. She was overruled. Then the event planner we had hired left due to pregnancy complications. Annie and Natalia (and Rose and everyone else) continued to step up and deal with everything. The conference was incredible.

Annie and I also became pals. We were, shall we say, the mature adults on the team. (But only from a chronological perspective.) Our Zoom one-on-ones tended to talk more about life than work. Sadly, Annie left in 2020 for what I thought was a better job. I found out after the events of Day 29 that it was more complicated than that. Not surprisingly she also poached Alicia (Annie's amazing right hand) who had been set to become my supervisor. That would have been *fan-fucking-tastic!*

Guess which way fate went?

Santa Fe

Day 28 Continued:
"Maybe I'm paralyzed"

Biden has experienced great tragedy in his life.

I wish he hadn't gone through those horrible things.
But I can say from personal experience
that great suffering
can make a person more compassionate,
realistic, and practical.

–Me, "I am enthusiastic for Joe Biden," April 23 2020

I was ready and *oh-so-eager* to make Biden's January 2021 inauguration a day of celebration for Team Green-Ball. (Covid had forced EK back to our house in March 2020.) But instead, I was sick that day with what felt like a low-to-moderate bout of Crohn's. We watched the inauguration with colleagues around the country. Then I worked the rest of the day. I ate a light supper and we went to bed a little early.

(Funny story: When reviewing my hospital admissions report several weeks later, Dr. C emailed to ask, "What were you drinking??" I showed the email to Anne, and we couldn't figure out what he was talking about. Turns out he had misread my 0.03 blood alcohol level as 0.3, which is *way* drunker than I have ever been – by a *lot*.)

A few hours after going to bed, I got up to use the bathroom in a Crohnsian way. I didn't think it would be *super*-violent, so I didn't rouse Anne. Since I'd be flushing, I closed the door and turned on the light.

But then, sitting on the pot, I felt so bad I thought, "I should call Anne."

The next thing I remember is coming to with my head against something hard and cold and wet. (Again, my memory is sure to be unreliable, but although most of it is dreamlike, some of it is quite vivid in its own strange way.) I couldn't really make out anything; I didn't have my glasses on (and wouldn't for days).

I couldn't move and I couldn't feel my legs. The thought formed: "Maybe I'm paralyzed." Then realization dawned that my head was in a pool of my own blood.

I don't really know what happened next. Anne may have been talking to me, very calmly, through the door. I may have passed out. I wasn't in pain. I was only vaguely conscious. Eventually, people were there in the bathroom with me. I don't know how long any of this took. I don't remember what anyone said. Soon I felt cold. (I was only in a pair of my "six for $10" briefs, and those would soon be cut off.)

I was lifted up and the blurry scenery changed. Someone said "St. Joseph's Hospital" which somehow woke me up. I croaked, "TMC?" (As far as I know, this was the only sound I made until I was in the Emergency Department crying for help.) I really wanted to go to Tucson Medical Center, knowing how good it was and just how bad other places could be. (See Day 30.) The voice – I couldn't see – there were just vague fuzzy shapes – said, "St. Joe's is the Trauma 1 center." (*That* didn't sound good, but I just fell back into fog.)

Rain fell on my face. I was lifted again. In a bright box. It rattled and bumped.

By seeming mutual unspoken agreement, Anne and I have never talked this through. (Not sharing is caring.) And I'll bet she'll just silently edit this chapter without comment or corrections. And she'll learn things I've never told her before, because she told me that I needed to write this honestly and with emotion, not clinically or with omissions.

Sorry.

Upper and Lower Yosemite Falls.
Doesn't really fit with the text, does it?
Except the "fall" part.

Day 28 Concluded: Free-Falling

Once, just by chance
I made a friend in an ambulance
I was half man, half broken glass
High in a trance
My life smeared right past

–Wilco, "Ambulance"

Edit: Well, we've broken our unspoken pact of "*We shall never speak of this.*" For her, Day 28 *far* exceeds Day 30 in Worstness; not surprisingly as she wasn't there for Lung II. It also surpasses Oregon, which she had to experience crammed into a cheap motel's bathroom. Given the power of endorphins, this day and its aftermath are also worse for her than July 1994, although she doesn't like "ranking" anything.

On these awful days in January 2021, Anne went through a lot that I don't remember.

I can never tell her how sorry I am.

Here is what I have pieced together. None of this is funny. Sorry.

My loud "crack" of free-falling face-first into the tile wakes Anne up. She calls out and comes over to the bathroom, but part of me (my legs?) is up against the door and she doesn't want to push on it. Once she determines I am unresponsive, she gets EK up. (E would be, *by far*, the most traumatized of the three of us, this being their first near-death experience. Oddly, I would be the *least* traumatized, at least until the second surgery.)

I have the impression Anne is very calm and focused.

One of them calls 911, and the ambulance and fire truck are there pretty quickly. (We're 3.1 miles from Station 37.) The firemen take the bathroom door off – a good trick, given that the hinges are on the inside. When examining me, one of the paramedics exclaims that my heart rate is only 60, but Anne and EK assure them that is just me. (Taking it

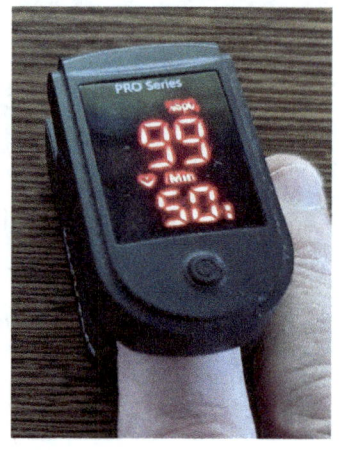

right now, my pulse varied between 48 and 57.) At least at that moment, lying on the bathroom floor realizing I might be paralyzed, I am not yet stressed out – my heart just beats along as normal.

Doo-dee-doo-dee-dooo.

It is raining, a rarity here in Tucson. It is not a torrent, just a chill January drizzle. I am cold in the ambulance. At some point, I can feel my legs again, but I don't remember when. The ride is very rough. My hands start to hurt. Especially my left.

I am taken out of the ambulance and wheeled inside. My hands start to really hurt. I don't know where I was in the hospital, but I'm not swarmed over like in a medical drama. I'm left alone. My hands are now screaming with pain.

The ambulance that took me, at a neighbor's house in 2022.

I sense other patients around me, or maybe just beds or gurneys. It is dark, darker than the ambulance, darker than Tucson Medical Center's Emergency Department. I call out. Someone says in passing they'll be with me soon. The pain in my hands – still moreso the left – takes over my consciousness.

After what seems like a long time of the pain going to 11, I start hollering. A very mean nurse comes over and says something like "Stop whining." Then she adds, "You're not going to die." I cry, "But I want to die!" She snaps, "Do I have to send you to suicide watch?"

The way she says it sounds so ominous – like it would somehow be even worse than my hands, which now feel like someone had taken a sledgehammer to them. (Not an exaggeration; I don't remember a lot, but I very distinctly remember that my hands felt like they had been pulverized.)

I shut up and fall back down the well, submersed in agony.

God I hate that nurse.

I don't remember what happened next. Except for my hands, I can't recall a lot of this entire event. Unlike Lungs I and II and other trips to the hospital, trying to remember this is like trying to remember a dream, interspersed with just a few certain memories.

(Writing "Day 29 Concluded" and "Day 30" were painful. Psychically and physically painful. But oddly, except for the end, this chapter is not. The worst part of this chapter is knowing what my fall did to Anne and especially EK.)

 the man of the group exclaims, "Holy shit."

At some point, I am given intravenous pain medicine that makes me no longer want to die, moving me down from pain level 10 to 9. Then I am given an additional intravenous nerve pain drug (gabapentin) that moves me to 8. I don't remember any of this at all. I just know the pain went down some.

There's one bit of awesome. Relative awesome. It is still gross. TMI, but we're way past that now. ███████████████████ ███████████████████ I'm sorry.

Since I have to be immobilized because of my broken neck (which I didn't know about yet) I am catheterized for the duration.

It is great. No bottle like Jim in his girlfriend's dorm room. Just lie back and think of the good of the empire.

I am put somewhere even darker. I don't know what was going on. Someone says, "...surgery in the morning...." For what? I don't remember anything until I am in that freakish amnesiac state I've already told you about in the "Stud" chapter, where I think I am home, and the hospital is just a bad dream. (Turns out there were *multiple* crazed calls. Mercifully, Anne is withholding details. Not sharing is caring.)

Covid means alone. Anne can't follow the ambulance. Anne can't be there in the morning. Sometime after the surgery, she gets my glasses to me, arranging with someone to do a handoff outside the hospital's entrance. Seeing but alone. Not even the familiar horrible cacophony of emergency.

I don't even know how long I was at St. Joe's.

St. Joe's was my school and parish in Tiffin.

Coincidence?

At some point, an actual hospital room. It has a weird shape, with glass windows that look out into the rest of the floor. Real or just a memory of *House*? Given food (days later?) and it hurts like Hades to chew. I eventually talk on the phone such that I remember, I think. (Again, I'm so sorry.)

After days or weeks or months, someone said "discharge." Then someone said "surgery." I ignored the latter and pushed the former, and they made me promise to ... something. Who cares? Anne and EK in our silver Honda outside the door.

(Nothing has been explained to Anne, despite repeated demands for explanations. She was just told, "He'll have to see the plastic surgeon," as though I just needed some cosmetic work.)

Still in the hard, immobilizing neck brace – the "cone of shame" that will be my home for months. A few days later, the dentist says my loose teeth should be OK, although they and the rest of my teeth need extensive work. (It will be a six-figure repair

– the most crushing out-of-pocket expense of this entire adventure – but that is a problem for Future Matt.)

Then the plastic surgeon.

Who didn't understand why I had been given solid food, much less released from the hospital. Upper *and* lower jaw broken. Facial reconstruction. Nose broken. (*My poor nose.*) Horizontal skull fracture nearly from ear-to-ear. Facial reconstruction? Eye socket fractured.

Facial reconstruction.

What?

Anne is with me, so it's real. Not a dream. Not a dream. Surgery center for plates and screws. No Anne. Under again. Wake up, jaw wired shut. Trapped. Drowning. No Anne.

Finally, a wheelchair. Home with Anne but still trapped. Can't move head, can't open mouth. Panic.

(Of everything from the fall, this panic attack is the most vivid; the hand pain is formless and overwhelming. The panic ties with Nurse Ratched as the most horrible memory from this event.)

Anne calls, gets valium.

Drugs good.

PS: Insurance good, too. Total medical bills for 2021, *not* including prescription drugs or out-of-pocket dental work: $530,544.56.

Billed

$530,544.56

Saguaro cactus flowers

Day 16 Revisited: Karma, Money, and a Bread Machine

And do you feel scared? I do
But I won't stop and falter
And if we threw it all away
Things can only get better

–Howard Jones

Yikes. This part of the book has been pretty heavy, and there is more to come. It gives a false impression that my life is entirely unrelenting misery. That's not true. Just intermittent misery.

My Kent State pal and homecoming date Dan (next page) used to say, "I hate [X] more than life itself." Or as Paul – who also has Crohn's, a terrible back, and a horror story from the Adventist Hospital we'll visit on Day 30 – regularly reminds me: "Life is suffering."

Not that I need to be reminded.

Paul also notes that my life seems to be an argument for karma. Every good thing is countered by a bad thing, and vice versa. Being tall – an advantage in this society – matched with a bad back. Good hair, terrible eyes. A childhood of bullying and intellectual repression and athletic embarrassment, three great years of basketball and a fantastic summer at Kent State. What felt like centuries of rejection by the opposite sex actually was followed by an interesting mix of partners. Not getting the full ride to Georgia Tech led to meeting my soulmate. Meeting Anne was followed by the onset of Crohn's.

Another of my yin/yangs has been money. As documented, I have had a very unhealthy relationship with money, one that caused me much more suffering than was necessary.

But the happiest I've ever been was also when I was the poorest. We not only had rent and car payments, but student debt. We lived in a shithole apartment with a rescued black cat that pissed *everywhere*. Strangers would beat on the door in the middle of the night, so we slept with a knife next to the bed. Being able to eat until sated was so rare that the single most memorable meal of my life is the "This is chow!" feast Best Man Mark paid for.

Now I certainly wouldn't want to live in those material circumstances again. I'm definitely *not* saying that poverty is the key to happiness. But I would give an awful lot to relive that year. (And to tell Young Matt to buy Amazon stock and Bitcoin.)

This goes back to my main financial tip: Don't buy things. Happiness won't come from purchases. Happiness comes from memorable events, alone and with your loved ones.

After we got legally married, someone at the university gave us a kitchen gadget which we returned. (Returning gifts was a source of income those years.) Since we only received store credit for this gadget, we got a bread machine instead. We ate almost an entire loaf a day for the first week – a week we still remember.

Turns out you *can* live on bread (and love) alone. It was fantastic.

Memories!

Cactus flowers

Mindfulness, Meaning, & More Drugs

I don't think that the main question in life
is the question of *meaning*.
I think that the main question in life
is the question of *suffering*.

You suffer, and you don't want to suffer.
What could be more simple than that?

–*Yuval Noah Harari on "People I Mostly Admire"*

The pain this afternoon was less than average (not as much typing?) so I wasn't as distracted during my 4 p.m. "Waking Up" guided meditation. (Only rarely can I dissociate from moderate-to-severe pain. I tried that with a Crohn's attack once and Anne found me collapsed on our cold kitchen tile. She basically had to drag me to the car to drive me to the hospital in – you guessed it – the middle of the night.)

The lesson part of today's meditation – "Mindfulness & Meaning" – was really good. In it, Sam Harris rightfully labeled "What is the meaning of life?" and "What is the purpose of it all?" as pseudo-questions. It is like asking, "Where is the real tooth fairy?" Or "On which epicycle does Jupiter's moon Europa ride?" (Or "Which are the true gods?")

Think about a wolf, experiencing the world through wolf consciousness. Does there have to be some meaning to the wolf's life? Some cosmic purpose? Or does she simply live, experiencing the ups and downs of day-to-day life?

So many have suffered so much because we are told that these pseudo-questions are both real and important. We are taught our parents' god(s) are the only answers to the made-up questions of meaning and purpose. Most people just stick with that. If they are straight, meet an acceptable mate, and have no intellectual curiosity, they can do fine – maybe even more than fine! (A strange quirk: Many of the least religious countries tend to be the happiest – e.g. Scandinavian countries – but the most religious communities *within* a country tend to be the happiest.) Those of us outside the norm in any way, however, are still hemmed in by this seemingly-necessary need to find "meaning" in life, to know what our "purpose" is.

We have to stop thinking that way. The Ann Leckie quote "The point is, there is no point. Choose your own!" isn't just pithy. It is entirely correct.

Mindfulness can help us recognize that these questions of "meaning" and "purpose" are, indeed, pseudo-questions. We can and should ignore these questions just as surely as we should ignore our horoscope. The meaning of life is to be alive. Our "purpose" is just to have our mind where we want it to be. This generally means being simply at ease, since for the most part, we are incapable of sustained bliss – we acclimate to any situation, no matter how good. (And then, of course, something else will come along to flap our not-unflappable minds.)

As you know, I'm all for using drugs to help us be more mindful, and thus more content in general. I can *seem* like a Zen master when the Wellbutrin is working well and life isn't too hard. But there are many other drugs in the world!

If you read Michael Pollan's *How To Change Your Mind* (great title; also on Netflix) you will find stories that range from psilocybin removing terminal patients' dread to ayahuasca providing wild, mind-bending trips that leave people feeling like they've been fundamentally changed. A friend of ours speaks very highly of MDMA helping to provide perspective.

Before I read Pollan's *Change*, I had tried marijuana three times. The first time, I smoked it and felt nothing. Years later, the second smoke made me feel lightheaded in an unpleasant way. I thought the third time would be the charm, as it was for Carl Sagan. (Uncle Carl was a *huge* dope fiend.) But that brownie left me feeling only nauseous.

Ugh.

When I got a stash of magic mushrooms – the most common source of psilocybin – I started low. The first two times, I didn't get to the minimum dosage to feel anything. The third time, I took enough.

The positive effect was how my brain interpreted visual stimuli. Walking outside, the mountains just looked … *different*. Better. Heightened.

Inside was where things were particularly striking. We have a big Van Gogh print in our living room, "Wheat Field with a Reaper" (1889). On 'shrooms, it had literal motion in it. Not surprising, given his painting style. But there was also a dog in the painting, clear as day, made up of different parts of the wheat and the reaper. I had never seen it before, and now I couldn't unsee it. I pointed it out to Anne ("This is the head, this is the tongue...") and she could then make it out.

Our O'Keeffe print, "Chama River, Ghost Ranch, New Mexico (Blue River)" (1935) became three dimensional. The river, but not the surrounding land, also had motion.

But the main impact was not visual. I felt nauseous. Not in a "I'm gonna hurl" way, but "Oh, I'm *really* not well." (This despite taking every precaution, including ginger and Ondansetron, the anti-nausea drug I have on hand for Crohn's attacks.) There was also an indescribable sense that I wasn't myself. Not in a good, "discovery" sense, but "Oh, I've been poisoned."

I very much wanted the trip to end, and after listening to me whine long enough, Anne did too. Won't be going back to that!

Because I have been willing to try anything to help cope with my pain (including acupuncture) I went back to Mary Jane, but this time in the "medical" sense. After consulting with someone who would know, I chatted extensively with a counselor at one of the biggest, most reputable places. We discussed my injury, my ongoing physical therapy, and the nature of my pain. She suggested trying one thing first, and then something else, all of which I ordered. I felt some things on the second product. When it was good, it was like having taken an anti-anxiety med. But I would generally just feel nauseous.

Sadly, none of it changed my pain at all.

Luckily, I am excellent at consuming good old ethanol, titrating it to relaxation and keeping it there. For me, it does quiet my monkey mind somewhat. (Or as Anne says, "Release all your worries and cares.") With a buzz,

I'm able to re-read more of Bob Wright's *Why Buddhism Is True* before becoming lost in thought.

Obviously, your mileage may vary! It is likely that you will have – or have had, or maybe are having right now! – better, more mind-opening and mind-changing trips on "illicit" substances. Or maybe approved mind-altering substances, from alcohol to Luvox, help you break out of bad patterns. Or maybe you don't need any "drug" to maximize your well-being.

As always, though, don't view your "natural" state as somehow sacred or untouchable. We go to school for decades to become "smarter." We should put in at least as much effort to become happier.

Hanging Gardens, Prague

Day 29: Good Times!
Literally. Not Sarcastically.

Oh my fair North Star
I have held to you dearly.

–Dar Williams, "The Mercy of the Fallen"

Two "Boss Annie" stories that aren't important to the narrative but are very memorable (and hopefully help lighten the mood).

Again, please be sure to distinguish soulmate Anne from boss Annie.

In 2018, at the first work retreat I was able to attend (I was too sick previously) Anne and I spent the first part of Karaoke night upstairs talking and drinking with Zak, another person who, in 30 years or so, will have a vastly better story to tell than mine.

(Sociologists have noted the important role singing together plays in bonding people together, which is why teams so often do karaoke and churches feature singing. Holy Jeebus, I could sing you so *many* Catholic hymns even today.)

After maybe an hour, Annie and Alicia came sneaking up the staircase to see where we were. They knew something was amiss because Zak hadn't participated in a song whose lyrics had been rewritten to cover effective altruism.

The five of us sat and laughed as other introverts (Keri [not Kari, but also from Phoenix] Jean, Rose) found their way up to our little gathering. Anne coveted Alicia's rowdy red curls.

As the only extrovert, Annie had a blast playing to the audience. She told a story that was so funny that I fell out of my chair laughing. Literally, not figuratively. I don't remember the story and it probably wouldn't be funny outside that context, but I hadn't laughed that hard since *Bigger, Longer, Uncut.*

My signature caused the next round of side-splitting hilarity.

I drafted a letter for all our media contacts and submitted it and a digital version of my signature for layout. Rose, our designer, then sent me a pdf of the letter to approve, copying Annie. After looking it over, I wrote back to both: "No, we can't use that signature. The reporters would wonder why a first-grader is writing to them." Anne forged an adult-looking signature for me.

The next day, I got a call from Annie. She was laughing. *Really* laughing. Laughing so hard she couldn't talk. I put her on speaker for Anne, and we also started to laugh. Annie croaked out, "Maaaaaaaaaaaaaaaatt."

That is when I figured her call was about my signature, which caused me to laugh even harder. I was doubled over before Annie caught her breath. She had seen my email about the cover letter and thought, "What is he talking about?" Then she opened the pdf, saw for herself, and couldn't stop laughing.

Good times!

There were more good times I won't list here. I was doing work I believed in. I was being useful and helpful. I was spending time with people I respected and admired. I was staying in my lane, head down. It had finally come together.

[M]y general happiness depends on my ability to accomplish good, productive work that does somebody some good.

–*Nick Offerman,* Where the Deer and the Antelope Play

And we all lived happily ever after.

Random Tucson photo. Pretty though, no?

Day 29 Concluded:
Even with a Soulmate,
Life Can Become Not Worth Living

As I lay sick and broken
My eyes just can't stay open.

And as you walk and as you breathe
You ain't no friend to me.

–*Lyle Lovett, "The Road to Ensenada"*

On Day 30, a different surgeon will accuse me of having loyal friends.

After Annie left, the politics and machinations started. Comms was reorganized into "teams" and I reported to Mary the Third (who I like very much). We didn't have a department head for many months, and the inmates running the asylum actually worked pretty well. Eventually, though, a ███████████████████ ███████████ was hired.

██

████████████████████

As the oldest and most tenured on the team, I emailed the new department head three times during her first few months, offering to chat, maybe provide some useful background. Whatever I could do to be helpful. She never replied. On our official "get to know you" one-to-one call, she spoke the entire time, repeating the bio she had already told the full Comms team.

During another full-team call, she asked, "What would you do if you didn't have to worry about money?" She then went off on a wistful monologue about being a volunteer at a park on the coast of Oregon. Fortunately, she didn't get to me. Afterwards, I told Jean (who worked in a different department) how weird it was; if I didn't have to worry about money, I would only change one thing: I'd volunteer instead of taking a salary. She agreed, replying, "Let's not let our colleagues know that we'd work for free."

The only other time I talked with that Comms' department head was a call that was supposed to be about how I saw my future. Having noted the pattern, I punched up my phone's stopwatch app. In the 70-minute call, I spoke for 17. None of those minutes were about me, simply replying to things she had said and asking her questions about herself.

After that, she stopped replying to *any* of my emails. At one point, I turned to Caroline the Second (also in another department) for advice. I was at a loss.

Then came Biden's inauguration and my free-falling face-plant, after which I was on disability for months.

It was a pretty lousy time. Even on oxy and the maximum dose of gabapentin, I was in constant pain. A slight breeze caused my hands to *scream*. When Anne would wash me, I sat on the old-man shower chair wearing thick ski gloves – the steady pain from the gloves was preferable to water hitting my hands, every drop of which felt like a nail being driven into them. As you might expect, trying to sleep in the Cone of Shame was a nightmare.

Anne made smoothies during the weeks and weeks I had my jaw wired shut. (Since I couldn't talk, she was mostly free from my smart-assery. Yay for her?) She got a chocolate protein drink from Amazon and mixed it with different flavors of Ben & Jerry's dairy-free ice cream. (Mint Chocolate is the best, but they're all good when you need calories.) Various friends sent food and gift cards.

When I could start to use my hands, they were very weak and uncoordinated. Every day, I spent hours doing physical therapy, including some things you wouldn't expect. I would have the Transcutaneous Electrical Nerve Stimulation (TENS) unit zapping my forearms while I lay in bed listening to podcasts. Three times a day, I would work my hands in a bin of chickpeas, and then in a bin of rice (both uncooked). I did the same with very hot and very cold – *painfully* cold – water, back and forth, back and forth.

These were efforts to teach my brain that my real, physical hands were there, transmitting valid signals. The trauma to my spine had short-circuited the wiring, and now my brain thought my hands had been mangled, smashed by sledgehammer. But as painful as they felt, my hands themselves were actually physically fine. (Well, as fine as they were before – they still have degenerative osteoarthritis. Today, a year-and-a-half later, it is hard to know what pain is the fall and what is the arthritis.)

After months of intensive physical therapy, the water baths revealed that things wouldn't always be (exactly) this way. One day, I took my hands out of the ice water and they felt ... better.

I couldn't believe it.

Praise Jeebus!

It only lasted 10-15 seconds, but at that moment I knew that it *could* get better.

One positive thing, which I noted at the time to several people, was that my relationship with Benedict reverted to its earlier state. We had enjoyed a great time together several years prior when I stayed with him and his wife for Paul's wedding.

Otherwise we had mostly talked shop since I had started at his nonprofit. This had changed a bit after Annie began easing me out of the media arena, but while I was on disability after the accident, Benedict and I talked and joked about other things, just like the old days.

But I thought about work often and badly wanted to get back. At one point while I was out, Comms had a four-hour mini-retreat, during which Alicia texted me (including humorous commentary that kept me laughing) so I could know what was going on.

After months of rehab, I came back part-time, then full-time. I wasn't given much to do and my emails often went unanswered. I told various people, "I appreciate that people want to treat me with kid gloves, but I want to get to work."

Then my new immediate supervisor emailed to say the department head and chief counsel would be joining our 1-on-1 later that morning. Obviously that was a bad sign in retrospect, but nothing occurred to me at the time. *Doo-dee-doo-dee-dooo.*

As I am wont to do, I was cluelessly asking people about themselves when they told me my position was terminated. I actually didn't get what they were saying. (I must have sounded simple-minded.) Eventually, I got it and sputtered, "Wait. You're firing me? You're *firing* me?"

After that, I did not speak with equanimity, although I don't regret anything I said.

I called Benedict immediately and left a message: "████████ ██ ██"

That was the last I will ever communicate to him.

Then came ███ ██ ██ ██ ███████████████████████████

In case it isn't obvious, ███████████████████████
███████████████████████████:

I was still *in bad pain* – on oxy and the top dose of the nerve
med. (At the time I returned to work, my doc had said I could stay
on disability for months longer, but I really wanted to get back to
work.) (A year after being terminated, and 18 months after the fall,
I'm *still* on the top dose of the nerve med.)

I sure as shit *do* care and have a lifetime of action to prove it.
It is just ... *cruel* to say I don't care.

Most importantly: Aren't these the types of issues you discuss
before ████████████████████████████████████
███████████████████████████?

That ████████, combined with being betrayed (to use a now-
former colleague's word) after such trauma and while still in such
pain – not to mention the loss of decades of incredibly close
friendship – that started Worst the Fourth. (I know I told you
there were only three. And that is a bad sentence. Sorry.)

I blocked his email address and phone number. If I never see
him again, it will be too soon. He and Judas are why I can't do
meta (loving-kindness) meditation. (Well, those two and any
number of Republicans.)

To this day – *to this very moment* – I have *no idea* why the
Comms head wanted me gone. I have no idea why ████████████
██
████████████████████████ during one of the worst periods of my
life. I only wanted to be as helpful as possible. I had oodles of skills
and knowledge, a proven work ethic, and a solid track record. I
wanted nothing for myself – no career advancement, no raise, no
accolades. Just to be helpful, especially for people I liked and
cared for so very much.

A few months later, the organization would lose its
recommendation by a charity evaluator. They didn't even make
the next tier down. This was a big deal: every previous year since

their founding, they had received the top rating, which brought in *big* bucks. Given the importance of their work and the wonderful people who work there, I can only hope this prompted change, that they no longer   .

Anne and I did our best to put on a good front for EK, who was still living with us. But we were spiraling down. (Won't get into all of it – part is Anne's story.)

So much bad had befallen us, almost entirely through me.

Crohn's. Lung I and Lung II. Fired by former friends. Heart surgery and the first bathroom fall. Crushed face and broken neck, followed by betrayal. I have brought the love of my life so much heartache, so much agony.

It was too much.

Late July 2021, lying in bed with the TENS electrodes on my arms. I was too despondent to listen to any podcast. Anne came in to check on me. I blurted out: "I don't see any reason to go on. E will be fine once they're back in their apartment. But I see no reason to continue. Why go on?"

She agreed.

You know, of course, that this is not how the story ends. As I conclude in the "Three Tips" chapter, "Things won't always be this way." And that's right! Not even a year later, I would be so happy it's scary.

But even though I *knew* that tip, it seemed impossible at the time.

It had seemed impossible before. Especially seven years before, in June 2014.

Day 30: "Where is his heart?"
The Foreshadowing Pays Off

All I wanna know: What's the god-damn pain?
Not what's in the medicine.

All I want to do is I want to breathe.

What's the latest way that a man can die?
The silence of the rotten, forgotten
Screaming at you.

–Green Day, "The Static Age"

Anne has missed out on several of my wonderful near-death experiences. For me, this one from 2014 is the ... least wonderful.

The only relative "highlight" of this story happened right before surgery. I had been writhing in agony all day, moaning out loud and screaming internally. Nothing helped. Not Dilaudid, not morphine, not fentanyl. The anesthesiologist took one look at me, glanced at my chart, and said, "Since you're about to go into surgery, you can have mbbledmir." (I couldn't process what he was saying. But I would have killed for some earlier, and I would have killed for some later. I honestly don't think that's hyperbole.)

Whatever he injected, it was magic. I was literally, not figuratively, a different man. It was literally, not figuratively, the greatest thirty seconds of my life. (This is more support for painism – the removal of pain is better than the World's Greatest Orgasm. [Sorry, can't tell you *that* story.])

Then this wonderful, compassionate, magical man asked, "Do you have any questions?"

Of course, we have to back up.

A quick timeline review: May 2013 = Lung I. March 2014 = Coup and firing.

Now it is late June 2014, a few months after being forcibly freed from the organization we had co-founded and which I had led for decades. Cut off from our reliable salary and our secure health insurance.

At Paul's invitation, I flew to DC to speak at HSUS's national advocacy conference. JL was leaving to go to Billionaire Island (he could tell you more, but then he'd have to kill you) but we met in passing at Dulles airport. As I had several years before, I was going to stay at his place with his wife, Jhini, who has a *vastly* more impressive and interesting story than mine. This is not false modesty. She has the most incredible story of anyone I have ever met, and that includes Peter Singer, Tom Scholz, Ingrid Newkirk, Andrew Tobias, and other famous people. Jhini was also one of EK's bosses for two years. In a moment, she's going to save my life. Although I make interest payments with chocolate crinkles (next page) every winter, I still owe her a Klingon Life-Debt.

JL and Jhini lived in an apartment in Silver Spring Maryland, where I slept on the most amazing air mattress I've ever encountered. The next morning I headed downtown to give my talk and meet with my remaining friends. Josh and Curt were exceptionally generous with their time and sympathy; Curt also with his concern, Josh with his jocularity.

The best cookies. Literally.

After my talk, I met Leslie, one of the many former Executive Directors of Animal Asylum. She was now the head of VegFund. (Which is just what it sounds like – a fund of veggies.) She had liked my talk, and I mentioned that I was going to apply for the job opening they had recently posted. (I would get the job, but never really found a groove. One Step for Animals, which Joe, Anne, and I had just founded earlier in 2014, still works with VegFund today – they enable a great deal of our outreach every month.)

After talking more that evening, Jhini and I said goodnight. (Although I'm sure she worked more in her room.)

Some hours later, I woke up with that funny sensation on the left side of my chest. This time, though, I thought "Aha. I know what *this* is."

I was wrong.

And that could have been my last mistake.

Instead of waking up Jhini or even driving myself to the hospital, I first emailed the people I was supposed to see the next day. Given that Anne and I had previously encountered nightmares in situations like this, I also called our Obamacare health insurance company.

Important side note: In addition to Jhini, everyone who fought to make Obamacare the law of the land literally saved my life. (Thanks!) If I hadn't had insurance, I might have waited even longer to go to the ER. Then I'd be *dead*. On the other hand, then you would have been saved from this book. So it goes.

Since I knew I'd been in the hospital for more than a day, I took a nice shower. By this time, my being up and about had awakened Jhini. (A mother's radar.) I calmly told her my lung had collapsed, and she calmly drove me to The Shittiest Hospital in America.

Slightly more than a year after my excellent experience at Tucson Medical Center for Lung I, I was about to enter the torture chamber. Jhini and the anesthesiologist were the only people in the entire building who cared.

Sadly, I could write a book about this time, and it would be horrible as hell. Not as horrible as Elie Wiesel's *Night*, but *pretty fucking bad.*

(A note before we get into this: Lung I took just over a day from start to finish. This time, I was almost always under the impression that things would be fine in a few days. This is part of why Anne never flew out. The other part is that I had more friends within six miles of that horrible hospital than anywhere else.)

I'll try to be brief, but a lot happened.

Remember Lung I, when everyone at TMC said how amazingly lucky I was not to have the giant side hole? Guess what happens this time.

At the same time the first guy is drilling me (I'm not put out, as anesthesia suppresses pulmonary function) a doc shows my x-rays to Jhini in the waiting room. She asks, "Where is his heart?"

Indeed. Where *is* my heart?

It turns out I *don't* have another "simple," partial pneumothorax. I have the deadly tension pneumothorax Dr. C had mentioned. The one where he sent the kid straight to surgery, do not pass go, do not write emails or take a shower.

They don't tell me that at the time, although it is why they start tunneling into my side right away. Before he starts, I tell the driller about the previous doc's difficulties boring into my upper chest. He assures me he's "all set." After what seemed like hours but was probably 10-15 minutes – during which time I was strangling the bed frame and wailing internally to avoid filling the ward with my screams (the last foreshadowing, I'm serious) – he calls another guy over to help him.

Good times.

I am in blinding agony. Except for the minutes before surgery and the hours under anesthesia, I will be at various heights of towering torment until Worst the Third.

The drillers finally finish and flee, replaced by Jhini, who keeps the heart news to herself.

After sitting with me for a long time, telling me amazing stories of her life, I agree Jhini needs to go home and get some sleep.

Now the miscommunications and fuck-ups commence – e.g., I am sent to a room when I'm supposed to be with the anesthesiologist. I can't process any of this, let alone try to address it. I don't understand what's going on or what's supposed to happen except something about surgery.

After Dr. Feelgood magically takes away the agony and asks, "Do you have any questions?" I can't answer. I don't know enough to ask anything. I'm gurneyed into a *freezing* cold ER and placed on what my memory says is an oddly-shaped bed that is … filled with beads? My memory, of course, is about as unreliable regarding this moment as it has ever been. They later tell me that they dislocated ribs and cut out a portion of my lung – the part they suspected of leaking. Then they basically glued the rest of the lung to the chest cavity so it can't collapse again. (As you know, it can, and it will.)

When I come to, Jhini is standing over me, along with Benedict and his wife. I can't speak. I can't move voluntarily. I'm in so much pain that I'm convulsing. Benedict goes out and confronts the surgeon: "Can't you see this? He's in so much pain he's shaking!" (I'm told about this exchange after the fact.) To which the doc replies, "That's what happens in these situations" and turns and walks away.

Weeks later, when I go to that surgeon's office to get his blessing to leave town, he says, "You have some loyal friends."

Oh doc, how I wish it were so.

In my intensive care room, another patient has his TV on 24/7 at an earplug-defeating volume. Even when he's playing reruns of M*A*S*H – one of my favorite shows – the sound is still torturous. I stare at the curtains.

Elsewhere in the ward, someone futilely cries out, over and over, at all hours, "Nurse! *Nurse!*"

I stare at the curtains.

Despite the overwhelming urge caused by quarts of IVs, I can't pee. I might die like Tycho Brahe. Eventually, a put-upon nurse catheterizes me for a stream that shocks even her.

There are now three elongated holes in my side – my dinosaur attack – one of which has a tube draining disgusting bile into a bag. I have an IV they say contains Dilaudid but may well just be only saline. For one, it has absolutely no effect. But also, given the level of incompetence I have encountered, not giving me any medicine would be par for the course.

With the astounding agony and the thundering television and the plaintive cries, I don't sleep that first night. I stare at the curtains. I'm at the bottom of the well. Despite my entreaties, the TV blares on.

The next day, I try to get some answers and any help. I get nothing. Over the phone, Paul tells me about a horrible experience he had at this same hospital. He *begged* them to put him under to escape the pain. (Probably one of his three Worsts; another might be one of his Crohn's stories, which I had partially listened to in real time.) I stare at the curtain in the depths of the damned.

Three nights of no sleep and uncontrolled pain brings about Worst the Third. That morning, whatever was left of me snaps.

Gradually and then suddenly I scream and shriek and sob. My cries are so ferocious and frenzied, nurses actually come into my area. It goes on and on and on. I'm inconsolable. I'm frantic. I have become despair, destroyer of worlds. My howls are fueled by agony and anger and anguish. It goes on and on and on. Multiple nurses are now congregating, gawking. Others gather up Mr. TV and hurry him from the room. A lifetime of pain wells up and breaks free. It goes on and on and on.

There is much more to tell. (I'm not joking about it being an entire book.) Sorry. I'll be brief this time, I'm serious:

Projectile-vomiting the first time out of bed, the physical therapist hurrying away. The first bathroom horror while pals chat a few feet away. Further incompetence, botched IVs, lost orders. A failed plot to get me transferred to GWU's hospital.

The delayed discharge and the further week of recovery. The July 4 party and parade of friends and friends of friends while I slouch on the couch. The Dogfish story, the bleb story. The Wimbledon story. The Ethiopian story. The car-return story. The bird murder crisis. The dog emergency. The weeks of ever-evolving blobs of bruises and blood and bile around my emaciated torso. (Anne vetoed including that picture here – "too disturbing.")

The cross-country trip with my sister and mom. (At *least* a short story in itself.) The second bathroom horror. The life-flashing-before-eyes as mom starts to merge into a tanker truck. The mesmerizing gaze over lush green Kentucky hills on a soft, silent summer evening. The urge to *drive on* when only four hours away. The tears at the Arizona state line. The painful but blessed long-dreamt-of embrace. The whispered near-sob of release, of understatement, of confession: "It was bad. It was *really* bad." The six nights spent gently, carefully, desperately making up for our longest, most horrific time apart.

I simply love you
More than I love life itself.

–Elton John / Bernie Taupin,
"I guess that's why they call it the blues"

And that's it. The last of the Worsts. I'm serious.

Lacebark Pine. Weird, huh?

Aspen, San Francisco Peaks, north of Flagstaff AZ.

Day 18 Revisited:
So Happy It's Scary

I may not have gone where I intended to go,
but I think I have ended up where I needed to be.

–Douglas Adams, The Long Dark Tea-Time of the Soul

Last night (still May 2022) I was strolling down San Francisco
Street here in Flagstaff, on my way to get takeout from Red Curry,
a plant-based Thai place in town.

We came to Arizona for the first time in the spring of 1994,
when Anne was five-and-a-half months pregnant. After five days,
she flew back to Pittsburgh. Before I went back, I gave a
presentation at a big climate change conference in Phoenix.

But before that, Judas, his college roommate (and future co-
conspirator) and I went to Flagstaff.

I was immediately enamored. The air was crisp but no colder
than back east. The sun was *brilliant*. The mountains – *oh, the
mountains!* Look up pictures of the San Francisco Peaks. They
were snow covered when first I saw them then, early April. (When
hiking in the San Fran Peaks today, toward the end of May, there
was still a pile of dirty snow at the end of the parking lot.) The

next morning, I woke up right at sunrise and drove around to simply stare at the Peaks.

If possible, we like to come to Flag twice a year – early summer (it is twenty-five to thirty degrees cooler here than in Tucson) and then October, when the dense aspen groves are in peak color. On July 14 2015, when the spacecraft New Horizons flew by Pluto, Team Green-Ball was at the Lowell Observatory, where Pluto had been discovered. It was, literally, not figuratively, Pluto-palooza – I have the picture to prove it.

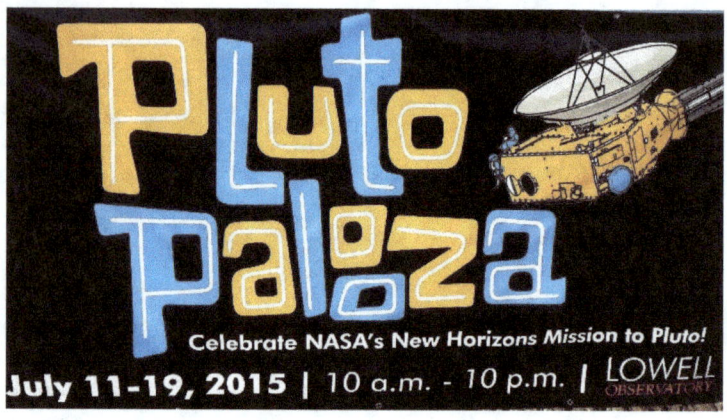

But we've not been here in over two years, since May 2019. Not just because of the pandemic – we're pretty good at avoiding people on Flag trips. No, other scheduled trips have been canceled for fire, flood, and frost. (Love Flag when Tucson is hot, but not going to drive four hours to actually be *cold*.)

Just as it had felt surreal to actually get on a plane to fly to Frankfurt four years after our previous Germany trip and three years after our previous flight and two years after covid canceled our Germany / Prague trip, it *also* felt surreal to actually pull into Flagstaff yesterday. (Yes, I realize that is quite a convoluted sentence. I'm too happy to care.) (Sorry for the emotional whiplash between this and the previous chapter.)

In a way, arriving in Flagstaff was *even more surreal* than Germany, given that our ability to come here has seemed repeatedly cursed.

Again, I know you aren't reading this book for my travel recommendations. (And again: Please read Bill Bryson for laughs and/or watch Rick Steves for sincerity.) But I get gushy about Flagstaff as a *place* more than anywhere else, including Tucson and Germany. (As an *experience*, Germany is the best, OMG.)

Flag is a groovy college town, bounded by National Forest and dominated by people who live to be outdoors. The hiking is fantastic and there are two plant-based restaurants. (Morning Glory Cafe, where Anne had tacos and I had pecan French toast *with whipped topping* after a four-hour-plus hike, makes the best plant-based sausage I've ever had. The secret ingredient is probably pork. [A joke! A joke!]) There are other good places, too, e.g., we got a big Mexican breakfast from MartAnne's. (Oooh, so close – only one letter off!)

Back to last night. I'm strolling down the street. The air is cool not cold, crisp and clear. Save for a few days back home between Germany and this trip, I have been traveling with Anne almost nonstop for weeks. And as I walked and as I breathed, this thought occurred to me:

"I am so happy, it's scary."

This is, of course, in large part because of the antidepressant. (Thanks again Wellbutrin!) But also because I have spent weeks with Anne in our favorite places. It is one of the best months of my life. The best in many, many, *many* years.

You might even say it is Time the Fourth, if one month is long enough to count.

Let the record show: Life *can* be Perfect.

At the last call

When it's time for us all

To say goodbye

I know I'm gonna cry

Because all in all

I'm just having a ball

Being alive

And I don't want to die

I don't want to die.

—*Jeff Tweedy with George Saunders,*
"A Robin or a Wren"

Day 31: And In the End

On and on and on
We'll stay together, yeah

And whether short or long
I will live in you
Or you will live in me
Until we disappear

Together in a dream

—Wilco

Last night, while out on an evening stroll here in Tucson, I ran into Alex, a neighbor who lives a few doors up the street. Not that much older than EK, but he's been a father for a while.

Back when he was in high school, living with his parents even farther up the street, Alex threw a senior party at our neighborhood pool. Exuberant with the immortality of youth, he tried to jump from the ramada roof into the pool. It went about as badly as possible without him actually dying or becoming paralyzed.

He now lives right by that pool. He can see the ramada roof from his backyard.

Alex knows that last year, I, too, almost died; for much of 2021, he and the other neighbors had gotten used to watching Anne or EK walk me in my Cone of Shame. When he saw me last night, he told me I looked good. (He was raised well – always flatter your elders.) I thanked him. Then, with great sincerity, he asked if it – almost dying, we both understood without saying – had changed me. If I "wake up with a sense of *carpe diem*."

Oh Alex, how I wish it were so.

In addition to being loathed – first by classmates and teachers and then by the vegan mob – three things have shaped my life: logic and love and suffering. Meeting Anne made me stronger, better looking, and above-average. Drugs further improved my life – and probably can yours!

While it would make a better story, a better pitch, a better ending, the reality is I am Homer Simpson: After his heart attack, Homer pleads, "But what doesn't kill me makes me stronger, right?"

"On the contrary," replies Dr. Hibbert. "The heart attack has left you weak as a kitten."

Almost dying multiple times – my hobby, it seems – and Crohn's and degenerative osteoarthritis and scoliosis and tinnitus – all of this has left me far weaker today than I was from, say, 1998-2012.

But to be totally straight with you, the betrayals broke me.

At least a large part of me. The ambitious part. The "let's-make-a-better-world" part. The optimistic, hopeful-for-the-future part.

Sorry.

Has this been an inspiring story that leaves you eager to change your life and the world? I hope so, although I doubt it.

But it is honest.

Does that count for something? Does that count for anything?

Seriously, I'm asking.

In my ethics, it counts for nothing.

Only consequences count. Only results matter.

On the one hand – and I've seen this be true for many kind and decent folk – Hell is other people.

On the other – and I've *not* seen *this* to be the case for many others – a soulmate exists for me. My fortune is *immense*. Despite everything, Life *can* be Perfect. I have been So Happy It's Scary, even after everything. It will remain possible to be happy again, for as long as Anne and I can be together.

Is that enough?

Seriously, I'm asking.

In the end, I hope this book has entertained you and made you laugh, at least a little. I hope there are some bits that will help you avoid my many mistakes. (So many mistakes.) I sincerely hope you want to change the world and reduce someone's suffering – that bastard Creator has really made a mess of this place.

I hope that no matter where you are now, you have a good life, that you can be So Happy It's Scary.

That's all I have. That's everything.

www.ingramcontent.com/pod-product-compliance
Lightning Source LLC
Chambersburg PA
CBHW060848120626
46553CB00001B/14